# Dynamic Programming in Python

*From Basics to Expert Proficiency*

# Contents

# Introduction

Dynamic Programming (DP) is a powerful algorithmic paradigm used to solve complex optimization problems. By breaking down a problem into simpler subproblems and solving each subproblem just once, DP facilitates the efficient use of computational resources. This book, "Dynamic Programming in Python: From Basics to Expert Proficiency," aims to provide a comprehensive guide to mastering dynamic programming techniques using Python.

Dynamic programming finds its roots in the 1950s, originating from the work of Richard Bellman. Since its inception, DP has transformed into an essential toolkit for software developers, data scientists, and researchers. By understanding the principles of dynamic programming, students and professionals can enhance their problem-solving capabilities and apply these techniques to a plethora of real-world scenarios.

Key concepts and terminologies relevant to dynamic programming are integral to this discipline. Terms such as "optimal substructure" and "overlapping subproblems" are fundamental, and their detailed understanding is critical to effectively implement DP solutions. This book will familiarize readers with these terminologies, providing clear and precise explanations.

Python, a versatile and widely-used programming language, is the medium of instruction in this book. Its readability, extensive libraries, and strong community support make Python an excellent choice for learning and implementing dynamic programming techniques. We will start with an introduction to Python programming, covering basic syntax, data structures, and setup instructions to ensure a smooth learning experience.

In the journey through this book, readers will be introduced to concepts starting from the basics of recursion, progressing through various dynamic programming principles, and culminating in advanced topics. The distinction between top-down and bottom-up approaches, combined with detailed sections on memoization and tabulation techniques, will provide a robust foundation. Practical implementation sections will offer real-world examples and case studies to demonstrate the applicability of dynamic programming.

Through carefully curated chapters and progressively challenging sections, this book aims to build a deep and nuanced understanding of dynamic programming. The inclusion of combinatorial problems, optimal substructure, and overlapping subproblems will prepare readers to tackle complex problems with confidence.

By the end of this book, readers will have acquired a proficient command of dynamic programming techniques. Equipped with both theoretical and practical knowledge, they will be well-prepared to address various computational challenges and optimize solutions effectively. We hope this book serves as a valuable resource in your journey to mastering dynamic programming with Python.

# Chapter 1

# Introduction to Dynamic Programming and Python

**Dynamic programming (DP) is a method for solving complex problems by breaking them down into simpler subproblems, solving each subproblem once, and storing their solutions. This chapter lays the groundwork for understanding DP by explaining its key concepts and terminologies, illustrating why DP is useful, and providing an introduction to Python programming. We cover how to set up your Python environment, basic syntax, and data structures, as well as the philosophy of Pythonic problem-solving. By comparing DP with other techniques and exploring real-world problems, this chapter prepares readers for the comprehensive study of dynamic programming that follows.**

## 1.1 What is Dynamic Programming?

Dynamic Programming (DP) is a methodical approach to solving optimization problems by breaking them into simpler subproblems and solving each subproblem only once, storing their solutions to avoid redundancy. This technique is particularly beneficial for problems exhibiting overlapping subproblems and optimal substructure, where a problem can be recursively broken down into smaller, similar problems.

DP essentially encapsulates two main strategies: memoization and tabulation. Memoization is a top-down approach where we store the results of expensive function calls and reuse them when the same inputs occur again. Tabulation, on the other hand, is a bottom-up approach where we solve all subproblems starting from the simplest up to the original problem.

Consider the classical problem of computing Fibonacci numbers to illustrate the concept. The Fibonacci sequence is defined as follows:

$$F(n) = \begin{cases} n & \text{if } n \leq 1, \\ F(n-1) + F(n-2) & \text{if } n > 1. \end{cases}$$

A naive recursive approach recomputes Fibonacci values, leading to exponential time complexity. By applying memoization, we significantly optimize the process. Below is a Python implementation using memoization:

```
def fibonacci_memo(n, memo={}):
    if n in memo:
        return memo[n]
    if n <= 1:
        return n
    memo[n] = fibonacci_memo(n-1, memo) + fibonacci_memo(n-2, memo)
    return memo[n]
```

In this code, we use a dictionary, 'memo', to store previously computed Fibonacci numbers, thereby reducing redundant calculations. Each required Fibonacci number is calculated once, achieving a time complexity of $O(n)$.

Tabulation, alternatively, uses an iterative bottom-up method. The following Python code demonstrates this approach:

```
def fibonacci_tab(n):
    if n <= 1:
        return n
    table = [0] * (n+1)
    table[1] = 1
    for i in range(2, n+1):
        table[i] = table[i-1] + table[i-2]
    return table[n]
```

Here, we create an array 'table' where each index represents the Fibonacci number at that position. Starting from known values, we build up the solutions for the larger subproblems. This iterative method also achieves $O(n)$ time complexity with additional $O(n)$ space complexity.

Crucially, an effective DP solution involves two primary steps: 1. **Define the structure of the optimal solution** - Understand the nature of the subproblems and how they contribute to the solution of the overall problem. 2. **Recursively define the value of optimal solutions** - Use recurrence relations to break the problem into subproblems, solving and storing them to avoid recomputation.

Let's consider another example - the Knapsack Problem, a classic optimization problem. Suppose we have a set of items, each with a weight and a value, and a knapsack with a weight capacity. The goal is to determine the maximum value that can be carried in the knapsack without exceeding its capacity.

The problem can be recursively defined as follows:

$$K(i, w) = \begin{cases} 0 & \text{if } i = 0 \text{ or } w = 0, \\ K(i-1, w) & \text{if } w_i > w, \\ \max(K(i-1, w), K(i-1, w - w_i) + v_i) & \text{if } w_i \leq w. \end{cases}$$

Where $K(i, w)$ represents the maximum value for the first $i$ items and capacity $w$, $w_i$ is the weight of item $i$, and $v_i$ is the value of item $i$.

Here is a Python solution using tabulation:

```
def knapsack(weights, values, capacity):
    n = len(values)
    table = [[0 for _ in range(capacity + 1)] for _ in range(n + 1)]

    for i in range(1, n + 1):
        for w in range(1, capacity + 1):
            if weights[i-1] <= w:
                table[i][w] = max(values[i-1] + table[i-1][w-weights[i-1]], table[i-1][w])
            else:
                table[i][w] = table[i-1][w]

    return table[n][capacity]
```

In this code, 'weights' and 'values' are lists of item weights and values respectively, and 'capacity' is the maximum weight the knapsack can carry. By filling up the 'table' using previous computations, we avoid redundant calculations.

To summarize, dynamic programming is a powerful technique for optimization problems characterized by overlapping subproblems and optimal substructure. Whether through memoization or tabulation, DP ensures efficient computation by storing intermediate results, reducing time complexities from exponential to polynomial, making previously intractable problems manageable.

## 1.2 History and Origins of Dynamic Programming

The concept of dynamic programming (DP) was introduced in the mid-20th century by Richard Bellman, an American mathematician who made significant contributions to various scientific fields. The term "dynamic programming" was carefully chosen by Bellman, where "dynamic" refers to the time-varying nature of problems it aims to solve and "programming" refers to the process of decision making. Contrary to what some might think, the term is not related to computer programming but to mathematical problem solving.

During the 1940s and early 1950s, Bellman was working at RAND Corporation, a research and development organization for the U.S. Air Force. The specific problem Bellman sought to address was to develop computational methods for multi-stage decision-making processes, relevant to a range of applications including logistics, resource allocation, and technology adoption. He observed that many of these real-world problems could be solved by breaking them down into simpler subproblems that could be solved independently.

Bellman's seminal work formally established the principle of optimality, which is a foundational concept in dynamic programming. The principle of optimality can be stated as follows:

> *An optimal policy has the property that, whatever the initial state and initial decision are, the remaining decisions must constitute an optimal policy regarding the state resulting from the first decision.*

This principle implies that the optimal solution to a problem can be recursively composed of optimal solutions to its subproblems, minimizing the need for re-computation and thereby reducing the complexity of solving the initial, more complex problem. Bellman proceeded to develop what are now known as Bellman equations, a set of recursive equations that form the core of dynamic programming methodology.

The development of dynamic programming paralleled the advancement of digital computing, providing the required computational support for numerically intense operations. Initially, dynamic programming was applied to inventory management, production control, and other industrial applications. Over time, with the growth of computational power and the emergence of new programming paradigms, its use expanded to other areas such as economics, operations research, bioinformatics, artificial intelligence, and telecommunications.

For example, one of the early applications of dynamic programming was in the field of economics, specifically in the context of optimization problems such as the "knapsack problem" where DP was used to determine the optimal combination of items to maximize the total value while adhering to constraints like weight or volume. Similarly, in bioinformatics, algorithms based on dynamic programming, such as the Needleman-Wunsch algorithm for sequence alignment, greatly advanced the field of genomics by enabling efficient comparison of DNA and protein sequences.

The evolution of programming languages, particularly the development of high-level languages such as FORTRAN, C, and eventually Python, has made dynamic programming more accessible and easier to implement. With Python's rich set of libraries and its emphasis on readability and simplicity, implementing complex dynamic programming algorithms has become more straightforward, which aids in broader adoption and further innovation.

Dynamic programming continues to evolve, particularly with the introduction of optimization techniques such as memoization and tabulation. Memoization is a top-down approach where function calls are stored to avoid redundant calculations, and tabulation is a bottom-up approach that involves solving all related subproblems iteratively and storing their results.

Today's vast repositories of computational resources and burgeoning fields such as data science, machine learning, and artificial intelligence are fostering further innovations in dynamic programming. Its utility in solving optimization problems ensures it remains an indispensable tool for academics, researchers, and professionals alike.

```
def fibonacci(n, memo={}):
    if n in memo:
        return memo[n]
    if n <= 1:
        return n
    memo[n] = fibonacci(n-1, memo) + fibonacci(n-2, memo)
    return memo[n]

print(fibonacci(10))
```

55

Dynamic programming's origins rooted in mathematics and its growth alongside computer science exemplify its interdisciplinary nature. Understanding its history not only provides context but also underscores its adaptability and enduring relevance in solving both theoretical and practical problems.

## 1.3 Key Concepts and Terminologies

Dynamic Programming (DP) is a powerful technique for solving optimization problems by breaking them down into simpler subproblems and storing the solutions to avoid redundant computations. Understanding the key concepts and terminologies in DP is crucial for applying this method effectively. This section delves into the fundamental concepts and the specific terminologies associated with DP.

**Optimal Substructure** is a property of a problem that indicates an optimal solution can be constructed efficiently from optimal solutions of its subproblems. For instance, consider the shortest path problem: If the shortest path from vertex $u$ to vertex $v$ passes through vertex $w$, then the path from $u$ to $w$ and from $w$ to $v$ must also be the shortest paths. This property forms the basis for recursive problem-solving approaches in DP.

**Overlapping Subproblems** refers to the scenario where the solution to a problem can be broken down into solutions of the same subproblems that occur multiple times. Recursive algorithms might solve these subproblems repeatedly. DP improves efficiency by storing the results of these subproblems, typically using a *memoization* technique or constructing a *DP table*. Take the Fibonacci sequence as an example, where $F(n) = F(n-1)+F(n-2)$. Calculating $F(n-1)$ and $F(n-2)$ involves recomputing previous Fibonacci numbers, which can be avoided by storing their values.

**Memoization** is a technique used to store the results of expensive function calls and reusing those result when the same inputs occur again. This strategy is implemented using a data structure (often a dictionary in Python) to store computed values, avoiding redundant calculations and significantly reducing computation time for problems with overlapping subproblems.

The **DP Table** (or DP array) is a table used to store solutions to subproblems in an iterative DP approach, which builds up the solution to the original problem step by step. Each entry in the DP table represents the solution to a subproblem, and by filling this table, one can derive the solution to the overall problem. The approach usually involves deciding the table dimensions, initializing the base cases, and filling the table based on the problem's recurrence relation.

**Recurrence Relation** expresses the solution of the problem in terms of solutions to smaller instances. It provides a mathematical formulation to derive a solution based on the optimal substructure property. For example, in the case of the Fibonacci sequence, the recurrence relation is $F(n) = F(n-1) + F(n-2)$.

**State** in DP represents a snapshot of the parameters and variables at a particular point in the problem-solving process. States are used to define subproblems and the relations between them. Identifying appropriate states is a crucial step in formulating a DP solution, as the states must be expressive enough to capture the essence of subproblems.

**State Transition** describes the process of moving from one state to another, typically defined by the recurrence relation. In other words, it represents how a solution to a subproblem transitions to a solution to another subproblem or the larger problem.

**Top-Down vs. Bottom-Up Approaches** are two methodologies in DP. The *Top-Down Approach* relies on recursion with memoization, where the main problem is solved by recursively solving and storing the subproblems. Conversely, the *Bottom-Up Approach* iteratively constructs the solution from the base cases, gradually build-up to the final solution using the DP table.

```
def fibonacci_memo(n, memo={}):
    if n in memo:
        return memo[n]
    if n <= 2:
        return 1
    memo[n] = fibonacci_memo(n-1, memo) + fibonacci_memo(n-2, memo)
    return memo[n]

# Example usage:
print(fibonacci_memo(10))
```

```
Output:
55
```

```
def fibonacci_bottom_up(n):
    if n <= 2:
        return 1
    fib = [0] * (n+1)
    fib[1], fib[2] = 1, 1
    for i in range(3, n+1):
        fib[i] = fib[i-1] + fib[i-2]
    return fib[n]

# Example usage:
print(fibonacci_bottom_up(10))
```

Output:
55

**Time and Space Complexity** in DP solutions often relate to the number of subproblems and the space used to store results. For instance, the naive recursive Fibonacci algorithm has exponential time complexity $O(2^n)$, whereas the memoized and bottom-up versions reduce it to linear time complexity $O(n)$. The space complexity generally relates to the size of the memoization structure or DP table.

**Memo Table or Memoization Dictionary** is used in top-down solutions to store the results of subproblems. For bottom-up solutions, this structure is called a *DP Table* and is typically implemented as an array or matrix.

**Initialization** involves setting up the base cases for the DP table or the memoization structure. These base cases often correspond to the simplest subproblems, which can be solved directly without recursion. For example, initializing 'fib[1]' and 'fib[2]' to 1 in the bottom-up Fibonacci solution.

Understanding and accurately implementing these key concepts and terminologies allows for the formulation of efficient DP solutions to complex problems.

## 1.4 Why Use Dynamic Programming?

Dynamic Programming (DP) is a powerful tool for solving a wide range of complex problems efficiently. It fundamentally relies on the principle of breaking down problems into a series of overlapping subproblems, solving each subproblem just once, and storing their solutions. This approach significantly reduces the amount of computation required compared to naive methods, making DP an essential technique in the field of algorithms and optimization.

Consider a simple recursive solution to the Fibonacci sequence:

```
def fibonacci(n):
    if n <= 1:
        return n
    return fibonacci(n-1) + fibonacci(n-2)
```

The above implementation, while straightforward, is highly inefficient for large values of $n$. Each call to fibonacci(n) results in two more calls: fibonacci(n-1) and fibonacci(n-2). This leads to an exponential growth in the number of calls, causing redundant computations.

For instance, computing fibonacci(5) involves computing fibonacci(3) and fibonacci(4), with fibonacci(3) itself requiring fibonacci(2) and fibonacci(1) to be recomputed multiple times.

To resolve this inefficiency, DP employs either a top-down approach with memoization or a bottom-up approach with tabulation. Let's transform the Fibonacci function using memoization:

```
def fibonacci_memo(n, memo={}):
    if n in memo:
        return memo[n]
    if n <= 1:
        return n
    memo[n] = fibonacci_memo(n-1, memo) + fibonacci_memo(n-2, memo)
    return memo[n]
```

Here, memo is a dictionary that stores the results of subproblems as they are computed. When fibonacci_memo(n) is called, it first checks if the result for $n$ is already computed and stored in memo. If so, it returns the stored value, avoiding redundant computations. This drastically reduces the number of recursive calls, ensuring each unique subproblem is solved only once.

Alternatively, the bottom-up approach to the Fibonacci sequence uses tabulation:

```
def fibonacci_tab(n):
    if n <= 1:
        return n
    fib_table = [0] * (n + 1)
    fib_table[1] = 1
    for i in range(2, n + 1):
        fib_table[i] = fib_table[i-1] + fib_table[i-2]
    return fib_table[n]
```

In this approach, we initialize an array fib_table to store the results of subproblems in a bottom-up manner, iteratively solving each subproblem from the smallest to the largest. This ensures that each problem is solved exactly once, providing a linear time complexity, $O(n)$. This is an exponential improvement from the naive recursive implementation, which has a time complexity of $O(2^n)$.

Dynamic Programming is not limited to the Fibonacci sequence; its applicability spans a wide range of domains. Some classic problems that benefit greatly from DP include:

- **Knapsack problems**: DP provides an efficient method to solve both the 0/1 knapsack problem and the fractional knapsack problem. The idea is to build up a table where each entry represents the maximum value that can be achieved with a given capacity.

- **Shortest path problems**: Algorithms like Floyd-Warshall and Bellman-Ford use DP concepts to find the shortest paths in weighted graphs, capable of handling negative weights.
- **String editing problems**: Edit distance (Levenshtein distance) and other string alignment problems utilize DP to efficiently compute the minimal number of operations required to transform one string into another.
- **Partition problems**: DP helps in solving subset sum, partition, and rod cutting problems by breaking them down into overlapping subproblems.

The key advantages of using DP are its ability to:

- **Optimize performance**: By storing solutions to subproblems, DP avoids redundant computations, leading to significant performance improvements and feasible solutions for otherwise intractable problems.
- **Ensure correctness**: The philosophy of building solutions from the ground up or top down ensures that all subproblems are solved correctly and only once.
- **General applicability**: DP applies to various domains beyond computer science, including operational research, economics, and bioinformatics, making it a versatile problem-solving tool.

## 1.5 Introduction to Python Programming

Python is a high-level, interpreted programming language known for its readability and simplicity. Its syntax is designed to be easy to understand and write, which makes it an excellent choice for both beginners and experienced programmers. In the context of dynamic programming, Python's flexible data structures and powerful libraries provide a robust environment for implementing and testing algorithms.

Python supports multiple programming paradigms, including procedural, object-oriented, and to some extent, functional programming. This flexibility makes it suitable for a wide range of applications, from web development to data science and artificial intelligence.

The core philosophy of Python is captured in "The Zen of Python," a collection of aphorisms that guide the design of the language. You can view these aphorisms by executing the following command in a Python interpreter:

```
import this
```

Some key principles from "The Zen of Python" include:

- Readability counts.
- Simple is better than complex.
- Complex is better than complicated.
- There should be one—and preferably only one—obvious way to do it.

### Python Installation and Environment Setup

Before writing Python programs, you need to install Python on your system. Python can be downloaded from the official website https://www.python.org/. It is recommended to download the latest stable version.

In addition to the Python interpreter, you will need an Integrated Development Environment (IDE) or a text editor to write your code. Popular choices include:

- **PyCharm**: A feature-rich IDE designed specifically for Python development.
- **VS Code**: A versatile text editor with a wide range of extensions, including excellent support for Python.
- **Jupyter Notebooks**: An interactive environment often used for data science and machine learning tasks.

Once Python is installed, you can verify the installation by opening a terminal or command prompt and typing:

```
python --version
```

This command should display the version of Python that you have installed.

### Basic Python Syntax

Python's syntax is clean and straightforward, making it easy to learn and use. Here are some fundamental aspects of Python syntax:

- **Indentation**: Python uses indentation to define blocks of code. All statements within the same block must be indented by the same amount.
- **Comments**: Comments in Python are denoted by the '#' symbol. They can be on their own line or at the end of a statement.
- **Variables**: Variables in Python do not require explicit declaration, and their types are inferred from the value assigned.
- **Basic Data Types**: Python supports several basic data types, including integers, floats, strings, and booleans.
- **Print Function**: The 'print()' function is used to output data to the console.

```
# This is a comment
x = 5 # Variable assignment
y = 3.14 # Float variable
str = "Hello, world!" # String variable
is_valid = True # Boolean variable

print(x, y, str, is_valid) # Output: 5 3.14 Hello, world! True
```

### Control Structures

Python provides several control structures for managing the flow of the program:

- **Conditional Statements**: 'if', 'elif', and 'else' are used to execute code based on a condition.
- **Loops**: 'for' and 'while' loops are used to repeat blocks of code.

```
# Conditional statement
if x > 0:
    print("x is positive")
elif x == 0:
    print("x is zero")
else:
    print("x is negative")

# For loop
for i in range(5):
    print(i)
```

```
# While loop
count = 0
while count < 5:
    print(count)
    count += 1
```

### Functions

Functions in Python are defined using the 'def' keyword. They can take parameters and return values.

```
# Function definition
def add(a, b):
    return a + b

# Function call
result = add(3, 4)
print(result) # Output: 7
```

### Data Structures

Python provides several built-in data structures that are particularly useful for dynamic programming:

- **Lists**: Ordered, mutable collections.
- **Tuples**: Ordered, immutable collections.
- **Dictionaries**: Key-value pairs.
- **Sets**: Unordered collections of unique elements.

```
# List
fruits = ["apple", "banana", "cherry"]
fruits.append("date")
print(fruits) # Output: ['apple', 'banana', 'cherry', 'date']

# Tuple
coordinates = (10, 20)
print(coordinates) # Output: (10, 20)

# Dictionary
student = {"name": "Alice", "age": 21}
print(student["name"]) # Output: Alice

# Set
unique_numbers = {1, 2, 3, 3, 2, 1}
print(unique_numbers) # Output: {1, 2, 3}
```

These basics provide a foundation for more advanced concepts that will be used in dynamic programming. Understanding Python syntax and its data structures is crucial for implementing efficient algorithms and solving complex problems effectively.

## 1.6 Setting Up Your Python Environment

Setting up an efficient Python development environment is a fundamental step toward mastering dynamic programming. A well-configured environment ensures that you can focus on problem-solving without being hindered by technical issues. This section provides a meticulous guide to setting up Python on your machine, including installation, configuring an Integrated Development Environment (IDE), and installing necessary packages.

### Installing Python

Python can be installed from the official website https://www.python.org/downloads/. It is crucial to download a version that is compatible with your operating system (Windows, macOS, or Linux). Python 3.x is recommended due to its extensive support and contemporary features.

- Navigate to https://www.python.org/downloads/.
- Click on the download link appropriate for your operating system.
- Run the downloaded installer.
- Ensure that the option "Add Python to PATH" is checked. This option is essential for running Python from the command line.
- Follow the installation prompts.

To verify the installation, open a terminal (Command Prompt on Windows, Terminal on macOS, or a shell prompt on Linux) and type the following command:

```
python --version
```

On some systems, you may need to use 'python3' instead:

```
python3 --version
```

You should see an output similar to:

```
Python 3.x.x
```

## Installing pip

'pip' is Python's package installer, which allows you to install and manage additional libraries that are not included in the standard library. It is typically included with Python 3.x installations. To verify 'pip' installation, you can run:

```
pip --version
```

If 'pip' is not installed, follow the instructions available at https://pip.pypa.io/en/stable/installation/.

## Setting Up a Virtual Environment

Using virtual environments is a best practice to maintain dependencies required by different projects separately. This isolation avoids conflicts between projects.

Create a virtual environment by navigating to your project directory and executing:

```
python -m venv env
```

Activate the virtual environment using:

- **Windows:**

  ```
  .\env\Scripts\activate
  ```

- **macOS and Linux:**

  ```
  source env/bin/activate
  ```

You will notice the prompt changes, indicating that the virtual environment is active. To deactivate the virtual environment, simply run:

```
deactivate
```

## Installing Necessary Packages

Several packages are fundamental for dynamic programming and general development tasks. Install them using 'pip'. Commonly used packages include:

- numpy - for numerical computations.
- pandas - for data manipulation and analysis.
- matplotlib and seaborn - for data visualization.
- jupyter - for interactive notebooks.

Install these packages by executing:

```
pip install numpy pandas matplotlib seaborn jupyter
```

## Choosing an Integrated Development Environment (IDE)

An IDE significantly enhances productivity by providing features such as syntax highlighting, code completion, debugging tools, and integrated terminal access. Popular Python IDEs include:

- **PyCharm:** A robust IDE with extensive support for professional developers. Downloadable from https://www.jetbrains.com/pycharm/.
- **VS Code:** A lightweight yet powerful editor from Microsoft. It supports Python through the Python extension. Available at https://code.visualstudio.com/.
- **Jupyter Notebook:** Primarily used for data analysis and academic purposes. It allows you to create and share documents containing live code, equations, visualizations, and explanatory text. Install it using the command pip install jupyter and launch with jupyter notebook.

## Configuring Your IDE

Each IDE has its configuration process. Below are key configurations for PyCharm and VS Code.

**PyCharm:**

- **Create a New Project:** Upon launching PyCharm, click on "Create New Project."

- **Configure Python Interpreter:** Select the interpreter for your virtual environment by navigating to File → Settings → Project: <Project Name> → Python Interpreter. Click on the gear icon and choose Add to select the interpreter from the virtual environment.

- **Install Packages:** You can install required packages within PyCharm by clicking on File → Settings → Project: <Project Name> → Python Interpreter → + and selecting the packages to be installed.

**VS Code:**

- **Install Python Extension:** Go to the Extensions view ('Ctrl+Shift+X'), search for "Python," and install the extension provided by Microsoft.

- **Select Python Interpreter:** Press Ctrl+Shift+P to open the command palette, then type and select Python: Select Interpreter. Choose your virtual environment's interpreter.

- **Install Packages:** Open a terminal in VS Code ('Ctrl+'), and use 'pip' commands to install packages as discussed earlier.

After setting up your environment, you are fully equipped to begin writing Python programs and tackling dynamic programming problems efficiently.

## 1.7 Basic Python Syntax and Data Structures

Understanding basic Python syntax and data structures is crucial for effectively implementing dynamic programming solutions. This section provides a detailed overview of Python's syntax, variables, data types, and core data structures such as lists, tuples, sets, and dictionaries.

Python is an interpreted, high-level, general-purpose programming language known for its readability and simplicity. Python programs are typically shorter and easier to write due to its well-defined syntax.

**Variables and Data Types**

Variables in Python do not require explicit declaration to reserve memory space. The declaration happens automatically when a value is assigned to a variable. Python also supports multiple data types including integers, floats, strings, and booleans.

```
x = 10 # An integer
y = 3.14 # A float
name = "Alice" # A string
is_valid = True# A boolean
```

Python's dynamic typing means that the same variable can hold values of different types at different times:

```
x = 10
x = "Now I'm a string"
```

### Basic Operators

Python supports various operators for arithmetic, comparison, assignment, bitwise operations, and logical operations.

- **Arithmetic Operators:** +, -, *, /, //, %, **
- **Comparison Operators:** ==, !=, >, <, >=, <=
- **Logical Operators:** and, or, not
- **Bitwise Operators:** &, |, ^, ~, «, »

### Lists

Lists are one of the most versatile data structures in Python. A list is an ordered collection of items, which can be of different types. Lists are defined using square brackets.

```
numbers = [1, 2, 3, 4, 5] # List of integers
mixed = [1, "Two", 3.0, True] # List of mixed data types
```

Common list operations include:

```
numbers.append(6) # Adds an item to the end of the list
numbers.remove(3) # Removes the first occurrence of an item
print(numbers[0]) # Accesses the first element, result: 1
print(numbers[-1]) # Accesses the last element, result: 6
print(numbers[1:3]) # Slices a list, result: [2, 4]
```

### Tuples

Tuples are similar to lists but are immutable, meaning once created, their values cannot be changed. Tuples are defined using parentheses.

```
point = (3, 4)
```

Tuples support indexing and slicing like lists, but they do not support item assignment.

```
print(point[0]) # Accesses the first element, result: 3
print(point[1:2]) # Slices a tuple, result: (4,)
# point[0] = 5 # This will raise a TypeError
```

### Sets

Sets are unordered collections of unique items. They are defined using curly braces or the set() function.

```
fruits = {"apple", "banana", "cherry"}
fruits.add("orange")
print(fruits) # Output includes "orange" but order may vary
```

Operations on sets include union (|), intersection (&), difference (-), and symmetric difference ˆ().

```
A = {1, 2, 3}
B = {3, 4, 5}
print(A | B) # Union: {1, 2, 3, 4, 5}
print(A & B) # Intersection: {3}
print(A - B) # Difference: {1, 2}
print(A ^ B) # Symmetric Difference: {1, 2, 4, 5}
```

### Dictionaries

Dictionaries are collections of key-value pairs. The keys must be unique and immutable, while the values can be of any type. Dictionaries are defined using curly braces with key-value pairs separated by colons.

```
student = {"name": "Alice", "age": 25, "courses": ["Math", "CompSci"]}
print(student["name"]) # Accesses the value associated with "name"
student["age"] = 26 # Updates the value associated with "age"
student["address"] = "123 Main St" # Adds a new key-value pair
del student["courses"] # Removes the key-value pair associated with "courses"
```

Dictionaries can also be traversed using loops to access keys and values.

```
for key, value in student.items():
    print(key, value)
```

Python's powerful data structures alongside its straightforward syntax make it especially suitable for implementing dynamic programming solutions. Mastery of these core elements allows for the construction of efficient, readable, and effective algorithms.

## 1.8 First Steps: Writing Your First Python Program

To start writing your first Python program, it is essential to have a firm grasp of both the theoretical and practical components of Python scripting. Python is an interpreted, high-level, and dynamically typed language that emphasizes readability and simplicity. For beginners, Python is an excellent choice due to its gentle learning curve and the wide range of available resources and community support.

A basic Python program generally comprises a sequence of statements, expressions, and possibly functions. The first program traditionally written in any new programming language is the "Hello, World!" program. Let's begin by writing this simple script and understanding its components.

```
print("Hello, World!")
```

The print() function is one of Python's built-in functions, which outputs the specified message to the console. The statement print("Hello, World!") consists of the function name print, followed by parentheses containing the string "Hello, World!".

To execute this program, follow these steps:

- Open your Python environment or text editor.
- Type the code as shown in the listing above.
- Save the file with a .py extension, for example, hello_world.py.
- Run the script by executing python hello_world.py from your command line or terminal.

Upon successful execution, the output will be:

```
Hello, World!
```

In this simple example, we've used a string, a built-in function, and saw how to run a Python script. Let's explore these components further.

**Strings**: In Python, strings are sequences of characters enclosed in quotation marks (either single ' or double "). Strings can be of arbitrary length. Some examples are:

```
'Singular'
```

```
"Double"
"This is a sentence."
'This string spans
multiple lines.'
```

**Functions**: A function is a reusable block of code that performs a single, related action. Python defines functions using the def keyword. Here's an example:

```
def greet(name):
    return "Hello, " + name + "!"

# Calling the function
print(greet("Alice"))
```

Executing this script will yield:

```
Hello, Alice!
```

Here, the function greet takes a parameter name and returns a greeting string. When called with the argument "Alice", it produces the expected greeting.

**Variables and Data Types**: Variables in Python are used to store data, which can be of various types such as integers, floats, strings, etc. Python determines the type of a variable based on the value assigned to it. Consider the following examples:

```
integer_var = 10
float_var = 20.5
string_var = "Dynamic Programming"
```

In the above example, integer_var is an integer, float_var is a floating-point number, and string_var is a string. Python is dynamically typed, meaning that the variable type is inferred at runtime.

**Comments**: Comments are essential in code for documentation and are ignored during execution. Single-line comments in Python start with the # symbol.

```
# This is a single-line comment
print("This will be printed")
```

**Basic Input and Output**: Interaction with the user can be handled via input and output functions. The input() function is used to read a line of text entered by the user.

```
name = input("Enter your name: ")
print("Hello, " + name + "!")
```

When executed, this script will prompt the user to enter their name and then greet them with a personalized message.

**Control Flow**: Python provides various control flow statements to handle decision-making (if, elif, else) and looping (while, for).

```
name = input("Enter your name: ")
if name == "Alice":
    print("Hello, Alice!")
elif name == "Bob":
    print("Greetings, Bob!")
else:
    print("Nice to meet you!")
```

In this script, different messages are printed based on the user's input.

By writing your first Python program and understanding its components, you've taken initial steps into Python programming. This foundational knowledge will be essential as we delve deeper into dynamic programming and more complex Python scripts in subsequent chapters.

## 1.9 Understanding the Pythonic Way of Thinking

The term *Pythonic* refers to the idiomatic conventions and stylistic guidelines that Python programmers adhere to. These conventions not only follow Python's design philosophy but also promote code readability, simplicity, and the efficiency of problem-solving. Understanding these conventions is critical for writing clean, robust, and maintainable code.

Python's design philosophy is summarized in the Zen of Python, which is a collection of aphorisms that capture the philosophy and ideals of the language. You can access it directly in the Python interpreter by typing:

```
import this
```

The output from this command is:

```
The Zen of Python, by Tim Peters

Beautiful is better than ugly.
Explicit is better than implicit.
Simple is better than complex.
Complex is better than complicated.
Flat is better than nested.
Sparse is better than dense.
Readability counts.
```

```
Special cases aren't special enough to break the rules.
Although practicality beats purity.
Errors should never pass silently.
Unless explicitly silenced.
In the face of ambiguity, refuse the temptation to guess.
There should be one-- and preferably only one --obvious way to do it.
Although that way may not be obvious at first unless you're Dutch.
Now is better than never.
Although never is often better than *right* now.
If the implementation is hard to explain, it's a bad idea.
If the implementation is easy to explain, it may be a good idea.
Namespaces are one honking great idea -- let's do more of those!
```

Each of these guiding principles plays an important role in defining what is considered *Pythonic* code. Let's explore these concepts in-depth.

The first principle, **"Beautiful is better than ugly."**, emphasizes the importance of code aesthetics. Python's syntax is designed to be clean and human-readable, which facilitates easier understanding and maintenance.

**"Explicit is better than implicit."** underscores the value of clarity in code. When writing functions, for example, it is better to pass parameters explicitly rather than relying on global variables or hidden states.

**"Simple is better than complex."** advocates for simplicity. This can be achieved by breaking down complex problems into smaller, more manageable functions or modules.

**"Complex is better than complicated."** while allowing for complexity when necessary, warns against making the code unnecessarily complicated. Complicated code is harder to understand and maintain.

**"Flat is better than nested."** suggests that reducing the level of nesting improves readability. Deeply nested code is harder to trace and understand.

**"Sparse is better than dense."** means that it is preferable to have a slightly less compact code that is easy to read than densely packed lines of code that can be unintelligible.

The principle **"Readability counts."** is central to the Pythonic way of thinking. Readable code is easier to debug and maintain, and Python's design emphasizes this aspect through its indentation rules and syntactic choices.

The principle **"Special cases aren't special enough to break the rules."** asserts that one should adhere to these guidelines consistently, as making exceptions can introduce confusion and errors.

Although **"practicality beats purity,"** practical considerations should not compromise the code's fundamental principles.

**"Errors should never pass silently."** highlights the importance of proper error handling. Silent errors can lead to bugs that are difficult to trace.

The principle **"In the face of ambiguity, refuse the temptation to guess."** means opting for explicit and clear code paths rather than relying on assumptions.

**"There should be one– and preferably only one –obvious way to do it."** suggests that among various possible solutions, there should be a clear, optimal approach to solving a problem. This principle is vital for maintaining a consistent style within the codebase.

**"Namespaces are one honking great idea – let's do more of those!"** encourages the use of namespaces in order to avoid name conflicts and to improve modularity.

Another critical aspect of writing Pythonic code is adhering to PEP 8, the Python Enhancement Proposal which outlines the conventions for Python code. PEP 8 covers everything: naming styles, indentation, comments, and more.

For example, PEP 8 recommends using 4 spaces per indentation level:

```
def my_function(x, y):
    if x > y:
        print("x is greater than y")
    else:
        print("x is not greater than y")
```

PEP 8 also encourages meaningful naming of variables and functions, using snake_case for variable and function names, and CapWords for class names:

```
# Good:
def calculate_area(radius):
    pass

class Circle:
    pass

# Bad:
def calculateArea(radius):
    pass

class circle:
    pass
```

Additionally, PEP 8 suggests limiting all lines to a maximum of 79 characters, which ensures readability across various devices and interfaces.

Comments should be used judiciously to explain why certain decisions were made in the code.

```
# Calculate the area of a circle
def calculate_area(radius):
    import math
    return math.pi * (radius ** 2)
```

Docstrings are another Pythonic practice and provide inline documentation for modules, classes, methods, and functions. The built-in **help()** function can be used to access the docstrings of any module, class, or function, which is handy. For example:

```
def calculate_area(radius):
    """
    Calculate the area of a circle.

    Parameters:
    radius (float): The radius of the circle

    Returns:
    float: The area of the circle
    """
    import math
    return math.pi * (radius ** 2)
```

By adhering to these principles, one not only writes efficient and functional code but also ensures that the codebase remains clean, consistent, and easy to understand for other contributors. The Pythonic way of thinking fosters collaborative coding, simplifies debugging, and enhances the development process.

## 1.10 Comparing Dynamic Programming with Other Techniques

Dynamic programming (DP) is a method used for solving problems by breaking them down into simpler subproblems and solving each one only once, storing their solutions. This paradigm is notably distinct from other problem-solving techniques. To understand the full utility and scope of dynamic programming, it is instructive to compare it with other techniques such as divide-and-conquer, greedy algorithms, and brute force methods.

**Divide-and-Conquer**

Divide-and-conquer algorithms work by recursively breaking down a problem into smaller subproblems, solving the subproblems, and combining their solutions to solve the original problem. This approach is highly effective for problems that can be naturally divided into non-overlapping subproblems. For instance, the merge sort algorithm employs divide-and-conquer by splitting the array into halves, recursively sorting each half, and finally merging the sorted halves.

In contrast, dynamic programming is particularly useful for problems where subproblems overlap and recursive decomposition leads to redundant computations. For example, the Fibonacci sequence can be solved by both divide-and-conquer and dynamic programming. However, the former leads to an exponential time complexity due to redundant calculations, while the latter harnesses memoization to achieve polynomial time complexity. Here is a comparison using Python code:

```
# Divide-and-Conquer approach to Fibonacci sequence
def fib_dc(n):
    if n <= 1:
        return n
    return fib_dc(n-1) + fib_dc(n-2)

# Dynamic Programming approach to Fibonacci sequence
def fib_dp(n, memo={}):
    if n in memo:
        return memo[n]
    if n <= 1:
        return n
    memo[n] = fib_dp(n-1, memo) + fib_dp(n-2, memo)
    return memo[n]
```

The time complexity of the divide-and-conquer approach is $O(2^n)$, while the dynamic programming approach reduces it to $O(n)$ due to the elimination of redundant calculations.

### Greedy Algorithms

Greedy algorithms work by making the locally optimal choice at each stage with the hope of finding a global optimum. This method is efficient and simple but only works for certain types of problems where a global optimum can be achieved through a series of local optima, known as greedy-choice property and optimal substructure.

A classical example where greedy algorithms and dynamic programming can both be applied is the knapsack problem. The fractional knapsack problem can be solved efficiently using a greedy algorithm, as items can be broken into smaller pieces, and the decision to include an item is straightforward.

For the 0/1 knapsack problem, a greedy approach may not always yield the optimal solution due to the binary nature of item inclusion. This problem is better suited for dynamic programming, which can evaluate all possible combinations of items to find the optimal solution. Here is a comparative implementation:

```
# Greedy approach to the fractional knapsack problem
def fractional_knapsack(items, capacity):
    items.sort(key=lambda x: x[1]/x[0], reverse=True) # Sort by value-to-weight ratio
    total_value = 0
    for weight, value in items:
        if capacity >= weight:
            capacity -= weight
            total_value += value
        else:
            total_value += value * (capacity / weight)
            break
    return total_value

# Dynamic Programming approach to the 0/1 knapsack problem
def knapsack_01(weights, values, capacity):
    n = len(weights)
    dp = [[0 for x in range(capacity + 1)] for x in range(n + 1)]
    for i in range(n + 1):
        for w in range(capacity + 1):
            if i == 0 or w == 0:
                dp[i][w] = 0
            elif weights[i-1] <= w:
                dp[i][w] = max(values[i-1] + dp[i-1][w-weights[i-1]], dp[i-1][w])
            else:
                dp[i][w] = dp[i-1][w]
    return dp[n][capacity]
```

The greedy approach is not suitable for the 0/1 knapsack problem as it can lead to suboptimal solutions. In contrast, the dynamic programming approach guarantees the optimal solution, but at the expense of higher computational overhead.

### Brute Force Methods

Brute force methods explore all possible solutions to a problem and select the best one. While this approach is straightforward and guarantees an optimal solution, it is often impractical for large problem instances due to its exponential time complexity.

Consider again the 0/1 knapsack problem. A brute force solution would involve evaluating all possible subsets of items to find the maximum value that can be accommodated in the knapsack. The time complexity for this brute force approach is $O(2^n)$, compared to $O(nW)$ for the dynamic programming approach, where $W$ is the capacity of the knapsack.

```
# Brute force approach to the 0/1 knapsack problem
def knapsack_brute_force(weights, values, capacity):
    def knapsack_recursive(n, W):
        if n == 0 or W == 0:
            return 0
        if weights[n-1] > W:
```

```
            return knapsack_recursive(n-1, W)
        else:
            return max(values[n-1] + knapsack_recursive(n-1, W-weights[n-1]),
                       knapsack_recursive(n-1, W))

    return knapsack_recursive(len(weights), capacity)
```

While brute force ensures an optimal solution, it is computationally infeasible for large $n$, making dynamic programming a more practical approach for many applications.

By comparing dynamic programming with divide-and-conquer, greedy algorithms, and brute force methods, it becomes clear that DP is particularly powerful when dealing with problems that have overlapping subproblems and require storing intermediate results. This distinguishes DP as an essential technique for optimizing recursive solutions in computationally intensive problems.

## 1.11 Examples of Real-World Problems Solved by Dynamic Programming

Dynamic programming (DP) is a powerful technique used to solve a wide variety of problems in diverse domains. In this section, we will explore several real-world problems addressed effectively using dynamic programming. These examples will illustrate the practical applicability of DP and provide insights into formulating and solving problems with this paradigm.

**1. The Knapsack Problem**

The knapsack problem is a classical optimization problem where the objective is to maximize the total value of items placed in a knapsack of fixed capacity. Given a set of items, each with a weight and value, the goal is to determine the combination of items to include in the knapsack such that the total weight does not exceed the knapsack's capacity while maximizing the total value.

```
def knapsack(weights, values, capacity):
    n = len(weights)
    dp = [[0 for _ in range(capacity + 1)] for _ in range(n + 1)]

    for i in range(1, n + 1):
        for w in range(1, capacity + 1):
            if weights[i - 1] <= w:
                dp[i][w] = max(values[i - 1] + dp[i - 1][w - weights[i - 1]], dp[i - 1][w])
            else:
                dp[i][w] = dp[i - 1][w]
```

```
    return dp[n][capacity]

weights = [1, 2, 3, 4]
values = [100, 300, 350, 500]
capacity = 5
print("Maximum value in knapsack:", knapsack(weights, values, capacity))
```

The above Python code demonstrates a dynamic programming solution to the knapsack problem. It constructs a 2D array 'dp' where 'dp[i][w]' represents the maximum value that can be obtained with the first 'i' items and a knapsack capacity of 'w'. The final solution is obtained at 'dp[n][capacity]'.

**2. The Longest Common Subsequence (LCS) Problem**

The Longest Common Subsequence problem involves finding the longest subsequence common to two given sequences. This problem has applications in bioinformatics for DNA sequence analysis and in text comparison tools.

```
def lcs(X, Y):
    m = len(X)
    n = len(Y)
    dp = [[0 for _ in range(n + 1)] for _ in range(m + 1)]

    for i in range(1, m + 1):
        for j in range(1, n + 1):
            if X[i - 1] == Y[j - 1]:
                dp[i][j] = 1 + dp[i - 1][j - 1]
            else:
                dp[i][j] = max(dp[i - 1][j], dp[i][j - 1])

    return dp[m][n]

X = "AGGTAB"
Y = "GXTXAYB"
print("Length of LCS:", lcs(X, Y))
```

The above code computes the length of the longest common subsequence between two strings 'X' and 'Y'. The 'dp' array is used to store the lengths of the longest common subsequences of substrings of 'X' and 'Y'. The value 'dp[m][n]' gives the length of the LCS for the input strings.

**3. The Matrix Chain Multiplication Problem**

Matrix Chain Multiplication is a problem of determining the most efficient way to multiply a given sequence of matrices. The task is to find the minimum number of multiplications needed to multiply the matrices.

```
def matrix_chain_order(p):
    n = len(p) - 1
    dp = [[0 for _ in range(n)] for _ in range(n)]
```

```
    for l in range(2, n + 1):
        for i in range(n - l + 1):
            j = i + l - 1
            dp[i][j] = float('inf')
            for k in range(i, j):
                q = dp[i][k] + dp[k + 1][j] + p[i] * p[k + 1] * p[j + 1]
                if q < dp[i][j]:
                    dp[i][j] = q
    return dp[0][n - 1]

p = [10, 20, 30, 40, 30]
print("Minimum number of multiplications:", matrix_chain_order(p))
```

This code finds the minimum number of scalar multiplications required to multiply a chain of matrices with dimensions defined in array 'p'. The 'dp' array stores the minimum cost for matrix multiplications.

**4. The Fibonacci Sequence**

The Fibonacci sequence is an excellent example of a problem that benefits significantly from dynamic programming. The sequence is defined as $F(n) = F(n-1) + F(n-2)$ with base cases $F(0) = 0$ and $F(1) = 1$.

```
def fibonacci(n):
    if n <= 1:
        return n
    dp = [0] * (n + 1)
    dp[1] = 1

    for i in range(2, n + 1):
        dp[i] = dp[i - 1] + dp[i - 2]

    return dp[n]

n = 10
print("Fibonacci number:", fibonacci(n))
```

In this implementation, the 'dp' array is used to store the Fibonacci numbers up to 'F(n)'. This approach ensures that each Fibonacci number is computed only once and stored for future reference.

**5. The Edit Distance Problem**

The Edit Distance (or Levenshtein Distance) problem computes the minimum number of operations required to convert one string into another. The allowed operations are insertion, deletion, and substitution.

```
def edit_distance(str1, str2):
    m = len(str1)
    n = len(str2)
    dp = [[0 for _ in range(n + 1)] for _ in range(m + 1)]

    for i in range(m + 1):
        for j in range(n + 1):
```

```
            if i == 0:
                dp[i][j] = j
            elif j == 0:
                dp[i][j] = i
            elif str1[i - 1] == str2[j - 1]:
                dp[i][j] = dp[i - 1][j - 1]
            else:
                dp[i][j] = 1 + min(dp[i][j - 1], dp[i - 1][j], dp[i - 1][j - 1])

    return dp[m][n]

str1 = "kitten"
str2 = "sitting"
print("Edit Distance:", edit_distance(str1, str2))
```

This dynamic programming solution utilizes a 2D array ‘dp‘ where ‘dp[i][j]‘ represents the edit distance between the first ‘i‘ characters of ‘str1‘ and the first ‘j‘ characters of ‘str2‘.

These examples demonstrate the versatility of dynamic programming in solving complex problems efficiently by breaking them into simpler subproblems, solving each subproblem once, and storing their solutions. This method not only optimizes the computational process but also enhances the understanding of problem structures and solutions.

## 1.12 Overview of the Book Structure

The structure of this book is meticulously designed to build a robust understanding of dynamic programming (DP) through Python, progressing from fundamental concepts to expert-level applications. Each chapter is strategically organized to introduce new topics while reinforcing previously covered material.

The book is organized into the following chapters:

- **Chapter 1: Introduction to Dynamic Programming and Python**
- **Chapter 2: Fundamental Concepts of Dynamic Programming**
- **Chapter 3: Recursive and Iterative Solutions**
- **Chapter 4: Memoization Techniques**
- **Chapter 5: Tabulation Method**
- **Chapter 6: Advanced Dynamic Programming Strategies**

- **Chapter 7: Dynamic Programming on Trees**
- **Chapter 8: Dynamic Programming in Graph Theory**
- **Chapter 9: String Processing with Dynamic Programming**
- **Chapter 10: Optimization Problems and Dynamic Programming**
- **Chapter 11: Real-World Applications of Dynamic Programming**
- **Chapter 12: Case Studies and Complex Problem-Solving**

Chapter 1 sets the stage by introducing what dynamic programming is, its historical context, key concepts, and terminologies. It underscores the significance of DP and provides an overview of Python programming, aiming to equip readers with the foundational tools necessary for subsequent chapters.

Chapter 2 dives into the core principles of DP, including overlapping subproblems and optimal substructure property. This chapter serves as the theoretical underpinning for all the practical implementations that follow. Careful attention is given to articulating why these principles are crucial in simplifying complex problems.

Chapter 3 examines the two primary styles of DP: recursive and iterative solutions. Through Python examples, readers will learn how to identify recursive relationships and convert them into iterative approaches when appropriate. Each code example is wrapped in the lstlisting environment, and the corresponding outputs are displayed in the FittedVerbatim environment for clarity.

In Chapter 4, memoization techniques are introduced. This approach to dynamic programming involves storing the results of expensive function calls and reusing them when the same inputs occur again. The chapter details various memoization strategies in Python, emphasizing both the functools.lru_cache and custom implementations.

Chapter 5 explores the tabulation method, another critical strategy in DP. Unlike memoization, which is top-down, tabulation is a bottom-up approach. Python implementations are provided for a range of problems, illustrating how to build a table to store results of subproblems and using this table to construct the solution to the overall problem.

Advanced strategies in DP are the focus of Chapter 6. Here, readers are introduced to techniques such as state-space reduction, dynamics on subsets, and more. This chapter bridges the gap between fundamental methods and more sophisticated problem-solving strategies.

Chapter 7 delves into dynamic programming on trees, a special data structure with unique properties. It covers Tree DP problems, such as finding the diameter of a tree, and includes thorough Python implementations to guide readers through these complex problems.

Chapter 8 extends the discussion to graph theory, addressing problems where dynamic programming can be applied to graphs. Topics such as shortest paths, longest paths, and other graph-based problems are examined. Detailed explanations and Python code snippets illustrate the practical applications of these methods.

String processing with DP is covered in Chapter 9. This chapter focuses on classic problems such as longest common subsequence, edit distance, and pattern matching. Python implementations for each problem help solidify the reader's understanding of these algorithms.

In Chapter 10, optimization problems and DP converge. Problems like the knapsack problem, coin change, and others are tackled. Emphasis is placed on formulating these problems in a DP framework and efficiently solving them using Python.

Real-world applications in Chapter 11 showcase how DP is used in various domains, such as bioinformatics, economics, and artificial intelligence. Each application is accompanied by a practical Python implementation that highlights DP's versatility and power.

Chapter 12 presents case studies and complex problem-solving. This chapter synthesizes the concepts learned throughout the book by examining detailed case studies. Each case study includes problem statements, theoretical analysis, and comprehensive Python solutions, serving as exemplars for tackling complex problems in practice.

By structuring the book in this manner, readers are equipped with a progressive understanding of dynamic programming and its applications in Python. Each chapter builds on the last, ensuring a cohesive and comprehensive learning experience.

# Chapter 2

# Fundamentals of Recursion

**This chapter introduces the foundational concepts of recursion, an essential technique for solving problems that can be broken down into smaller, similar subproblems. We will explore how recursion works, the significance of base and recursive cases, and the differences between recursive and iterative solutions. The chapter includes practical examples in Python, discussions on common pitfalls, and debugging strategies for recursive programs. Additional topics such as stack frames and tail recursion are covered to provide a comprehensive understanding of recursion's role in problem-solving.**

## 2.1 Introduction to Recursion

Recursion is a fundamental programming technique employed to solve problems that can be broken down into simpler, similar subproblems. A recursive function is one that calls itself to compute its result, typically by reducing the problem into smaller instances each time. This concept, although straightforward in its definition, often requires a deep understanding to implement efficiently and correctly in practical scenarios.

At its core, recursion involves two key components: the base case and the recursive case. The base case serves as the stopping criterion, preventing the function from calling itself indefinitely and thereby avoiding infinite loops. The recursive case is the part of a function where the function calls itself with reduced or transformed arguments, gradually progressing towards the base case.

To illustrate the idea of recursion, consider the classic example of computing the factorial of a number. The factorial of a non-negative integer $n$ is the product of all positive integers less than or equal to $n$, denoted as $n!$. The factorial function can be defined recursively as follows:

$$n! = \begin{cases} 1 & \text{if } n = 0 \\ n \times (n-1)! & \text{if } n > 0 \end{cases}$$

Here, the base case is when $n = 0$ and the result is 1. The recursive case is when $n > 0$, where the function calls itself with the argument $n - 1$.

In Python, a recursive implementation of the factorial function can be written as:

```
def factorial(n):
    if n == 0:
        return 1
    else:
        return n * factorial(n - 1)

# Example usage
print(factorial(5)) # Output: 120
```

Executing the above code with $n = 5$, the recursive function calls can be visualized as follows:

```
factorial(5)
= 5 * factorial(4)
= 5 * (4 * factorial(3))
= 5 * (4 * (3 * factorial(2)))
= 5 * (4 * (3 * (2 * factorial(1))))
= 5 * (4 * (3 * (2 * (1 * factorial(0)))))
= 5 * (4 * (3 * (2 * (1 * 1))))
= 120
```

This example demonstrates the process of breaking down the problem (computing factorial of 5) into smaller subproblems (computing factorial of 4, 3, 2, 1, 0) and combining their results to obtain the final answer.

While recursion provides an elegant and natural way to solve certain problems, it is crucial to assess whether it is the most efficient approach for a given problem. Recursive solutions may lead to significant overhead in terms of memory and execution time due to repeated function calls and stack frame management. Therefore, it is important to consider the potential drawbacks and explore alternative solutions, such as iterative approaches, when appropriate.

Understanding the recursive approach requires an appreciation of how function calls are managed in a stack data structure. Each recursive call creates a new stack frame encapsulating the function's execution context, including its parameters and local variables. Once the base case is reached, the stack frames are unwound in reverse order, each returning a result to its caller until the entire computation is completed.

In the context of recursion, the concept of stack overflow represents a critical pitfall where excessive recursive calls exhaust the limited stack space available, leading to a program crash. Establishing a correct and efficient base case is paramount to preventing such issues.

Moreover, common pitfalls include infinite recursion due to incorrect base conditions and handling large input sizes where iterative approaches might be more efficient. These aspects will be discussed in greater detail in subsequent sections.

An in-depth understanding of recursion provides a powerful tool for algorithm design and problem-solving. Mastery of recursive thinking enhances the ability to decompose complex problems, leading to elegant and efficient solutions across various domains.

## 2.2 How Recursion Works

Recursion operates on the principle of breaking a complex problem into smaller subproblems, each of which resembles the original. Understanding the mechanics of recursion requires familiarity with the two crucial components of any recursive function: the base case and the recursive case. The base case provides the condition under which the function stops calling itself, preventing infinite recursion. The recursive case involves the function calling itself with a modified argument that progressively brings it closer to the base case.

In practical terms, every recursive function must ensure two things: it must handle a base case to avoid infinite loops, and it must modify its state in each recursive call to approach the base case.

Consider the classic example of calculating the factorial of a number $n$. The factorial of $n$ (denoted as $n!$) is defined as the product of all integers from 1 to $n$. The mathematical definition is as follows:

$$n! = \begin{cases} 1 & \text{if } n = 0 \\ n \times (n-1)! & \text{if } n > 0 \end{cases}$$

In this definition, the base case is $n = 0$, where $0! = 1$, and the recursive case is $n \times (n-1)!$.

A Python implementation of this recursive definition is straightforward:

```
def factorial(n):
    if n == 0:
        return 1
    else:
        return n * factorial(n - 1)
```

To deepen our understanding, let us analyze how this function executes with $n = 3$:

- The initial call is 'factorial(3)'.
- Inside 'factorial(3)', 'n' is not '0', so the function returns $3 \times factorial(2)$.
- The call 'factorial(2)' is made. Again, 'n' is not '0', so the function returns $2 \times factorial(1)$.
- The call 'factorial(1)' is made. Yet again, 'n' is not '0', so the function returns $1 \times factorial(0)$.
- The call 'factorial(0)' is made. This time 'n = 0', so the function returns '1'.

The call stack during this execution would resemble the following:

```
factorial(3)
  factorial(2)
    factorial(1)
      factorial(0)
```

As each recursive call returns, the stack unwinds, yielding:

```
factorial(0) returns 1
factorial(1) computes 1 * 1 = 1 and returns 1
factorial(2) computes 2 * 1 = 2 and returns 2
factorial(3) computes 3 * 2 = 6 and returns 6
```

The final return value of 'factorial(3)' is '6'. This step-by-step progression shows how recursion reduces the complexity of the original problem by solving progressively smaller instances until reaching the simplest possible problem, the base case.

Understanding recursion requires carefully tracking function calls and the stack frames they generate. Each invocation of the function creates a new stack frame, maintaining its own independent execution context containing parameters and local variables. This separation is crucial for preventing variable overlap and ensuring correct logic flow.

The recursive Fibonacci sequence calculation offers another example to examine:

$$F(n) = \begin{cases} 0 & \text{if } n = 0 \\ 1 & \text{if } n = 1 \\ F(n-1) + F(n-2) & \text{if } n > 1 \end{cases}$$

Here is the Python code for the Fibonacci sequence:

```
def fibonacci(n):
    if n == 0:
        return 0
    elif n == 1:
        return 1
    else:
        return fibonacci(n - 1) + fibonacci(n - 2)
```

Analyzing ‘fibonacci(4)‘ helps clarify the recursive process:

- ‘fibonacci(4)‘ returns ‘fibonacci(3) + fibonacci(2)‘.
- ‘fibonacci(3)‘ returns ‘fibonacci(2) + fibonacci(1)‘.
- ‘fibonacci(2)‘ returns ‘fibonacci(1) + fibonacci(0)‘.
- ‘fibonacci(1)‘ returns 1 (base case).
- ‘fibonacci(0)‘ returns 0 (base case).

Constructing the call tree visualizes the recursive breakdown:

```
fibonacci(4)
|---fibonacci(3)
|   |---fibonacci(2)
|   |   |---fibonacci(1) returns 1
|   |   |---fibonacci(0) returns 0
|   |---fibonacci(1) returns 1
|---fibonacci(2)
    |---fibonacci(1) returns 1
    |---fibonacci(0) returns 0
```

Combining returns provides:

```
fibonacci(2) returns 1 (1+0)
fibonacci(3) returns 2 (1+1)
fibonacci(4) returns 3 (2+1)
```

The recursive definition effectively showcases how problems decompose into manageable subproblems, which resolve to yield the final solution.

## 2.3 Base Case and Recursive Case

The foundation of any recursive function is built upon two fundamental components: the **base case** and the **recursive case**. Understanding these elements is vital for crafting efficient and effective recursive solutions.

A correctly formulated recursion must always make progress towards the base case, which ensures the function does not continue to call itself indefinitely. To illustrate these concepts, we can analyze the classic example of computing the factorial of a number $n$.

The **factorial** of a non-negative integer $n$ is the product of all positive integers less than or equal to $n$ and is denoted as $n!$. Mathematically, it can be expressed as:

$$n! = \begin{cases} 1 & \text{if } n = 0 \\ n \cdot (n-1)! & \text{if } n > 0 \end{cases}$$

In the definition above, the factorial of $0$ is given as $1$. This forms our **base case**. For $n > 0$, the function is defined in terms of itself, representing the **recursive case**.

### Base Case

The **base case** is a critical stopping condition in a recursive function. This case specifies the scenario where the function returns a value directly without making further recursive calls. It ensures the recursion will eventually terminate. In our factorial example, the base case is $0! = 1$. In practice, this translates to:

```
def factorial(n):
    if n == 0:
        return 1
```

This segment of code checks if $n$ is $0$ and returns $1$, effectively stopping further recursion. Without a base case, a recursive function would enter an infinite loop, ultimately leading to a stack overflow error.

### Recursive Case

The **recursive case** implements the logic where the function calls itself with arguments that progressively approach the base case. It should reduce the problem's size with each call, converging towards the base case. In our factorial function, for $n > 0$, the function returns $n$ times the factorial of $n - 1$:

```
def factorial(n):
    if n == 0:
        return 1
    else:
        return n * factorial(n - 1)
```

In this example, each call to factorial(n) will lead to a subsequent call to factorial(n-1), continuing until $n$ reaches $0$, the base case.

By running this piece of code,

```
print(factorial(5))
```

we observe the following steps:

```
factorial(5)
  -> 5 * factorial(4)
    -> 4 * factorial(3)
      -> 3 * factorial(2)
        -> 2 * factorial(1)
          -> 1 * factorial(0)
            -> 1
```

Combining these steps yields $5! = 5 \times 4 \times 3 \times 2 \times 1 = 120.$

### Ensuring Progress

The structure of recursive functions must guarantee progress towards the base case. Each recursive call should modify the input arguments in such a way that they steadily converge towards the base condition. In our factorial example, $n$ is decremented by $1$ in each call until it reaches $0$.

Improper recursive definitions that do not approach a base case will result in infinite recursion. For instance,

```
def faulty_factorial(n):
    return n * faulty_factorial(n)
```

Running this faulty function,

```
print(faulty_factorial(5))
```

would cause infinite recursion, eventually leading to a *RecursionError* due to exceeding the maximum recursion depth.

The meticulous design of base and recursive cases ensures efficient recursive solutions. The synergy between these two components underpins the elegance and power of recursion, enabling the decomposition of complex problems into manageable sub-problems, ultimately converging to a solution.

## 2.4 Simple Recursive Functions

Understanding the core mechanics of recursion begins with examining simple recursive functions. These functions encapsulate the fundamental principles of recursion: calling a function from within itself to solve progressively smaller instances of the same problem. This section will illustrate these principles through basic Python examples.

A quintessential example of a simple recursive function is computing the factorial of a number. The factorial of a non-negative integer $n$ is the product of all positive integers less than or equal to $n$. This can be defined recursively as follows:

$$\text{factorial}(n) = \begin{cases} 1 & \text{if } n = 0 \\ n \times \text{factorial}(n-1) & \text{if } n > 0 \end{cases}$$

In Python, this recursive definition translates into the following code:

```
def factorial(n):
    if n == 0:
        return 1
    else:
        return n * factorial(n - 1)
```

When we call $\text{factorial}(5)$, the following sequence of function calls and returns occurs:

- $\text{factorial}(5)$ calls $\text{factorial}(4)$
- $\text{factorial}(4)$ calls $\text{factorial}(3)$
- $\text{factorial}(3)$ calls $\text{factorial}(2)$
- $\text{factorial}(2)$ calls $\text{factorial}(1)$
- $\text{factorial}(1)$ calls $\text{factorial}(0)$
- $\text{factorial}(0)$ returns 1 (base case)
- $\text{factorial}(1)$ returns $1 \times 1 = 1$

- factorial(2) returns $2 \times 1 = 2$
- factorial(3) returns $3 \times 2 = 6$
- factorial(4) returns $4 \times 6 = 24$
- factorial(5) returns $5 \times 24 = 120$

By breaking down the problem into smaller subproblems and leveraging the base case to terminate the recursion, this function effectively computes the factorial of any non-negative integer.

Another well-known example is computing the $n$-th Fibonacci number. The Fibonacci sequence is defined recursively as:

$$F(n) = \begin{cases} 0 & \text{if } n = 0 \\ 1 & \text{if } n = 1 \\ F(n-1) + F(n-2) & \text{if } n \geq 2 \end{cases}$$

The corresponding Python implementation is:

```
def fibonacci(n):
    if n == 0:
        return 0
    elif n == 1:
        return 1
    else:
        return fibonacci(n - 1) + fibonacci(n - 2)
```

When fibonacci(5) is invoked, it breaks down into a series of recursive calls as follows:

- fibonacci(5) calls fibonacci(4) and fibonacci(3)
- fibonacci(4) calls fibonacci(3) and fibonacci(2)
- fibonacci(3) calls fibonacci(2) and fibonacci(1)
- fibonacci(2) calls fibonacci(1) and fibonacci(0)
- fibonacci(1) returns 1
- fibonacci(0) returns 0
- fibonacci(2) returns $1 + 0 = 1$
- fibonacci(3) returns $1 + 1 = 2$

- $\text{fibonacci}(2)$ returns $1 + 0 = 1$
- $\text{fibonacci}(4)$ returns $2 + 1 = 3$
- $\text{fibonacci}(3)$ returns $1 + 1 = 2$
- $\text{fibonacci}(5)$ returns $3 + 2 = 5$

These examples underscore two key components of any recursive function:

- **Base Case:** The condition under which the recursion terminates. Without a base case, the function will continue to call itself indefinitely, leading to a stack overflow.
- **Recursive Case:** The part of the function that includes the recursive call. This typically involves breaking down the problem into smaller instances.

In writing recursive functions, one must ensure that each recursive call brings the problem closer to the base case to prevent infinite recursion. The core simplicity of these functions lies in their structure and clarity, making them valuable tools for solving a variety of problems in a granular, step-by-step manner without loop constructs.

## 2.5 Recursive vs. Iterative Solutions

When solving computational problems, two primary strategies are often considered: recursion and iteration. Both techniques can be used to achieve the same results, but they offer unique advantages and drawbacks. This section delves into the distinctions, use cases, and practical considerations for choosing between recursive and iterative solutions.

**Recursion** involves solving a problem by breaking it down into smaller instances of the same problem. A recursive function calls itself with modified parameters until reaching a base case where the problem can be solved directly. Mathematically, this is often represented as:

$$f(n) = \begin{cases} base\_case & \text{if } n \text{ is the base case,} \\ recursive\_relation & \text{otherwise.} \end{cases}$$

**Iteration**, on the other hand, uses looping constructs to repeat operations until a certain condition is met. Algorithms are expressed using for loops, while loops, or similar constructs. The process is generally explicit, with clear control over the execution flow.

### Factorial Example (Recursive Solution)

```
def factorial_recursive(n):
    if n == 0:
        return 1 # base case
    else:
        return n * factorial_recursive(n - 1) # recursive case
```

### Factorial Example (Iterative Solution)

```
def factorial_iterative(n):
    result = 1
    for i in range(1, n + 1):
        result *= i
    return result
```

When comparing recursive and iterative solutions, several key factors must be evaluated:

**1. Readability and Maintainability:** Recursive algorithms often provide a clearer and more intuitive representation of the problem, especially when dealing with problems that have a natural recursive structure (e.g., tree traversal, Fibonacci sequence). They closely match the mathematical or logical definition of the problem. However, deeply recursive solutions can be harder to debug due to the implicit flow of execution.

Iterative solutions, while potentially more verbose, make the flow of execution explicit, often resulting in code that is easier to follow and debug. Loop invariants can also be explicitly stated and verified.

**2. Time Complexity:** Both recursive and iterative algorithms can have similar time complexity if designed correctly. However, careless use of recursion can lead to excessive recomputation of values and exponential time complexity. For example, the naive recursive Fibonacci algorithm:

```
def fibonacci_recursive(n):
    if n <= 1:
        return n
    else:
        return fibonacci_recursive(n-1) + fibonacci_recursive(n-2)
```

has exponential time complexity, making it impractical for large $n$.

In contrast, an iterative solution with linear time complexity:

```
def fibonacci_iterative(n):
    a, b = 0, 1
    for _ in range(n):
        a, b = b, a + b
    return a
```

is much more efficient.

**3. Space Complexity:** Recursive solutions can incur a significant space overhead due to the function call stack. Each recursive call adds a new frame to the call stack until the base case is reached. This can lead to stack overflow errors if the recursion depth is too large. For example, trying to compute the factorial of a very large number recursively can exceed the stack size limit.

Iterative solutions generally use a fixed amount of memory, regardless of the input size. This is because they do not rely on the call stack but rather on looping constructs and a finite set of variables. Thus, iterative algorithms often have lower space complexity, making them suitable for memory-constrained environments.

**4. Tail Recursion:** Tail recursion is a specific case of recursion where the recursive call is the last operation in the function. Compilers and interpreters can optimize tail-recursive functions to avoid adding a new call frame to the stack, thereby mitigating some of the space overheads. Here is an example of a tail-recursive factorial function:

```
def factorial_tail_recursive(n, acc=1):
    if n == 0:
        return acc
    else:
        return factorial_tail_recursive(n - 1, n * acc)
```

Conversely, if the language or runtime environment does not support tail call optimization (TCO), tail-recursive functions will still suffer from the same stack overflow risks as non-tail-recursive functions.

**5. Recursion Depth:** Python's default recursion depth limit can result in a RecursionError for highly recursive functions. This limitation requires either optimization of the recursive algorithm or adjusting the recursion limit via the sys.setrecursionlimit() function, which has its own risks and drawbacks.

Understanding the fundamental differences in performance, readability, and application constraints makes it easier to determine when to use recursion versus iteration. While recursion aligns naturally with many problem formulations, iteration offers control and efficiency that are often necessary in real-world applications.

## 2.6 Understanding Stack Frames

Understanding how stack frames work is pivotal to mastering recursion and effectively debugging recursive programs. A stack frame is a data structure that contains information about a function call, including the function's parameters, local variables, return address, and the point at which the function's execution should continue after it returns. Each time a function is called, a new stack frame is allocated on the call stack.

In recursive functions, the call stack grows with each recursive call, adding a new stack frame for each invocation. This section delves into the mechanics of stack frames, providing a comprehensive analysis of their role in recursion using detailed examples.

```
def factorial(n):
    if n == 0:
        return 1
    else:
        return n * factorial(n-1)

factorial(3)
```

When the function factorial(3) is called, the sequence of stack frames is as follows:

1. The call to factorial(3) creates a stack frame with $n = 3$. 2. factorial(3) calls factorial(2), adding a new stack frame with $n = 2$. 3. factorial(2) calls factorial(1), adding a new stack frame with $n = 1$. 4. factorial(1) calls factorial(0), adding a new stack frame with $n = 0$. 5. factorial(0) reaches the base case and returns 1.

The return values are then propagated back up the call stack:

```
factorial(0) returns 1
factorial(1) returns 1 * 1 = 1
factorial(2) returns 2 * 1 = 2
factorial(3) returns 3 * 2 = 6
```

To visualize the stack frames, consider the following diagram where each box represents a stack frame and the arrow indicates the function call sequence:

factorial(3) $\rightarrow$ factorial(2) $\rightarrow$ factorial(1) $\rightarrow$ factorial(0)

As each function call returns, its corresponding stack frame is popped off the call stack, and execution continues in the previous frame.

Stack frames are essential because they maintain the state of each function call in terms of its parameters and local variables. Any changes to variables in one stack frame do not affect other stack frames, providing isolation between function calls. This isolation is what allows recursive functions to operate correctly, independently handling each recursive subproblem.

To further understand stack frames, consider the following Python code that includes debugging print statements to illustrate the creation and destruction of stack frames:

```
def factorial(n):
    print(f"Entering factorial({n})")
    if n == 0:
        result = 1
    else:
        result = n * factorial(n-1)
    print(f"Leaving factorial({n}) with result {result}")
    return result

factorial(3)
```

The output of this program clearly shows the sequence of calls and returns:

```
Entering factorial(3)
Entering factorial(2)
Entering factorial(1)
Entering factorial(0)
Leaving factorial(0) with result 1
Leaving factorial(1) with result 1
Leaving factorial(2) with result 2
Leaving factorial(3) with result 6
```

Each Entering factorial(n) line corresponds to the creation of a new stack frame. Each Leaving factorial(n) line indicates that the function has completed execution and its stack frame will be removed from the call stack.

Recursive functions can lead to stack overflow if the depth of recursion exceeds the maximum stack size. This is because each recursive call consumes additional stack space. To illustrate a stack overflow, consider the following code:

```
def infinite_recursion(n):
    print(n)
    infinite_recursion(n+1)

infinite_recursion(1)
```

Running this code would eventually result in a RecursionError: maximum recursion depth exceeded. This outcome emphasizes the importance of having a base case in any recursive function to ensure that it terminates.

Understanding stack frames also sheds light on why certain optimizations, such as tail recursion, can be beneficial. Tail recursion is a specific form of recursion where the recursive call is the last action in the function. In some programming languages, tail recursion can be optimized by the compiler to reuse the current function's stack frame for the next function call, minimizing stack growth. Unfortunately, Python does not perform tail call optimization, so tail recursive functions in Python will still create new stack frames for each call.

By comprehensively grasping how stack frames function and their impact on recursive calls, programmers can write more efficient and debuggable recursive functions, making the most of recursion's powerful problem-solving capabilities.

## 2.7 Common Pitfalls in Recursion

When working with recursion, certain pitfalls are frequently encountered by both novice and experienced programmers. These issues can lead to excessive computational overhead, stack overflow errors, and incorrect results. In this section, we will delve into these common pitfalls to aid in identifying and mitigating them.

**Infinite Recursion:**

Infinite recursion occurs when the base case is either absent or incorrectly specified, causing the recursive calls to continue indefinitely until a stack overflow occurs. Each recursive call consumes a new stack frame, and without termination, the system's stack memory will be exhausted.

```
def infinite_recursion(n):
    print("Recursing with n =", n)
    infinite_recursion(n + 1)

# Calling the function causes infinite recursion
infinite_recursion(1)
```

The output of running this code:

```
Recursing with n = 1
Recursing with n = 2
Recursing with n = 3
...
Recursing with n = 999998
Recursing with n = 999999
Traceback (most recent call last):
...
RecursionError: maximum recursion depth exceeded
```

To prevent infinite recursion, it is essential to identify and correctly implement a base case, which acts as the stopping condition.

**Incorrect Base Case:**

An incorrectly defined base case can yield misleading results or fail to stop the recursion. It is crucial to ensure that the base case correctly represents the simplest instance of the problem.

```
def incorrect_base_case(n):
    if n == 1:
        return 1
    return n + incorrect_base_case(n - 2)

# Possible unintended behavior or runtime error
result = incorrect_base_case(10)
print(result)
```

The expected output does not match the recursion logic, leading to incorrect results. The correct base case must be identified according to the problem's requirements. For instance, if we want to perform the summation, a corrected version would be:

```
def corrected_base_case(n):
    if n <= 0:
        return 0
    return n + corrected_base_case(n - 2)

# Correct behavior as per the logical problem
result = corrected_base_case(10)
print(result)
```

**Excessive Recursion:**

Recursion may lead to excessive overhead when the function calls are too frequent or handle large dataset sizes, causing performance degradation. The Fibonacci sequence is a classic example where naive recursion performs inefficiently.

```
def fibonacci(n):
    if n <= 1:
        return n
    return fibonacci(n - 1) + fibonacci(n - 2)

# Inefficiency arises due to repeated calculations
print(fibonacci(30))
```

The naive recursive approach recalculates the same Fibonacci numbers multiple times, resulting in exponential time complexity $O(2^n)$. Optimizing it using memoization improves efficiency:

```
def fibonacci_memoization(n, memo={}):
    if n in memo:
        return memo[n]
    if n <= 1:
        memo[n] = n
    else:
        memo[n] = fibonacci_memoization(n - 1, memo) + fibonacci_memoization(n -
            2, memo)
    return memo[n]

print(fibonacci_memoization(30))
```

**Stack Overflow:**

Deep recursive calls without optimization can lead to stack overflow even when the logic is correct. This commonly occurs with large input sizes. Python has a recursion limit defined to prevent infinite recursion, which defaults to 1000.

```
import sys
print(sys.getrecursionlimit()) # Default recursion limit
def deep_recursion(n):
    if n == 0:
        return 0
    return 1 + deep_recursion(n - 1)

# Exceeding the recursion limit
deep_recursion(1001)
```

The output will show:

```
1000
Traceback (most recent call last):
...
RecursionError: maximum recursion depth exceeded in comparison
```

To prevent stack overflow, algorithms can be revisited to ensure they are efficient, possibly by converting them to iterative forms when deep recursion is unnecessary, or by increasing the recursion limit judiciously if necessary.

```
import sys
sys.setrecursionlimit(2000)
deep_recursion(1001)
```

While increasing the recursion limit, it is crucial to understand the consequences as it may lead to higher memory consumption and potential crashes.

By acknowledging and addressing these common pitfalls, one can significantly enhance the robustness and efficiency of recursive solutions.

## 2.8 Recursion Examples with Python

To solidify our understanding of recursion, we will consider several illustrative examples in Python. Each example will demonstrate the fundamental aspects of recursive function design, namely, identifying the base case and the recursive case. The examples have been carefully selected to highlight different characteristics and applications of recursion.

### Factorial Calculation

The factorial of a non-negative integer $n$ is the product of all positive integers less than or equal to $n$. The factorial function, denoted as $n!$, can be defined recursively because $n! = n \times (n-1)!$, with $0! = 1$ as the base case.

```
def factorial(n):
    if n == 0:
        return 1 # Base case
    else:
        return n * factorial(n-1) # Recursive case

# Test the function
print(factorial(5)) # Output: 120
```

### Fibonacci Sequence

The Fibonacci sequence is a classic example of a problem that can be approached recursively. The sequence is defined as follows: $F(0) = 0$, $F(1) = 1$, and $F(n) = F(n-1) + F(n-2)$ for $n \geq 2$.

```
def fibonacci(n):
    if n <= 1:
        return n # Base cases
    else:
        return fibonacci(n-1) + fibonacci(n-2) # Recursive case

# Test the function
print(fibonacci(6)) # Output: 8
```

### Sum of Digits

This function calculates the sum of the digits of a non-negative integer $n$. The base case occurs when $n$ is a single digit. Otherwise, the function splits $n$ into its last digit and the remaining part of the number, and then recursively sums these parts.

```
def sum_of_digits(n):
```

```
    if n < 10:
        return n # Base case
    else:
        return n % 10 + sum_of_digits(n // 10) # Recursive case

# Test the function
print(sum_of_digits(1234)) # Output: 10
```

### Reverse a String

Reversing a string can also be accomplished through recursion. The base case occurs when the string is empty or consists of a single character. Otherwise, the function takes the first character and appends it to the reverse of the remaining string.

```
def reverse_string(s):
    if len(s) <= 1:
        return s # Base case
    else:
        return reverse_string(s[1:]) + s[0] # Recursive case

# Test the function
print(reverse_string("hello")) # Output: "olleh"
```

### Palindrome Check

A string is a palindrome if it reads the same forward and backward. This can be checked recursively by comparing the first and last characters and then checking the substring that excludes these characters.

```
def is_palindrome(s):
    if len(s) <= 1:
        return True # Base case
    else:
        return s[0] == s[-1] and is_palindrome(s[1:-1]) # Recursive case

# Test the function
print(is_palindrome("radar")) # Output: True
```

### Tower of Hanoi

The Tower of Hanoi is a classic problem in which the goal is to move a set of disks from one peg to another, obeying specific rules. This problem is best understood through its recursive solution, where disks are moved between pegs in a particular sequence.

```
def tower_of_hanoi(n, source, target, auxiliary):
    if n == 1:
        print(f"Move disk 1 from {source} to {target}") # Base case
        return
    tower_of_hanoi(n - 1, source, auxiliary, target) # Recursive case
    print(f"Move disk {n} from {source} to {target}")
    tower_of_hanoi(n - 1, auxiliary, target, source)

# Test the function
```

```
tower_of_hanoi(3, 'A', 'C', 'B')
```

```
Move disk 1 from A to C
Move disk 2 from A to B
Move disk 1 from C to B
Move disk 3 from A to C
Move disk 1 from B to A
Move disk 2 from B to C
Move disk 1 from A to C
```

The provided examples demonstrate a variety of ways in which recursive techniques can be applied to solve common computational problems. The key takeaway from these examples is the importance of clearly defining base cases and recursive cases to ensure proper function termination and correct computation.

## 2.9 Debugging Recursive Programs

Debugging recursive programs can be particularly challenging due to the complexity introduced by multiple instances of the function running concurrently on the call stack. To effectively debug recursive programs, a systematic approach must be employed to trace the logical flow and isolate issues. Common techniques include understanding stack traces, using debugging tools, and strategic insertion of print statements. Here, we will explore these methods with detailed explanations and practical examples.

To begin, a stack trace is an essential tool for understanding the flow of recursion. When an error occurs, the stack trace provides a snapshot of the call stack, showing the sequence of function calls that led to the error. Let us consider a simple example that calculates the factorial of a number recursively:

```
def factorial(n):
    # Base case
    if n == 0:
        return 1
    # Recursive case
    else:
        return n * factorial(n - 1)

# Example call
factorial(5)
```

Suppose there is an error, such as a negative input, that causes infinite recursion. Python will raise a RecursionError, and the stack trace will show the repeated calls to the factorial function:

```
RecursionError: maximum recursion depth exceeded in comparison
```

The stack trace helps identify the last function call and the sequence leading up to it. Review the arguments at each call to locate the erroneous logic.

Debugging tools integrated within IDEs (Integrated Development Environments) or standalone debuggers like pdb (Python Debugger) are invaluable. The pdb tool allows developers to set breakpoints, step through code, and inspect variables. Here is how to use pdb to debug our factorial function:

```
import pdb

def factorial(n):
    pdb.set_trace() # Set a breakpoint
    if n == 0:
        return 1
    else:
        return n * factorial(n - 1)

factorial(5)
```

Running the above code will start the debugger at pdb.set_trace(). You can then step through each call with commands like s (step), n (next), and p (print) to inspect variable values:

```
> <string>(4)factorial()
-> if n == 0:
(Pdb) p n
5
(Pdb) n
```

Strategic insertion of print statements provides another effective method for tracing recursive calls, particularly for simple debugging tasks. By printing the parameters on entry and before return, you can track the function's behavior:

```
def factorial(n):
    print(f"Entering factorial with n = {n}")
    if n == 0:
        result = 1
    else:
        result = n * factorial(n - 1)
    print(f"Returning {result} for factorial({n})")
    return result

factorial(5)
```

The output will trace the recursive calls and unwinding sequence, offering insights into potential logic errors:

```
Entering factorial with n = 5
Entering factorial with n = 4
Entering factorial with n = 3
Entering factorial with n = 2
Entering factorial with n = 1
Entering factorial with n = 0
Returning 1 for factorial(0)
Returning 1 for factorial(1)
Returning 2 for factorial(2)
Returning 6 for factorial(3)
Returning 24 for factorial(4)
Returning 120 for factorial(5)
```

Another crucial aspect of debugging recursive programs involves understanding the relationship between base cases and recursive cases. Errors often arise when the base case does not correctly terminate the recursion for all possible inputs. Consider testing edge cases, such as zero and negative inputs, to ensure the function handles them appropriately.

Suppose we modify our factorial function to handle negative inputs by raising a ValueError:

```
def factorial(n):
    if n < 0:
        raise ValueError("Negative input not allowed")
    if n == 0:
        return 1
    else:
        return n * factorial(n - 1)

factorial(-1)
```

The stack trace will now indicate the point of error with clarity:

```
ValueError: Negative input not allowed
```

Complex recursive functions benefiting from memoization can introduce additional debugging complexity. Memoization involves storing previously computed results to avoid redundant calculations, enhancing efficiency but requiring validation of the caching mechanism. Here's an example using a memoized Fibonacci sequence calculator:

```
def memoize(f):
    cache = {}
    def memoized_function(n):
        if n not in cache:
            cache[n] = f(n)
        return cache[n]
    return memoized_function

@memoize
def fibonacci(n):
    if n < 0:
```

```
        raise ValueError("Negative input not allowed")
    elif n <= 1:
        return n
    else:
        return fibonacci(n - 1) + fibonacci(n - 2)

fibonacci(5)
```

To debug, you can inspect the cache content and trace its usage:

```
@memoize
def fibonacci(n):
    if n < 0:
        raise ValueError("Negative input not allowed")
    elif n <= 1:
        return n
    else:
        result = fibonacci(n - 1) + fibonacci(n - 2)
    print(f"fibonacci({n}) = {result}")
    return result

fibonacci(5)
```

The printed values help verify that cached results are correctly utilized and identify any anomalies in the recursive logic.

Additionally, tools like visual debuggers (e.g., PyCharm, Visual Studio Code) provide graphical representations of call stacks and variable states, facilitating a deeper understanding of recursive behavior.

Proficiency in debugging recursive programs derives from a combination of theoretical insights and practical experience. By systematically employing stack trace analysis, utilizing debugging tools, and strategically inserting print statements, one can effectively isolate and rectify issues in recursive logic.

## 2.10 Tail Recursion

Tail recursion is a specific kind of recursion where the recursive call is the last operation in the function. This implies that the function returns the result of the recursive call directly without any further computation. Tail recursion is significant because it allows for optimizations by the compiler or interpreter, specifically an optimization known as Tail Call Optimization (TCO). TCO can convert recursive calls into a loop, minimizing the risk of stack overflow and improving performance.

In a conventional recursive function, each call adds a new frame to the call stack. For a deeply recursive function, this can lead to a stack overflow as the call stack becomes excessively large. Tail recursion, when optimized, can reuse the current function's stack frame for the next function call, thus not increasing the stack size.

To illustrate tail recursion, consider the classic example of the factorial function. A non-tail-recursive version of the factorial function is as follows:

```
def factorial(n):
    if n == 0:
        return 1
    else:
        return n * factorial(n - 1)
```

In the above function, the multiplication operation occurs after the recursive call, hence it is not tail-recursive. To convert this to a tail-recursive function, an additional parameter (usually called an accumulator) can be introduced to carry the intermediate result:

```
def tail_recursive_factorial(n, accumulator=1):
    if n == 0:
        return accumulator
    else:
        return tail_recursive_factorial(n - 1, n * accumulator)
```

Here, the recursive call to tail_recursive_factorial is the last operation, making it tail-recursive. The accumulator holds the ongoing product of the numbers from $n$ down to 1. Each recursive call effectively updates the value of the accumulator without the need for additional computations post-recursion.

To understand the mechanics:

```
print(tail_recursive_factorial(5))
```

120

Each call to tail_recursive_factorial reduces $n$ by 1 and multiplies the current value of $n$ with the accumulator, propagating this value through each level of recursion until $n$ reaches 0. At this point, the accumulated product is returned.

Many languages implement TCO, but Python does not inherently support this optimization due to design decisions prioritizing stack traces for debugging. However, understanding tail recursion is valuable as the concept extends easily to schemes and languages that do optimize tail calls, like Scheme and Haskell.

Let's consider another example, the computation of the Fibonacci sequence. A naive recursive implementation for Fibonacci is as follows:

```
def fibonacci(n):
    if n <= 1:
        return n
    else:
        return fibonacci(n - 1) + fibonacci(n - 2)
```

This implementation is neither efficient nor tail-recursive. It leads to excessive recalculations and a rapidly growing call stack. We can reframe the Fibonacci computation in a tail-recursive manner using additional parameters to keep track of the two preceding numbers in the sequence.

```
def tail_recursive_fibonacci(n, a=0, b=1):
    if n == 0:
        return a
    elif n == 1:
        return b
    else:
        return tail_recursive_fibonacci(n - 1, b, a + b)
```

With this approach, the recursive call to tail_recursive_fibonacci is the last operation, ensuring it is tail-recursive. The parameters $a$ and $b$ maintain the two most recent Fibonacci numbers, facilitating the progression without additional calculations post-return.

Testing this implementation:

```
print(tail_recursive_fibonacci(10))
```

```
55
```

The tail-recursive Fibonacci function provides the same result as the naive implementation but does so more efficiently by minimizing redundant calculations and avoiding potential stack overflow for large $n$.

In practical applications, converting a recursive function into a tail-recursive form where possible and understanding its optimizations can lead to more efficient and robust code. While Python does not optimize tail calls, the principles underlying tail recursion remain crucial in computational theory and in languages that facilitate such optimizations. Understanding these principles equips programmers with the skills to write recursive functions that are both effective and efficient, adhering to best practices in software development.

## 2.11 Recursion in Data Structures

Recursion serves as a powerful tool for handling complex data structures that can be recursively defined, such as linked lists, trees, and graphs. These data structures inherently possess recursive properties, making recursive algorithms a natural fit for traversing, modifying, and querying them. This section delves into the practical application of recursion in these data structures, enhancing our comprehension by solidifying theoretical concepts with practical Python examples.

To begin with, consider the fundamental structure of a linked list. A linked list consists of nodes, where each node contains a value and a reference to the next node in the sequence. This self-referential structure lends itself well to recursive approaches.

```
class ListNode:
    def __init__(self, value=0, next=None):
        self.value = value
        self.next = next

def print_linked_list(node):
    if node is not None:
        print(node.value)
        print_linked_list(node.next)
```

The function print_linked_list recursively prints each element of a linked list until it reaches the end (i.e., until node is None). This example provides a clear illustration of how recursion is employed to traverse each element of the linked list by invoking the function on the next node.

More complex data structures, such as trees, also benefit from recursive methods. Binary trees, a prevalent data structure in computer science, are a particularly illustrative example. Each node in a binary tree has at most two children, commonly referred to as the left child and the right child. Various operations, such as traversals (in-order, pre-order, post-order), are naturally implemented using recursion.

Consider the following Python implementation for in-order traversal of a binary tree:

```
class TreeNode:
    def __init__(self, value=0, left=None, right=None):
        self.value = value
        self.left = left
        self.right = right

def in_order_traversal(node):
    if node:
        in_order_traversal(node.left)
        print(node.value)
```

```
        in_order_traversal(node.right)
```

The in_order_traversal function visits the left subtree, processes the current node, and then visits the right subtree, leveraging recursion to handle each subtree. This method highlights the elegance and simplicity recursion brings to binary tree algorithms.

Beyond traversal, recursive strategies are effective for more complex tree manipulations, such as searching, insertion, and deletion operations in binary search trees (BSTs).

```
def search_bst(node, target):
    if node is None or node.value == target:
        return node
    if target < node.value:
        return search_bst(node.left, target)
    else:
        return search_bst(node.right, target)
```

In the search_bst function, the tree's structure dictates whether the search should proceed to the left or right subtree, efficiently narrowing down the target node search path.

Recursion also facilitates operations on non-binary trees and more complex graph structures. The concept of depth-first search (DFS) for graphs mirrors the traversal techniques discussed for trees, utilizing a recursive approach to explore graph components.

```
def dfs(graph, start, visited=None):
    if visited is None:
        visited = set()
    visited.add(start)
    print(start)
    for neighbor in graph[start]:
        if neighbor not in visited:
            dfs(graph, neighbor, visited)
```

Here, the dfs function recursively visits all nodes in a graph component starting from a given node. It ensures that each node is visited once, using a visited set to track the visitation status.

Additionally, recursion is instrumental in solving problems built on dynamic data structures, such as balanced trees (e.g., AVL trees, Red-Black trees), n-ary trees, and more. Recursive algorithms help maintain balance criteria, restructure trees, and manage various complex conditions integral to these advanced structures.

These practical implementations underscore recursion's versatility in data structure operations, aiding in tasks that range from basic traversals to sophisticated manipulations. By leveraging recursion, we can simplify complex algorithms, achieving clarity and efficiency in our programs.

## 2.12 Recursion in Problem Solving

Recursion plays an indispensable role in problem-solving by allowing complex problems to be broken down into simpler subproblems, which can be addressed more easily. By fostering a divide-and-conquer approach, recursion helps in formulating solutions that are both intuitive and efficient. This section delves into various problem-solving paradigms where recursion proves to be highly effective, supported by detailed Python code examples.

### Factorial Computation

The factorial of a non-negative integer $n$, denoted as $n!$, is defined as the product of all positive integers less than or equal to $n$. The recursive definition of the factorial function can be expressed as:

$$n! = \begin{cases} 1 & \text{if } n = 0, \\ n \times (n-1)! & \text{if } n > 0. \end{cases}$$

The following Python function illustrates this recursive definition:

```
def factorial(n):
    if n == 0:
        return 1
    else:
        return n * factorial(n - 1)

# Testing the recursive function
print(factorial(5)) # Output: 120
```

```
120
```

### Fibonacci Sequence

The Fibonacci sequence is another classic example where recursion is used to solve a problem with clear subproblem structure. Each term in the Fibonacci sequence is the sum of the two preceding terms, starting from 0 and 1. The sequence is defined recursively as:

$$F(n) = \begin{cases} 0 & \text{if } n = 0, \\ 1 & \text{if } n = 1, \\ F(n-1) + F(n-2) & \text{if } n > 1. \end{cases}$$

The following Python function implements this recursive definition:

```
def fibonacci(n):
    if n == 0:
        return 0
    elif n == 1:
        return 1
    else:
        return fibonacci(n - 1) + fibonacci(n - 2)

# Testing the recursive function
print(fibonacci(6)) # Output: 8
```

8

### Solving Towers of Hanoi

The Towers of Hanoi is a puzzle that demonstrates the power of recursion in problem-solving. The puzzle consists of three pegs and a number of disks of various sizes, which can slide onto any peg. The puzzle starts with the disks neatly stacked in ascending order of size on one peg, the smallest at the top, making a conical shape. The objective of the puzzle is to move the entire stack to another peg, obeying the following simple rules: 1. Only one disk can be moved at a time. 2. Each move consists of taking the upper disk from one of the stacks and placing it on top of another stack or on an empty peg. 3. No disk may be placed on top of a smaller disk.

The recursive algorithm to solve this puzzle can be defined as: 1. Move $(n-1)$ disks from source peg to auxiliary peg. 2. Move the nth disk from source peg to destination peg. 3. Move the $(n-1)$ disks from auxiliary peg to destination peg.

Below is the Python function that implements this recursive solution:

```
def towers_of_hanoi(n, source, auxiliary, destination):
    if n == 1:
        print(f"Move disk 1 from {source} to {destination}")
        return
    towers_of_hanoi(n - 1, source, destination, auxiliary)
    print(f"Move disk {n} from {source} to {destination}")
    towers_of_hanoi(n - 1, auxiliary, source, destination)

# Testing the recursive function
towers_of_hanoi(3, 'A', 'B', 'C')
```

```
Move disk 1 from A to C
Move disk 2 from A to B
Move disk 1 from C to B
Move disk 3 from A to C
Move disk 1 from B to A
Move disk 2 from B to C
Move disk 1 from A to C
```

### Permutations of a String

Generating permutations of a string involves arranging the characters of the string in all possible orders. This is another problem that can be elegantly solved using recursion. The recursive approach can be outlined as: 1. For each character in the string, set it as the first character and recursively concatenate it with the permutations of the remaining characters.

The Python code for generating the permutations of a string is as follows:

```
def permutations(string):
    if len(string) == 1:
        return [string]

    perm_list = []
    for char in string:
        remaining_elements = [c for c in string if c != char]
        z = permutations(''.join(remaining_elements))
        for t in z:
            perm_list.append(char + t)
    return perm_list

# Testing the recursive function
perm_result = permutations('ABC')
print(perm_result) # Output: ['ABC', 'ACB', 'BAC', 'BCA', 'CAB', 'CBA']
```

['ABC', 'ACB', 'BAC', 'BCA', 'CAB', 'CBA']

### Solving Maze Problems

Recursive algorithms can also be utilized to navigate maze-like structures. The objective is to find a path from the start point to the end point. The recursive strategy involves: 1. Mark the current cell as part of the path. 2. Try all possible directions from the current cell (up, down, left, right). 3. Recursively explore each direction. 4. If a direction leads to the solution, the path is found. 5. If no direction is viable, backtrack by unmarking the cell as part of the path.

Here is the Python implementation to solve a simple maze problem:

```
def is_safe(maze, x, y):
    return 0 <= x < len(maze) and 0 <= y < len(maze[0]) and maze[x][y] == 1

def solve_maze_util(maze, x, y, solution):
    if x == len(maze) - 1 and y == len(maze[0]) - 1:
        solution[x][y] = 1
        return True

    if is_safe(maze, x, y):
        solution[x][y] = 1

        # Move forward in x direction
        if solve_maze_util(maze, x + 1, y, solution):
```

```
            return True

        # Move down in y direction
        if solve_maze_util(maze, x, y + 1, solution):
            return True

        solution[x][y] = 0
        return False

    return False

def solve_maze(maze):
    solution = [[0] * len(maze[0]) for _ in range(len(maze))]

    if not solve_maze_util(maze, 0, 0, solution):
        return []

    return solution

# Testing the recursive function
maze = [[1, 0, 0, 0],
        [1, 1, 0, 1],
        [0, 1, 0, 0],
        [1, 1, 1, 1]]

solution = solve_maze(maze)
for row in solution:
    print(row)
```

```
[1, 0, 0, 0]
[1, 1, 0, 0]
[0, 1, 0, 0]
[0, 1, 1, 1]
```

These examples demonstrate how recursion can be effectively employed to simplify and solve computational problems, offering both clarity of implementation and efficiency when correctly applied.

# Chapter 3

# Principles of Dynamic Programming

**This chapter delves into the core principles of dynamic programming, focusing on the concepts of overlapping subproblems and optimal substructure. Readers will learn to break down problems into manageable subproblems, identify and define these subproblems, and formulate recursive relations. The chapter also covers state transitions, base cases, and evaluating time complexity. Practical examples and common patterns in DP problems are provided to illustrate these principles, along with strategies to avoid typical mistakes. This foundational knowledge is crucial for effectively applying dynamic programming techniques in various problem-solving scenarios.**

## 3.1 Introduction to the Principles of Dynamic Programming

Dynamic programming (DP) is a method used in computer science and mathematics to solve problems by breaking them down into simpler subproblems and solving these subproblems just once. The key idea is to store the solutions of subproblems to avoid redundant computations. This technique is especially useful when the problem has overlapping subproblems and an optimal substructure.

Overlapping subproblems occur when a problem can be broken down into subproblems which are reused multiple times. Optimal substructure means that the optimal solution of the problem can be constructed efficiently from optimal solutions of its subproblems. Dynamic programming is distinguished from other methods by its systematic approach and use of memoization or tabulation.

Memoization involves storing the results of expensive function calls and reusing the cached result when the same inputs occur again. Tabulation, on the other hand, is a bottom-up approach where you solve all possible small problems and use those solutions to build up solutions to bigger problems.

Consider the Fibonacci sequence, defined as:

$$F(n) = \begin{cases} 0 & \text{if } n = 0 \\ 1 & \text{if } n = 1 \\ F(n-1) + F(n-2) & \text{if } n > 1 \end{cases}$$

A naive recursive implementation would look like this:

```
def fibonacci(n):
    if n == 0:
        return 0
    elif n == 1:
        return 1
    else:
        return fibonacci(n-1) + fibonacci(n-2)
```

This approach is highly inefficient due to repeated calculations of the same subproblems. The time complexity of this naive implementation is $O(2^n)$.

With dynamic programming, we significantly improve efficiency by storing intermediate results. Here is the memoized version:

```
def fibonacci_memo(n, memo={}):
    if n in memo:
        return memo[n]
    if n == 0:
        return 0
    elif n == 1:
        return 1
    memo[n] = fibonacci_memo(n-1, memo) + fibonacci_memo(n-2, memo)
    return memo[n]
```

The time complexity of the memoized version is $O(n)$, as it computes the nth Fibonacci number in linear time by reducing redundant calls.

In DP's tabulation approach, the problem is solved iteratively:

```
def fibonacci_tabulation(n):
    if n == 0:
        return 0
    elif n == 1:
        return 1
    fib = [0] * (n+1)
    fib[1] = 1
    for i in range(2, n+1):
        fib[i] = fib[i-1] + fib[i-2]
    return fib[n]
```

This approach iteratively builds up the solution and also runs in $O(n)$ time complexity.

To grasp dynamic programming, one must understand two critical aspects:

1. **Optimal Substructure**: This property signifies that the optimal solution to a problem can be constructed from optimal solutions to its subproblems. For instance, in the Fibonacci example, the optimal solution for $F(n)$ is directly derived from the optimal solutions of $F(n-1)$ and $F(n-2)$.

2. **Overlapping Subproblems**: This is the essence of why dynamic programming is effective. In the Fibonacci sequence, the subproblems $F(n-1)$ and $F(n-2)$ overlap as both $F(n)$ and $F(n-1)$ require $F(n-2)$.

Understanding these principles allows us to design efficient algorithms to solve complex problems that would otherwise be computationally prohibitive. Incrementally building solutions to more extensive problems by relying on those of smaller subproblems is the characteristic methodology within dynamic programming, making it a powerful tool in algorithm design.

## 3.2 Understanding Overlapping Subproblems

Dynamic programming (DP) leverages the concept of overlapping subproblems, which is integral to its efficiency in solving complex problems. To understand overlapping subproblems, consider problems that can be divided into smaller subproblems, which are solved recursively. In many instances, these subproblems repeat themselves multiple times during the computation process, leading to redundancy. By storing the results of these subproblems, dynamic programming facilitates efficient problem-solving by avoiding redundant computations.

Let us delve into a classic problem to elucidate this concept: the Fibonacci sequence. The $n$-th Fibonacci number is given by the recurrence relation:

$$F(n) = \begin{cases} 0 & \text{if } n = 0, \\ 1 & \text{if } n = 1, \\ F(n-1) + F(n-2) & \text{if } n > 1. \end{cases}$$

A naive recursive implementation to compute $F(n)$ is as follows:

```
def fibonacci(n):
    if n == 0:
        return 0
    elif n == 1:
        return 1
    else:
        return fibonacci(n-1) + fibonacci(n-2)
```

To illustrate the overlapping nature of subproblems, consider calculating $F(5)$. The recursion tree for this computation is depicted in Figure 3.1.

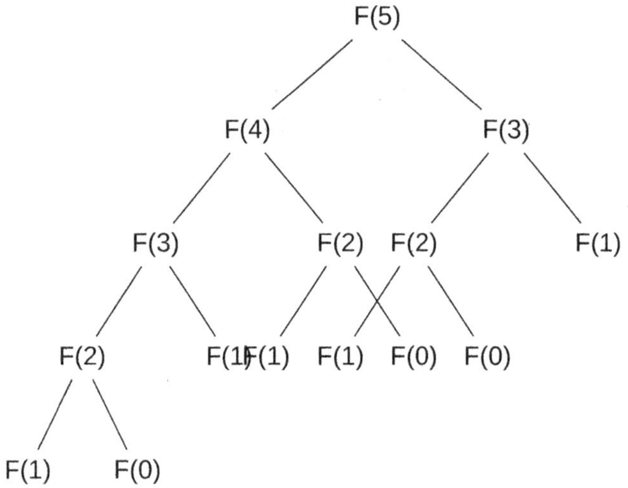


Figure 3.1: Recursion tree for computing $F(5)$

Observe that the computation of $F(3)$ and $F(2)$ is repeated multiple times, leading to redundant calculations. By storing the intermediate results, we can avoid this redundancy using a technique called memoization. The enhanced approach involves caching results of subproblems in a data structure, typically a dictionary or a list, and reusing these results whenever the same subproblem recurs.

The dynamic programming approach for computing Fibonacci numbers using memoization is given below:

```
def fibonacci_memo(n, memo={}):
    if n in memo:
        return memo[n]
    if n == 0:
        return 0
    elif n == 1:
        return 1
    memo[n] = fibonacci_memo(n-1, memo) + fibonacci_memo(n-2, memo)
    return memo[n]
```

Alternatively, an even more space-efficient method is called tabulation, which uses an iterative approach to fill up a table of results. Here's how the tabulation method computes the Fibonacci sequence:

```
def fibonacci_tab(n):
    if n == 0:
        return 0
    elif n == 1:
        return 1

    fib = [0] * (n + 1)
    fib[1] = 1

    for i in range(2, n + 1):
        fib[i] = fib[i-1] + fib[i-2]

    return fib[n]
```

The tabulation method constructs the solution iteratively, building from the base cases up to the desired result, thus ensuring that each subproblem is solved only once. This guarantees a time complexity of $O(n)$ as opposed to the exponential time complexity of the naive recursive approach.

Overlapping subproblems are common in various problems beyond the Fibonacci sequence. Let us consider another illustrative example: the problem of finding the length of the longest common subsequence (LCS) of two sequences. Suppose we have sequences $X$ and $Y$ of lengths $m$ and $n$ respectively. The LCS problem can be formulated as follows:

$$\text{LCS}(X[1..m], Y[1..n]) = \begin{cases} 0 & \text{if } m = 0 \text{ or } n = 0, \\ \text{LCS}(X[1..(m-1)], Y[1..(n-1)]) + 1 & \text{if } X[m] = Y[n], \\ \max(\text{LCS}(X[1..m], Y[1..(n-1)]), \text{LCS}(X[1..(m-1)], Y[1..n])) & \text{if } X[m] \neq Y[n]. \end{cases}$$

A recursive Python function to compute the LCS follows:

```
def lcs_recursive(X, Y, m, n):
    if m == 0 or n == 0:
        return 0
    elif X[m-1] == Y[n-1]:
        return 1 + lcs_recursive(X, Y, m-1, n-1)
    else:
        return max(lcs_recursive(X, Y, m, n-1), lcs_recursive(X, Y, m-1, n))
```

Similar to the Fibonacci example, the LCS computation using a naive recursive approach encounters redundant subproblems. By memoizing the results of subproblems, we can optimize the computation as illustrated below:

```
def lcs_memo(X, Y, m, n, memo):
    if memo[m][n] is not None:
        return memo[m][n]
    if m == 0 or n == 0:
        result = 0
    elif X[m-1] == Y[n-1]:
        result = 1 + lcs_memo(X, Y, m-1, n-1, memo)
    else:
        result = max(lcs_memo(X, Y, m, n-1, memo), lcs_memo(X, Y, m-1, n, memo))
    memo[m][n] = result
    return result

def lcs(X, Y):
    m = len(X)
    n = len(Y)
    memo = [[None] * (n + 1) for _ in range(m + 1)]
    return lcs_memo(X, Y, m, n, memo)
```

By structuring and storing subproblem solutions in a memoization table, the LCS solution runs in $O(m \times n)$ time, leading to substantial performance improvement.

Understanding and identifying overlapping subproblems is crucial when applying dynamic programming, as it enables the reusability of solutions for recurring subproblems, thereby significantly enhancing computational efficiency.

## 3.3 Exploring Optimal Substructure

Optimal substructure is a fundamental concept in dynamic programming. A problem exhibits optimal substructure if an optimal solution to the problem can be constructed efficiently from optimal solutions of its subproblems. This property is crucial for the applicability of dynamic programming techniques, as it allows a large problem to be broken down into smaller, manageable components which can be solved independently and then combined to form an overall solution.

Consider the classic example of the shortest path problem in graph theory. Suppose we have a graph $G = (V, E)$ with vertex set $V$ and edge set $E$. The task is to find the shortest path from a source vertex $s$ to a destination vertex $t$. This problem exhibits optimal substructure because the shortest path from $s$ to $t$ can be decomposed into two subproblems: finding the shortest path from $s$ to an intermediate vertex $u$, and finding the shortest path from $u$ to $t$. If these subproblems are solved optimally, they can be combined to solve the original problem optimally.

To better understand optimal substructure, we can formalize it using mathematical notation. Let $C[i, j]$ denote the cost of the shortest path from vertex $i$ to vertex $j$. Then the optimal substructure can be expressed as:

$$C[s, t] = \min_{u \in V}\{C[s, u] + C[u, t]\}$$

This recursive relation highlights that the shortest path from $s$ to $t$ is the minimum of the sum of the costs from $s$ to some intermediate vertex $u$ and from $u$ to $t$.

To illustrate this concept further, consider the problem of finding the minimum cost to multiply a chain of matrices. The matrix chain multiplication problem is defined as follows: given a sequence of matrices $A_1, A_2, \ldots, A_n$, the task is to find the most efficient way to multiply these matrices together. The efficiency is measured by the number of scalar multiplications required. For matrices $A_i$ of dimensions $p_{i-1} \times p_i$, the cost of multiplying two matrices $A = p \times q$ and $B = q \times r$ is $p \times q \times r$.

The optimal substructure property here implies that to compute the optimal solution for multiplying matrices $A_i$ through $A_j$ (with $i < j$), we need to consider the optimal solutions of its subproblems. Specifically, for some $k$ such that $i \leq k < j$, we compute the cost of:

$$\text{Cost}(A_i \cdots A_j) = \text{Cost}(A_i \cdots A_k) + \text{Cost}(A_{k+1} \cdots A_j) + p_{i-1} \times p_k \times p_j$$

Hence, the matrix chain multiplication problem demonstrates optimal substructure because the solution to the problem of multiplying $A_i$ to $A_j$ depends on the optimal solutions of the subproblems of multiplying $A_i$ to $A_k$ and $A_{k+1}$ to $A_j$.

We are now in a position to represent this as a dynamic programming solution. We let $m[i, j]$ represent the minimum number of scalar multiplications needed to compute the matrix product $A_i \cdots A_j$. The recursive formula based on the optimal substructure property is:

$$m[i,j] = \begin{cases} 0 & \text{if } i = j \\ \min_{i \leq k < j}\{m[i,k] + m[k+1,j] + p_{i-1} \times p_k \times p_j\} & \text{otherwise} \end{cases}$$

In a practical Python implementation, we fill a two-dimensional list with these values as shown below:

```
def matrix_chain_order(p):
    n = len(p) - 1 # number of matrices
    m = [[0] * (n + 1) for _ in range(n + 1)]

    for length in range(2, n + 1): # length of the chain
        for i in range(1, n - length + 2):
            j = i + length - 1
            m[i][j] = float('inf')
            for k in range(i, j):
                q = m[i][k] + m[k+1][j] + p[i-1] * p[k] * p[j]
                if q < m[i][j]:
                    m[i][j] = q

    return m[1][n]

p = [30, 35, 15, 5, 10, 20, 25]
print(matrix_chain_order(p))
```

```
15125
```

Another classical problem that exemplifies optimal substructure is the longest common subsequence (LCS) problem. Given two sequences, $X = x_1, x_2, \ldots, x_m$ and $Y = y_1, y_2, \ldots, y_n$, the task is to find the longest subsequence common to both sequences. A subsequence is derived by deleting zero or more elements from a sequence without changing the order of the remaining elements.

The optimal substructure property is observed as follows: let $L(X, Y)$ represent the length of the LCS of $X$ and $Y$. If $x_m = y_n$, then $L(X, Y)$ is 1 plus the length of LCS of the two sequences minus their last elements, i.e., $L(X[1 : m-1], Y[1 : n-1])$. Otherwise, $L(X, Y)$ is the maximum LCS length obtained by either dropping the last element of $X$ or $Y$:

$$L(X,Y) = \begin{cases} 0 & \text{if } m = 0 \text{ or } n = 0 \\ 1 + L(X[1:m-1], Y[1:n-1]) & \text{if } x_m = y_n \\ \max(L(X[1:m-1], Y), L(X, Y[1:n-1])) & \text{otherwise} \end{cases}$$

This recursive formulation translates naturally into a dynamic programming solution as follows:

```
def lcs(X, Y):
    m = len(X)
    n = len(Y)
    L = [[0] * (n + 1) for _ in range(m + 1)]

    for i in range(m + 1):
        for j in range(n + 1):
            if i == 0 or j == 0:
                L[i][j] = 0
            elif X[i - 1] == Y[j - 1]:
                L[i][j] = L[i - 1][j - 1] + 1
            else:
                L[i][j] = max(L[i - 1][j], L[i][j - 1])

    return L[m][n]

X = "AGGTAB"
Y = "GXTXAYB"
print(lcs(X, Y))
```

4

These illustrative examples highlight how optimal substructure is leveraged in dynamic programming to break down complex problems, solve simpler subproblems, and combine those solutions to form the overall optimal solution.

## 3.4 Breaking Down Problems

Breaking down problems into manageable subproblems is a fundamental technique in dynamic programming. This section explores how to decompose complex problems systematically and methodically, ensuring that each subproblem is both solvable independently and reusable. The goal is to simplify problem-solving by dividing the original problem into smaller, less complicated pieces that can be tackled one at a time, then combining their solutions to resolve the entire problem effectively.

At the core of breaking down problems are two key concepts: *overlapping subproblems* and *optimal substructure*. Let's revisit these concepts briefly in the context of problem decomposition.

First, consider the classic example of the Fibonacci sequence. The problem can be stated as finding the $n$-th Fibonacci number, where each number is the sum of the two preceding ones, usually starting with 0 and 1. The recursive definition is given by:

$$F(n) = \begin{cases} 0 & \text{if } n = 0 \\ 1 & \text{if } n = 1 \\ F(n-1) + F(n-2) & \text{if } n > 1 \end{cases}$$

In this scenario, both $F(n-1)$ and $F(n-2)$ are subproblems of $F(n)$. This elegant self-similarity, where the problem resembles a combination of its subproblems, demonstrates the overlapping subproblems principle.

To systematically break down a problem, follow these steps:

1. **Identify the subproblems:** Determine smaller instances of the original problem that can be solved independently. The key is to ensure that these smaller problems overlap, which means that their solutions are reused multiple times in solving the larger problem.

2. **Define the state:** Clearly define what constitutes a state in your problem. This involves specifying the parameters that uniquely identify subproblems. For example, in the Fibonacci sequence, the state is defined by the single parameter $n$.

3. **Formulate the state transition:** Determine how to transition from one state to another. This involves defining a recurrence relation or a state transition equation that captures the relationship between a state and its subsequent states.

4. **Establish the base cases:** Identify the simplest instances of the problem, which can be solved directly without further decomposition. These form the foundation for building solutions to more complex problems.

To illustrate these steps more concretely, let's consider the problem of calculating the minimum cost path in a grid from the top-left corner to the bottom-right corner. Each cell in the grid has a cost associated with it, and you can only move either right or down.

```
def minCost(cost, m, n):
    min_cost = [[0 for x in range(n+1)] for y in range(m+1)]

    min_cost[0][0] = cost[0][0]

    for i in range(1, m+1):
        min_cost[i][0] = min_cost[i-1][0] + cost[i][0]

    for j in range(1, n+1):
        min_cost[0][j] = min_cost[0][j] + cost[0][j]

    for i in range(1, m+1):
        for j in range(1, n+1):
```

```
            min_cost[i][j] = min(min_cost[i-1][j], min_cost[i][j-1]) + cost[i][j]

    return min_cost[m][n]

cost = [[1, 2, 3], [4, 8, 2], [1, 5, 3]]
print(minCost(cost, 2, 2))
```

Executing the code snippets yields:

```
Output: 8
```

**Step 1: Identify the Subproblems**. In this problem, a subproblem can be defined as finding the minimum cost to reach a particular cell $(i, j)$ from the starting cell $(0, 0)$.

**Step 2: Define the State**. The state can be represented by a 2D array $\text{min\_cost}[i][j]$, where $\text{min\_cost}[i][j]$ denotes the minimum cost to reach cell $(i, j)$.

**Step 3: Formulate the State Transition**. To transition between states, consider how you arrive at cell $(i, j)$. There are two possibilities: you can either come from the cell above it $(i-1, j)$ or from the cell to the left $(i, j-1)$. Thus, the state transition can be defined as:

$$\text{min\_cost}[i][j] = \text{cost}[i][j] + \text{min}(\text{min\_cost}[i-1][j], \text{min\_cost}[i][j-1])$$

**Step 4: Establish the Base Cases**. The simplest cases are reaching cells in the first row or first column:

- The minimum cost to reach any cell in the first row $(0, j)$ is the sum of the costs of all previous cells in that row.

- The minimum cost to reach any cell in the first column $(i, 0)$ is the sum of the costs of all previous cells in that column.

By following these steps, we efficiently break down the problem, solve each subproblem, and combine their solutions to form the final answer. This methodical decomposition is central to dynamic programming and ensures scalability and reusability of solutions.

Through examples and systematic techniques, learners can develop the skills to decompose any complex problem into manageable subproblems, laying the groundwork for effective dynamic programming solutions.

## 3.5 Identifying Subproblems

Identifying subproblems is a crucial step in the dynamic programming approach. It involves breaking down the original problem into smaller, more manageable components that can be solved individually. These subproblems are then used to build up the solution to the original problem. Each subproblem should ideally be independent and solvable on its own, and the solution to the larger problem should be a combination of these subproblem solutions.

At the onset, it is important to recognize that not all problems can be efficiently tackled using dynamic programming. The problems best suited for dynamic programming are those that exhibit the properties of overlapping subproblems and optimal substructure. Let's explore these concepts through a detailed example.

Consider the classic problem of computing the Fibonacci sequence, where each term is the sum of the two preceding ones, with the sequence starting from 0 and 1. The nth Fibonacci number can be defined using the following recurrence relation:

$$F(n) = F(n-1) + F(n-2)$$

with the base cases:

$$F(0) = 0, \quad F(1) = 1$$

The goal is to determine $F(n)$. To achieve this using dynamic programming, we follow these steps:

1. **Define the Subproblems**: A subproblem in this context would be finding the Fibonacci number for an integer i where $0 \leq i \leq n$. Thus, our subproblems are $F(0), F(1), \ldots, F(n)$.

2. **Formulate the Recurrence Relation**: The Fibonacci problem inherently defines its subproblems through the recurrence relation $F(n) = F(n-1) + F(n-2)$. This relation indicates how to build the solution for $F(n)$ using the solutions for the subproblems $F(n-1)$ and $F(n-2)$.

3. **Identify Base Cases**: Our base cases are directly provided: $F(0) = 0$ and $F(1) = 1$. These serve as the starting point for building up the solution to $F(n)$.

4. **Implementing the Solution Using a Bottom-Up Approach**: The next step is to implement the solution in a way that builds from the base cases up to the desired solution. This is often done using iterations to fill in an array (or other data structure) where each entry corresponds to a subproblem's solution.

Here is a Python implementation:

```
def fibonacci(n):
    # If n is 0 or 1, return n
    if n <= 1:
        return n

    # Create an array to store the subproblem results
    dp = [0] * (n + 1)
    dp[0] = 0
    dp[1] = 1

    # Fill the array with results of subproblems
    for i in range(2, n + 1):
        dp[i] = dp[i-1] + dp[i-2]

    return dp[n]

# Example usage
print(fibonacci(10)) # Output: 55
```

55

In this implementation, the array 'dp' is used to store the Fibonacci numbers for each subproblem from '0' to 'n'. By iterating from '2' to 'n', we fill in the array using the previously computed values.

Another approach employs memoization, which is a top-down technique to store solutions of already solved subproblems to avoid redundant computations. Here is an example:

```
def fibonacci_memo(n, memo=None):
    if memo is None:
        memo = {}

    # If n is 0 or 1, return n
    if n <= 1:
        return n

    # Check if the result is already in the memo dictionary
    if n not in memo:
        memo[n] = fibonacci_memo(n-1, memo) + fibonacci_memo(n-2, memo)

    return memo[n]

# Example usage
print(fibonacci_memo(10)) # Output: 55
```

55

In this memoization implementation, the dictionary 'memo' is used to store the results of subproblems. When a new subproblem is solved, its result is added to 'memo'. This ensures that each subproblem is computed at most once, resulting in a significant efficiency gain.

Identifying subproblems correctly is fundamental not only for the Fibonacci sequence but also in more complex dynamic programming problems. The process involves a systematic examination of the problem's structure, determining how it can be divided into smaller parts, and ensuring that each part can be independently solved and combined. This translates to most dynamic programming solutions across various domains, including optimization, combinatorial problems, and sequence analysis. Proper identification and structuring of subproblems lay the groundwork for an efficient and correct dynamic programming implementation.

## 3.6 Recursive Formulations

A critical step in solving problems with dynamic programming is constructing effective recursive formulations. In this process, the problem at hand is expressed as a function defined in terms of simpler instances of the same problem. This section will provide an in-depth understanding of how to derive recursive formulations and the significance of each component in this process.

To begin, let us consider the essential elements of a recursive formulation. Any recursive solution involves:

- **Base Case(s):** Conditions under which the problem has a trivial solution. These serve to terminate the recursion and prevent infinite loops.

- **Recursive Case(s):** The relationships that express larger problem instances in terms of smaller, more manageable ones.

- **Combining Results:** Methods for aggregating the solutions of subproblems to solve the original problem.

We illustrate these concepts with the example of the Fibonacci sequence. The Fibonacci sequence is defined as:

$$F(n) = \begin{cases} 0, & \text{if } n = 0 \\ 1, & \text{if } n = 1 \\ F(n-1) + F(n-2), & \text{if } n > 1 \end{cases}$$

Here, $0$ and $1$ are the base cases since the Fibonacci sequence is known directly for $n = 0$ and $n = 1$. The recursive case $F(n) = F(n-1) + F(n-2)$ expresses the $n$-th Fibonacci number as the sum of the two preceding numbers.

Implementing this in Python using a straightforward recursive approach looks like this:

```
def fibonacci(n):
    if n == 0:
        return 0
    elif n == 1:
        return 1
    else:
        return fibonacci(n-1) + fibonacci(n-2)
```

Despite the clarity of such straightforward recursion, it has significant inefficiencies. In particular, it repeatedly solves the same subproblems, leading to exponential time complexity $O(2^n)$. Hence, for larger values of $n$, this approach becomes impractical.

To improve upon this, dynamic programming techniques utilize memoization or tabulation, optimizing subproblem computations. First, consider the memoized version:

```
def fibonacci_memo(n, memo={}):
    if n in memo:
        return memo[n]
    if n == 0:
        result = 0
    elif n == 1:
        result = 1
    else:
        result = fibonacci_memo(n-1, memo) + fibonacci_memo(n-2, memo)
    memo[n] = result
    return result
```

The memoized approach stores previously computed results in a dictionary to avoid redundant computations. Next, we can explore tabulation:

```
def fibonacci_tab(n):
    if n == 0:
        return 0
    if n == 1:
        return 1
    fib = [0] * (n+1)
    fib[1] = 1
    for i in range(2, n+1):
```

```
        fib[i] = fib[i-1] + fib[i-2]
    return fib[n]
```

Tabulation builds an array bottom-up, rendering the solution more efficient than naive recursion. The time complexity is now $O(n)$ with an $O(n)$ space complexity. However, further optimization can yield a space complexity $O(1)$:

```
def fibonacci_optimized(n):
    if n == 0:
        return 0
    elif n == 1:
        return 1
    prev, curr = 0, 1
    for _ in range(2, n+1):
        prev, curr = curr, prev + curr
    return curr
```

In this optimized version, only two variables track the last two Fibonacci numbers, achieving both $O(n)$ time complexity and $O(1)$ space complexity.

Understanding recursive formulations is foundational for mastering dynamic programming. They guide the problem decomposition, ensuring that subproblems are both representative of the larger problem and manageable in size. Correctly defining the base cases ensures that recursion terminates appropriately without unnecessary computation.

Recursive formulations with dynamic programming exploit the principle of storing and reusing subproblem solutions, avoiding recomputation, and significantly enhancing efficiency. This methodology not only optimizes classic problems like Fibonacci sequence but also adapts to more complex scenarios, with recursion providing a clear, logical structure for problem solving.

## 3.7 State Transition and Recurrence Relations

State transitions and recurrence relations are fundamental components of dynamic programming (DP). These constructs provide a systematic approach to solving complex problems by breaking them down into simpler subproblems. State transitions explain how one state of a problem evolves into another, while recurrence relations define the principle way of computing the solution of a problem using its subproblems.

To understand state transitions, consider that any dynamic programming problem can be described by its state. A state typically represents a partial solution to the problem at hand. This partial solution generally corresponds to some subset or sub-configuration of the input data. The role of the state transition is to describe how to move from one state to another, thereby gradually progressing towards the complete solution.

One effective way to form these state transitions is to formulate them recursively. The recurrence relation is essentially a recursive formula that expresses the solution to the overall problem in terms of solutions to its smaller subproblems.

**Example: Fibonacci Sequence**

Let us consider a classic example to illustrate these concepts: the Fibonacci sequence.

The Fibonacci sequence is defined as follows:

$$F(n) = \begin{cases} 0 & \text{if } n = 0 \\ 1 & \text{if } n = 1 \\ F(n-1) + F(n-2) & \text{if } n > 1 \end{cases}$$

In this scenario: - The **state** can be defined by the integer $n$. - The **state transition** describes moving from $n-1$ to $n$ or from $n-2$ to $n$. - The **recurrence relation** is $F(n) = F(n-1) + F(n-2)$.

This transition and relation effectively break down the computation of $F(n)$ to computations of $F(n-1)$ and $F(n-2)$.

**Example: Longest Common Subsequence (LCS)**

Consider the problem of finding the length of the longest common subsequence (LCS) between two strings $X$ of length $m$ and $Y$ of length $n$.

The state can be represented by two indices $i$ and $j$ signifying the last elements considered in strings $X$ and $Y$, respectively. Let $L(i, j)$ denote the length of the LCS of the substrings $X[0..i]$ and $Y[0..j]$.

The state transition is defined as:

$$L(i, j) = \begin{cases} 0 & \text{if } i = 0 \text{ or } j = 0 \\ L(i-1, j-1) + 1 & \text{if } X[i-1] = Y[j-1] \\ \max(L(i-1, j), L(i, j-1)) & \text{if } X[i-1] \neq Y[j-1] \end{cases}$$

Here: - States are defined by pairs $(i, j)$. - Transitioning from $(i, j)$ can be accomplished via $(i-1, j-1)$ if the characters match, otherwise via $(i-1, j)$ or $(i, j-1)$. - The recurrence relation captures these transitions.

To implement this recurrence relation, one may use the following Python code:

```
def lcs(X, Y):
    m = len(X)
    n = len(Y)
    dp = [[0] * (n + 1) for _ in range(m + 1)]

    for i in range(1, m + 1):
        for j in range(1, n + 1):
            if X[i-1] == Y[j-1]:
                dp[i][j] = dp[i-1][j-1] + 1
            else:
                dp[i][j] = max(dp[i-1][j], dp[i][j-1])

    return dp[m][n]
```

In this code, the 2D list 'dp' stores LCS values for substrings. The recurrence relations are applied to fill the matrix, ultimately providing the LCS length for strings $X$ and $Y$.

**Example: Knapsack Problem**

For another illustrative example, consider the 0/1 Knapsack problem. Given a set of items, each with a weight and a value, determine the number of each item to include in a collection so that the total weight is less than or equal to a given limit and the total value is as large as possible.

Let $W$ be the maximum weight capacity of the knapsack, and let $w_i$ and $v_i$ represent the weight and value of the $i$-th item, respectively.

Define the state by two parameters: the index $i$, which indicates the items being considered, and $w$, the remaining weight capacity. Let $K(i, w)$ represent the maximum value that can be attained with the remaining capacity $w$ using the first $i$ items.

The recurrence relation is formulated as:

$$K(i, w) = \begin{cases} 0 & \text{if } i = 0 \text{ or } w = 0 \\ K(i-1, w) & \text{if } w_i > w \\ \max(K(i-1, w), K(i-1, w-w_i) + v_i) & \text{if } w_i \leq w \end{cases}$$

In the knapsack problem: - States are represented by pairs $(i, w)$. - Transitioning occurs either by excluding the $i$-th item or including it if its weight does not exceed the current capacity $w$. - The recurrence relation dictates choosing the maximum value achievable.

The implementation in Python might appear as follows:

```
def knapsack(values, weights, W):
    n = len(values)
    dp = [[0] * (W + 1) for _ in range(n + 1)]

    for i in range(1, n + 1):
        for w in range(W + 1):
            if weights[i-1] <= w:
                dp[i][w] = max(dp[i-1][w],
                               dp[i-1][w-weights[i-1]] + values[i-1])
            else:
                dp[i][w] = dp[i-1][w]

    return dp[n][W]
```

This implementation fills a DP table based on the formulated recurrence relation, allowing it to determine the maximum value achievable within the specified weight capacity.

Incorporating these examples shows how fundamental principles of state transitions and recurrence relations can be systematically applied to solve problems using dynamic programming. As these examples demonstrate, defining the states appropriately and formulating accurate recurrence relations are crucial steps in developing correct and efficient dynamic programming solutions.

## 3.8 Defining Base Cases

The concept of defining base cases in dynamic programming (DP) is fundamental for ensuring correct problem-solving processes. Base cases can be considered the simplest subproblems which have direct or trivial solutions. These are essential because they serve as stopping conditions for recursive algorithms and provide the initial values required to build solutions to larger subproblems in iterative algorithms.

In a dynamic programming context, every time we break down a problem into smaller subproblems, we eventually reach the smallest ones, which are our base cases. Properly defining base cases helps in correctly initializing the solution space, ensuring that the recursive or iterative process has a solid foundation to build upon.

**Example: Fibonacci Sequence** The Fibonacci sequence is a classical example used to illustrate base cases. The sequence is defined recursively as:

$$F(n) = F(n-1) + F(n-2), \quad \text{for } n > 1$$
$$F(0) = 0$$
$$F(1) = 1$$

Here, $F(0)$ and $F(1)$ are the base cases. They provide the initial values for constructing further values of the sequence using the recursive relation.

```
def fibonacci(n):
    if n == 0:
        return 0
    if n == 1:
        return 1
    return fibonacci(n - 1) + fibonacci(n - 2)
```

In this recursive implementation, the base cases $F(0)$ and $F(1)$ are explicitly defined to return the immediate results.

**Iterative Approach** An iterative approach in dynamic programming relies equally on accurately defined base cases. Consider the iterative computation of the Fibonacci sequence:

```
def fibonacci_iterative(n):
    fib = [0, 1]
    for i in range(2, n + 1):
        fib.append(fib[-1] + fib[-2])
    return fib[n]
```

In this example,

$$\text{fib[0]} = 0$$

and

$$\text{fib[1]} = 1$$

are the base cases, initializing the list to allow the iteration to build subsequent values correctly.

**Memorization Approach** Dynamic programming often utilizes memoization to store and reuse previously computed values, improving the efficiency of recursive solutions. Memoization also hinges on correctly defining and storing base cases. For the memoized Fibonacci sequence, we define base cases as follows:

```
def fibonacci_memo(n, memo={}):
    if n in memo:
        return memo[n]
    if n == 0:
        return 0
    if n == 1:
```

```
        return 1
    memo[n] = fibonacci_memo(n - 1, memo) + fibonacci_memo(n - 2, memo)
    return memo[n]
```

**Significance of Base Cases in General DP Problems** Proper base case definition is not only a characteristic of the Fibonacci sequence but also a general necessity for DP solution frameworks. Dynamic programming problems, whether one-dimensional, two-dimensional, or multi-dimensional, fundamentally depend on their base cases.

**Example: Coin Change Problem** In the coin change problem, one must find the minimum number of coins required to make a given amount from a set of denominations. Base cases here serve as the foundation for constructing solutions for larger amounts.

```
def coin_change(coins, amount):
    dp = [float('inf')] * (amount + 1)
    dp[0] = 0

    for coin in coins:
        for x in range(coin, amount + 1):
            dp[x] = min(dp[x], dp[x - coin] + 1)

    return dp[amount] if dp[amount] != float('inf') else -1
```

In this example,

$$\text{dp[0]} = 0$$

is the base case, indicating that no coins are needed to make the amount of zero. This setup enables the iterative calculation of the minimum number of coins for progressively larger amounts.

**Role of Base Cases in Avoiding Redundant Calculations** Base cases implicitly dictate the termination of recursive calculations, significantly reducing redundant computations. Consider the factorial function defined recursively:

$$\begin{aligned} n! &= n \times (n-1)!, \quad \text{for } n > 1 \\ 0! &= 1 \end{aligned}$$

Without a base case, a recursive call such as factorial(0) would result in an infinite loop or maximum recursion depth exceeded error. Defining $0! = 1$ as the base case ensures a definitive stopping point.

```
def factorial(n):
    if n == 0:
        return 1
    return n * factorial(n - 1)
```

Base cases not only prevent infinite recursion but also initialize dynamic tables in iterative solutions, enabling progressive computation of solutions.

**Ensuring Correctness and Completeness** Defining base cases is an integral step ensuring the dynamic programming solution's correctness and completeness. They cater to edge cases and ensure that all possible subproblem states are covered, preventing erroneous outcomes or incomplete computations.

When designing a dynamic programming solution, identify the smallest subproblems that have straightforward solutions, then establish these solutions explicitly as base cases. This foundational step is critical to building correct and efficient dynamic programming solutions. Properly defined base cases facilitate the accurate initialization of the dynamic structures and allow the recursive or iterative processes to function seamlessly, constructing the desired solution incrementally.

## 3.9 Evaluating Time Complexity

Analyzing the time complexity of dynamic programming algorithms is essential for understanding their efficiency. Time complexity gives us an approximation of the running time of an algorithm based on the size of its input. This section will cover the basics of evaluating time complexity in dynamic programming, focusing on common techniques and patterns.

Dynamic programming algorithms typically involve two key components: the number of subproblems to be solved and the time required to solve each subproblem. The total time complexity is the product of these two factors.

To begin, consider a dynamic programming problem, and let $n$ represent the size of the input, which could be the number of elements in an array, the length of a sequence, etc. Suppose the algorithm solves $P(n)$ subproblems. Let $T(n)$ denote the time required to solve each subproblem. Thus, the overall time complexity $C(n)$ can be represented as:

$$C(n) = P(n) \times T(n)$$

Evaluating $P(n)$ involves determining the total number of distinct subproblems the algorithm needs to solve. Often, this count depends on parameters like the length of the input sequence or the dimensions of the problem's state space. For instance, in a problem involving two dimensions, such as a grid, $P(n)$ might be expressed in terms of two parameters, e.g., $n$ and $m$.

Next, $T(n)$ represents the computational work needed per subproblem. This usually involves basic operations like addition, comparison, or function calls, which can often be considered $O(1)$ if they take constant time. However, some subproblems might involve more substantial computations, especially if they require iterating over multiple dimensions or recursive calls.

Let's consider a typical example to illustrate evaluating time complexity in practice. Suppose we have a dynamic programming solution to the classic Fibonacci sequence problem. The recursive formulation is:

$$F(n) = F(n-1) + F(n-2)$$

When expressed as a dynamic programming problem, we use a table to store the results of previously computed terms:

```
def fibonacci_dp(n):
    if n <= 1:
        return n
    dp = [0] * (n + 1)
    dp[1] = 1
    for i in range(2, n + 1):
        dp[i] = dp[i - 1] + dp[i - 2]
    return dp[n]
```

For the Fibonacci sequence problem, the number of subproblems $P(n)$ is directly related to the value of $n$. Each term from $F(0)$ to $F(n)$ is computed exactly once. Thus, $P(n) = n$.

The time to solve each subproblem, $T(n)$, involves a constant number of operations (specifically, a simple addition). Therefore, $T(n) = O(1)$.

Combining these components, the overall time complexity is:

$$C(n) = P(n) \times T(n) = n \times O(1) = O(n)$$

Consider another example involving a two-dimensional table, such as the Longest Common Subsequence (LCS) problem. The recursive relationship for LCS is:

$$LCS(X, Y) = \begin{cases} 0 & : i = 0 \text{ or } j = 0 \\ LCS(X_{i-1}, Y_{j-1}) + 1 & : X[i] = Y[j] \\ \max(LCS(X_{i-1}, Y), LCS(X, Y_{j-1})) & : X[i] \neq Y[j] \end{cases}$$

The dynamic programming approach involves filling a 2D table of size $m \times n$, where $m$ and $n$ are the lengths of sequences $X$ and $Y$:

```
def lcs_dp(X, Y):
    m, n = len(X), len(Y)
    dp = [[0] * (n + 1) for _ in range(m + 1)]
    for i in range(1, m + 1):
        for j in range(1, n + 1):
            if X[i - 1] == Y[j - 1]:
                dp[i][j] = dp[i - 1][j - 1] + 1
            else:
                dp[i][j] = max(dp[i - 1][j], dp[i][j - 1])
    return dp[m][n]
```

For the LCS problem, the number of subproblems $P(n)$ is related to both dimensions $m$ and $n$, giving $P(n) = m \times n$.

Solving each subproblem takes constant time, as it involves basic comparisons and assignments. Hence, $T(n) = O(1)$.

Thus, the overall time complexity for the LCS problem is:

$$C(n) = P(n) \times T(n) = m \times n \times O(1) = O(mn)$$

Evaluating time complexity also requires an understanding of the algorithm's reliance on previously computed values. For top-down approaches with memoization, time complexity similarly reflects the number of unique states visited and the time taken per state. Consider the top-down memoization version of the Fibonacci sequence:

```
def fibonacci_memo(n, memo={}):
    if n in memo:
        return memo[n]
    if n <= 1:
        return n
    memo[n] = fibonacci_memo(n-1, memo) + fibonacci_memo(n-2, memo)
    return memo[n]
```

Here, memoization ensures each state is computed only once, thus yielding $P(n) = n$ and $T(n) = O(1)$, resulting in an overall $O(n)$ time complexity.

In more complex problems, factors affecting the time complexity include the dimensionality of the problem space, the structure of the recurrence relation, and whether the problem's constraints influence the number of computed subproblems. Understanding these aspects enables precise time complexity analysis, paving the way for optimizing and comparing various dynamic programming solutions.

```
Output for fibonacci_dp(10):
55

Output for lcs_dp("ABCBDAB", "BDCAB"):
4
```

These examples illustrate the process of decomposing the overall time complexity into understandable components and fitting those together to grasp the efficiency of dynamic programming algorithms. Effective time complexity analysis allows one to anticipate performance issues and apply necessary optimizations, crucial for real-world problem-solving.

## 3.10 Comparing Recursion and DP Formulations

Recursion and dynamic programming (DP) are closely related concepts, yet they differ fundamentally in their approach toward solving complex problems. Understanding these differences and knowing when to utilize each methodology is essential for designing efficient algorithms.

Recursion is a method where the solution to a problem depends on solutions to smaller instances of the same problem. It often manifests as a function that calls itself directly or indirectly. With dynamic programming, we explicitly store the solutions to subproblems to avoid redundant calculations, transforming an exponential time complexity solution into a polynomial one.

Consider a classic example, the Fibonacci sequence, where each term is the sum of the two preceding ones. A naive recursive approach to compute the nth Fibonacci number can be implemented as follows:

```
def fibonacci_recursive(n):
    if n <= 1:
        return n
    return fibonacci_recursive(n-1) + fibonacci_recursive(n-2)
```

The above function is simple but highly inefficient for large values of $n$. This inefficiency arises because the same subproblems are solved multiple times. For instance, to compute $fibonacci\_recursive(5)$, the subproblem $fibonacci\_recursive(3)$ is solved twice, once for $fibonacci\_recursive(5)$ and once for $fibonacci\_recursive(4)$.

To illustrate this redundancy, consider the recursive calls tree for $fibonacci\_recursive(5)$:

```
fibonacci_recursive(5)
  -> fibonacci_recursive(4)
    -> fibonacci_recursive(3)
      -> fibonacci_recursive(2)
        -> fibonacci_recursive(1)
        -> fibonacci_recursive(0)
      -> fibonacci_recursive(1)
    -> fibonacci_recursive(2)
      -> fibonacci_recursive(1)
      -> fibonacci_recursive(0)
  -> fibonacci_recursive(3)
    -> fibonacci_recursive(2)
      -> fibonacci_recursive(1)
      -> fibonacci_recursive(0)
    -> fibonacci_recursive(1)
```

In contrast, dynamic programming optimizes this process by storing already computed values, thereby eliminating redundant calculations. There are two common approaches in dynamic programming: top-down with memoization and bottom-up with tabulation.

**Top-Down Approach:** Here, we use recursion but store the results of subproblems to avoid redundant computations.

```
def fibonacci_memoization(n, memo=None):
  if memo is None:
    memo = {}
  if n in memo:
    return memo[n]
  if n <= 1:
    return n
  memo[n] = fibonacci_memoization(n-1, memo) + fibonacci_memoization(n-2,
     memo)
  return memo[n]
```

In the top-down approach with memoization, we store the results of each subproblem in a dictionary (or an array) called 'memo'. This prevents redundant calculations. The call tree now only computes each Fibonacci number once:

```
fibonacci_memoization(5)
  -> fibonacci_memoization(4)
    -> fibonacci_memoization(3)
      -> fibonacci_memoization(2)
        -> fibonacci_memoization(1) -> 1
        -> fibonacci_memoization(0) -> 0
      -> 1 + 0 = 1
    -> fibonacci_memoization(2) -> 1
  -> 1 + 1 + 1 = 2
  -> fibonacci_memoization(3) -> 2
2 + 1 + 1 = 3
```

**Bottom-Up Approach:** Here, we iteratively compute the values starting from the base cases to the desired result.

```
def fibonacci_bottom_up(n):
  if n <= 1:
    return n
```

```
fib = [0] * (n + 1)
fib[1] = 1
for i in range(2, n + 1):
    fib[i] = fib[i - 1] + fib[i - 2]
return fib[n]
```

In the bottom-up approach, we use an array 'fib' to store our results. We iteratively compute the Fibonacci numbers from the base cases up to $n$. This approach ensures that each subproblem is solved once in a straightforward manner.

When comparing recursion and dynamic programming, several key differences emerge:

- **Time Complexity:** Recursive solutions like $fibonacci\_recursive$ often exhibit exponential time complexity, $O(2^n)$, due to redundant calculations. In contrast, both memoized and tabulated DP approaches reduce the time complexity to $O(n)$ by storing intermediate results.

- **Space Complexity:** Recursive solutions involve a call stack that can go up to $O(n)$ in depth. Memoization adds a $O(n)$ auxiliary space for storing intermediate results. Tabulation typically uses $O(n)$ space for storage and constant space for the iterative variables.

- **Duplication of Work:** Recursive methods without memoization redundantly solve the same subproblems multiple times. Memoization and tabulation store intermediate results to ensure each subproblem is solved only once.

- **Ease of Implementation:** Recursive methods can be easier to implement and understand due to their direct reflection of the problem's definition. However, dynamic programming tends to be more efficient by avoiding redundant work.

Recognizing the superiority of dynamic programming in handling overlapping subproblems and ensuring optimal substructure is crucial. This knowledge empowers the developer to switch from simple recursive solutions to more efficient, DP-based methods when required, thus effectively managing computational resources.

## 3.11 Examples of Principle Applications

Dynamic Programming (DP) can be illustrated through numerous classical examples that encapsulate its core principles: overlapping subproblems and optimal substructure. This section presents several such examples, demonstrating the concepts discussed earlier in the chapter with concrete implementations and detailed explanations.

### 1. Fibonacci Sequence

A fundamental example of DP is computing the Fibonacci sequence. Traditionally, the Fibonacci numbers are defined by the recurrence relation:

$$F(n) = F(n-1) + F(n-2) \quad \text{with base cases} \quad F(0) = 0, F(1) = 1$$

A naive recursive approach unnecessarily recomputes values, leading to exponential time complexity. By storing intermediate results using dynamic programming, we reduce this to linear time complexity.

```
def fibonacci(n):
    if n <= 1:
        return n
    fib = [0] * (n + 1)
    fib[1] = 1
    for i in range(2, n + 1):
        fib[i] = fib[i - 1] + fib[i - 2]
    return fib[n]
```

Output for $n = 10$:

```
55
```

### 2. Longest Common Subsequence (LCS)

The LCS problem is to find the longest subsequence common to two sequences. It exhibits optimal substructure: if $X[i] = Y[j]$, then $LCS(X,Y) = LCS(X[1\ldots i-1], Y[1\ldots j-1]) + 1$. Otherwise, $LCS(X,Y) = \max(LCS(X[1\ldots i], Y[1\ldots j-1]), LCS(X[1\ldots i-1], Y[1\ldots j]))$.

```
def lcs(X, Y):
    m = len(X)
    n = len(Y)
    L = [[0] * (n + 1) for i in range(m + 1)]
    for i in range(m + 1):
        for j in range(n + 1):
            if i == 0 or j == 0:
                L[i][j] = 0
            elif X[i - 1] == Y[j - 1]:
```

```
            L[i][j] = L[i - 1][j - 1] + 1
        else:
            L[i][j] = max(L[i - 1][j], L[i][j - 1])
return L[m][n]
```

Running the function with $X =' AGGTAB'$ and $Y =' GXTXAYB'$ yields:

```
4
```

### 3. Knapsack Problem

The 0/1 Knapsack Problem conveys the fundamental nature of DP in optimization problems. Given weights and values of $n$ items and a knapsack capacity $W$, maximize the total value without exceeding the capacity. Define $dp[i][w]$ as the maximum value for the first $i$ items with a total weight limit $w$.

```
def knapsack(W, wt, val, n):
    K = [[0 for x in range(W + 1)] for i in range(n + 1)]
    for i in range(n + 1):
        for w in range(W + 1):
            if i == 0 or w == 0:
                K[i][w] = 0
            elif wt[i - 1] <= w:
                K[i][w] = max(val[i - 1] + K[i - 1][w - wt[i - 1]], K[i - 1][w])
            else:
                K[i][w] = K[i - 1][w]
    return K[n][W]
```

For weights $wt = [1, 3, 4, 5]$, values $val = [1, 4, 5, 7]$ and capacity $W = 7$:

```
9
```

### 4. Matrix Chain Multiplication

Another instructive example is the Matrix Chain Multiplication problem, which seeks to determine the most efficient way to multiply a given sequence of matrices. The goal is to minimize the total number of scalar multiplications.

$$m[i, j] = \min_{i \leq k < j} \{m[i, k] + m[k + 1, j] + p_{i-1} \cdot p_k \cdot p_j\}$$

```
def matrix_chain_order(p):
    n = len(p) - 1
    m = [[0 for x in range(n)] for x in range(n)]
    for length in range(2, n + 1):
        for i in range(n - length + 1):
            j = i + length - 1
            m[i][j] = float('inf')
            for k in range(i, j):
```

```
            q = m[i][k] + m[k+1][j] + p[i]*p[k+1]*p[j+1]
            if q < m[i][j]:
                m[i][j] = q
    return m[0][n-1]
```

With dimensions array $p = [1, 2, 3, 4]$:

18

### 5. Edit Distance

Edit Distance measures the minimum number of operations required to convert string $A$ to string $B$. The possible operations are insertion, deletion, or substitution of a single character. Define $dp[i][j]$ as the edit distance between $A[0 \ldots i-1]$ and $B[0 \ldots j-1]$.

```
def edit_distance(A, B):
    m = len(A)
    n = len(B)
    dp = [[0 for x in range(n + 1)] for x in range(m + 1)]
    for i in range(m + 1):
        for j in range(n + 1):
            if i == 0:
                dp[i][j] = j
            elif j == 0:
                dp[i][j] = i
            elif A[i - 1] == B[j - 1]:
                dp[i][j] = dp[i - 1][j - 1]
            else:
                dp[i][j] = 1 + min(dp[i][j - 1], dp[i - 1][j], dp[i - 1][j - 1])
    return dp[m][n]
```

For $A =' kitten'$ and $B =' sitting'$:

3

These examples demonstrate the application of dynamic programming principles to various computational problems. Implementing these examples aids in grasping complex DP concepts while establishing a foundation for solving more intricate DP problems efficiently. Each example illustrates the transition from a recursive relation to an iterative dynamic program, emphasizing storage and reuse of intermediate results.

## 3.12 Common Mistakes and How to Avoid Them

When solving dynamic programming (DP) problems, there are several common mistakes that learners and even experienced practitioners often encounter. These errors can lead to incorrect solutions, inefficient algorithms, or increased difficulty in problem-solving. Recognizing these mistakes and understanding how to avoid them is crucial for mastering dynamic programming.

**1. Improperly Defining the State:**

One of the most frequent errors is not correctly defining the state of the DP. The state should represent the subproblems in such a way that solving these subproblems leads to solving the original problem.

- *Mistake:* Defining the state too broadly or too narrowly, which makes it difficult to relate the subproblems to the overall problem.
- *Solution:* Ensure that the state is neither too general nor too specific. The state should capture only the necessary information required to compute the solution.

Consider the following example where we try to find the number of ways to reach the $n$th step if we can take either 1 or 2 steps at a time:

```
# Incorrect State Definition

def count_ways(n):
    if n == 0 or n == 1:
        return 1
    return count_ways(n-1) + count_ways(n-2)
```

Correcting the state definition would involve using memoization to store the results of subproblems:

```
# Correct State Definition

def count_ways(n, memo={}):
    if n == 0 or n == 1:
        return 1
    if n not in memo:
        memo[n] = count_ways(n-1, memo) + count_ways(n-2, memo)
    return memo[n]
```

**2. Ignoring Base Cases:**

The base cases are critical in dynamic programming as they provide the termination condition for the recursive calls. Without well-defined base cases, the recursion could end up in infinite loops or stack overflow.

- *Mistake:* Omitting or incorrectly defining the base cases, leading to incorrect results or infinite recursion.
- *Solution:* Clearly identify and define base cases before addressing the recursive or iterative steps of the solution.

In the example above, the base cases are correctly defined as $n = 0$ and $n = 1$.

**3. Overlapping Subproblems Missing Memoization:**

Failing to save the results of already computed subproblems, causing redundant calculations and inefficiencies.

- *Mistake:* Recomputing the same subproblems multiple times.
- *Solution:* Use a memoization table to store results of subproblems as soon as they are computed.

```
# Without Memoization (Inefficient)

def fib(n):
    if n <= 1:
        return n
    return fib(n-1) + fib(n-2)

# With Memoization (Efficient)

def fib_memo(n, memo={}):
    if n <= 1:
        return n
    if n not in memo:
        memo[n] = fib_memo(n-1, memo) + fib_memo(n-2, memo)
    return memo[n]
```

**4. Misinterpreting the Problem Requirements:**

Misunderstanding the problem requirements or constraints can lead to incorrect state definitions, missed base cases, and wrong transition relations.

- *Mistake:* Not fully grasping the problem constraints and requirements.
- *Solution:* Carefully read and understand the problem statement and constraints before attempting to write the DP solution.

**5. Not Accounting for All State Transitions:**

State transitions form the backbone of the recurrence relation. Failing to account for all possible transitions leads to incomplete or incorrect results.

- *Mistake:* Missing out on potential transitions between states.

- *Solution:* Thoroughly analyze the problem to ensure all state transitions are incorporated.

For a problem where we want to find the minimum cost path in a grid from the top-left to the bottom-right, each cell can be reached either from the cell to its left or the one above it:

```
def min_cost_path(cost, m, n):
    dp = [[0 for _ in range(n+1)] for _ in range(m+1)]

    dp[0][0] = cost[0][0]

    # Initialize the first column
    for i in range(1, m+1):
        dp[i][0] = dp[i-1][0] + cost[i][0]

    # Initialize the first row
    for j in range(1, n+1):
        dp[0][j] = dp[0][j-1] + cost[0][j]

    # Fill the dp array
    for i in range(1, m+1):
        for j in range(1, n+1):
            dp[i][j] = min(dp[i-1][j], dp[i][j-1]) + cost[i][j]

    return dp[m][n]
```

**6. Inefficient Space Utilization:**

Many DP solutions can be optimized for space by recognizing that not all previously computed values need to be stored.

- *Mistake:* Using excessive memory by retaining all intermediate computations.

- *Solution:* Optimize space using techniques such as sliding window or reduction of dimensions.

The classic 0/1 Knapsack problem can be solved with space optimization as shown:

```
# Without Space Optimization

def knapsack(w, wt, val, n):
    K = [[0 for _ in range(w+1)] for _ in range(n+1)]
    for i in range(n+1):
        for W in range(w+1):
            if i == 0 or W == 0:
                K[i][W] = 0
            elif wt[i-1] <= W:
                K[i][W] = max(val[i-1] + K[i-1][W-wt[i-1]], K[i-1][W])
            else:
                K[i][W] = K[i-1][W]
    return K[n][w]
```

```
# With Space Optimization

def knapsack_opt(w, wt, val, n):
    K = [0 for _ in range(w+1)]
    for i in range(n):
        for W in range(w, wt[i]-1, -1):
            K[W] = max(K[W], K[W-wt[i]] + val[i])
    return K[w]
```

Understanding these common mistakes and learning strategies to avoid them will enhance your proficiency in applying dynamic programming techniques effectively. This section serves as a guide to recognizing pitfalls and optimizing your approach to DP problems. Think critically about the problem at hand, validate your states and transitions, and ensure efficient memory use for improved problem-solving.

# Chapter 4

# Top-Down vs. Bottom-Up Approaches

**In this chapter, we explore the two main approaches to dynamic programming: top-down and bottom-up. We examine how each approach works, their advantages and disadvantages, and when to use one over the other. The chapter includes detailed explanations of memoization in the top-down approach and tabulation in the bottom-up approach, along with case studies and practical examples. We also discuss converting solutions between the two approaches to highlight their flexibility. Understanding these strategies will enable readers to choose the most effective method for a given problem.**

## 4.1 Introduction to Top-Down and Bottom-Up Approaches

Dynamic programming is a powerful technique used to solve complex problems efficiently by breaking them down into simpler subproblems. The two primary strategies for implementing dynamic programming algorithms are the top-down approach with memoization and the bottom-up approach with tabulation. Understanding these two methodologies is crucial for selecting the appropriate technique based on the problem's characteristics and constraints.

The **top-down approach**, also known as memoization, involves solving the problem using a recursive strategy and storing the results of subproblems to avoid redundant calculations. This strategy starts with the overall problem and breaks it down into smaller subproblems. Each subproblem is solved and the result is stored, typically in a dictionary or an array, so that it can be reused when needed. This method is particularly effective when the recursive tree of the problem has overlapping subproblems, which, if calculated repeatedly, would result in unnecessary computation and increased time complexity.

An illustrative example of the top-down approach can be seen in the computation of the Fibonacci sequence. The naive recursive solution exhibits exponential time complexity due to the repeated calculation of the same Fibonacci numbers. By employing memoization, we can significantly reduce the computational overhead as follows:

```
def fibonacci(n, memo={}):
    if n in memo:
        return memo[n]
    if n <= 1:
        return n
    memo[n] = fibonacci(n-1, memo) + fibonacci(n-2, memo)
    return memo[n]
```

The **bottom-up approach**, or tabulation, in contrast, involves solving the problem by iteratively solving smaller subproblems and using these solutions to build up the solution to the overall problem. This approach typically uses an iterative process and a table (often an array) to store the solutions to subproblems. By starting with the smallest subproblems and solving them in an ascending order, this method ensures that each subproblem is solved only once, and solutions to smaller subproblems are always available when needed for solving larger subproblems.

Consider the same Fibonacci sequence problem implemented using the bottom-up approach:

```
def fibonacci(n):
    if n <= 1:
        return n
    fib = [0] * (n + 1)
    fib[1] = 1
    for i in range(2, n + 1):
        fib[i] = fib[i - 1] + fib[i - 2]
    return fib[n]
```

The core idea behind both approaches is the reusability of solutions to subproblems, but they differ in their execution and storage strategies. The top-down approach uses a recursive structure and stores results as the recursion unwinds, whereas the bottom-up approach iteratively builds solutions from the smallest subproblems up to the main problem.

Analyzing the time and space complexity of these approaches reveals interesting insights. With memoization, assuming we store already computed results, each subproblem is solved exactly once, reducing time complexity to $O(n)$ for the Fibonacci problem. However, the space complexity includes the recursion stack, potentially leading to $O(n)$ additional stack space. In the bottom-up approach, time complexity is similarly $O(n)$, with space complexity depending primarily on the storage of subproblem solutions, also resulting in $O(n)$.

Selecting between the top-down and bottom-up approaches often involves considering factors such as recursion depth, stack space limitations, and the nature of the problem's subproblems. Memoization and recursion can be more intuitive for problems with a naturally recursive structure, while the iterative nature of tabulation simplifies managing subproblem dependencies. By mastering both techniques, one can choose the most appropriate strategy for optimizing the dynamic programming solution to a given problem.

## 4.2 Understanding Top-Down Approach

The top-down approach, often referred to as the memoization technique, begins solving the problem from the highest level, breaking it down into simpler sub-problems. This method is both intuitive and recursive, making it easier to identify and solve sub-problems dynamically. The primary concept revolves around a recursive function that makes decisions based on solving smaller, more manageable problems and storing their results to avoid repeated computation.

To illustrate this, consider the classic Fibonacci sequence, where each number is the sum of the two preceding ones, starting from 0 and 1. The naive recursive solution has an exponential time complexity, which can be drastically reduced using the memoization technique.

We define a recursive function, say $\mathrm{fib}$, for calculating the $\mathrm{n}$-th Fibonacci number. Without memoization, the same Fibonacci numbers are recalculated multiple times leading to redundant computations. By storing the results of these intermediate calculations, we enhance the efficiency significantly. Here's how you implement memoization in Python:

```
def fib(n, memo={}):
    if n in memo:
        return memo[n]
```

```
    if n <= 2:
        return 1
    memo[n] = fib(n-1, memo) + fib(n-2, memo)
    return memo[n]

# Example usage
print(fib(10)) # Output: 55
print(fib(50)) # Output: 12586269025
```

In this example, the memo dictionary is used to store previously computed Fibonacci numbers. Each time the function fib is called, it first checks if the result is already in the dictionary. If so, it returns the cached value, avoiding redundant calculations. This reduces the time complexity to $O(n)$, a significant improvement over the naive approach.

**Key Characteristics of Top-Down Approach**

- **Recursion**: At its core, the top-down approach utilizes recursion. Each problem is divided into sub-problems, which are further broken down until the base case is reached.
- **Memoization**: An essential feature of this approach is storing the results of recursive calls. This is often implemented using hash tables, dictionaries, or arrays.
- **Intuitiveness**: The recursive nature of this method closely mirrors the problem definition, making it easier to understand and implement.
- **Optimal Substructure**: For the memoization technique to be effective, the problem must exhibit optimal substructure, meaning the optimal solution to the problem comprises optimal solutions to its sub-problems.

Consider another example: the problem of computing the minimum cost of climbing stairs, where each step i has a certain cost associated with it, cost[i]. You can either take one step or two steps at a time. To find the minimum cost to reach the top, we can use a similar memoization technique.

```
def minCostClimbingStairs(cost, n, memo={}):
    if n <= 1:
        return 0
    if n in memo:
        return memo[n]
    takeOneStep = cost[n-1] + minCostClimbingStairs(cost, n-1, memo)
    takeTwoSteps = cost[n-2] + minCostClimbingStairs(cost, n-2, memo)
    memo[n] = min(takeOneStep, takeTwoSteps)
    return memo[n]
```

```
# Example usage
cost = [10, 15, 20]
n = len(cost)
print(minCostClimbingStairs(cost, n)) # Output: 15
```

In this code, the recursive function minCostClimbingStairs calculates the minimum cost to reach the top of the stairs given a list of costs. The function maintains a memo to store the results of previously computed sub-problems, ensuring each sub-problem is solved only once.

**Benefits and Limitations**

**Benefits**:

- **Reduced Computation Time**: By storing intermediate results, memoization avoids redundant calculations, significantly reducing computation time for overlapping sub-problems.
- **Ease of Implementation**: The recursive nature aligns with the problem's natural definition, making the implementation straightforward, especially for problems with complex dependencies.
- **Memory Efficiency**: Memoization only stores required intermediate results, making it memory efficient compared to some iterative methods which might need to store entire tables or matrices.

**Limitations**:

- **Stack Overflow**: Deep recursion in the top-down approach can lead to a stack overflow, especially for problems with a large input size or depth.
- **Memory Consumption**: While generally memory efficient, the top-down approach still requires additional memory for storing intermediate results, which may be a constraint in memory-limited environments.

Given these characteristics, the top-down approach is particularly useful for problems where sub-problems overlap and can be reused. It provides a clear and efficient method once the recursive relationship is known and helps in developing a close understanding of the problem's structure, aiding in the identification of reusable sub-problems.

This approach seamlessly integrates with Python due to its built-in support for recursion and data structures like dictionaries, which facilitate quick and efficient storage and retrieval of intermediate results. The decision to use the top-down approach often hinges on the problem's specific constraints and the relative importance of computational time versus memory usage.

## 4.3 Understanding Bottom-Up Approach

The bottom-up approach to dynamic programming solves problems by starting from the simplest subproblems and building up to the solution of the original problem. This method is also known as the iterative or tabulation approach. Unlike the top-down approach, which relies on the recursive computation of subproblems and memoization, the bottom-up approach iteratively fills a table (or array) based on the previously computed values.

The key steps to implementing the bottom-up approach are as follows:

- Define the structure of the table that will hold intermediate results.
- Initialize the table with base cases.
- Fill the table in a manner that each cell is computed based on the values of cells that have already been filled.
- Retrieve the result for the desired problem from an appropriate table cell.

To illustrate this process, consider the classic example of computing the $n$-th Fibonacci number, defined as:

$$F(n) = \begin{cases} 0 & \text{if } n = 0 \\ 1 & \text{if } n = 1 \\ F(n-1) + F(n-2) & \text{if } n > 1 \end{cases}$$

Using the bottom-up approach, we first create an array to hold the Fibonacci numbers up to the $n$-th number. The size of the array will be $n+1$, where the $i$-th entry will store $F(i)$. The critical insight here is that each Fibonacci number only depends on the two preceding numbers, allowing us to fill the array iteratively from the base cases up to the desired $n$-th Fibonacci number.

Here is the corresponding Python implementation:

```
def fibonacci_bottom_up(n):
    if n == 0:
        return 0
    elif n == 1:
        return 1

    fib_table = [0] * (n + 1)
    fib_table[0] = 0
    fib_table[1] = 1

    for i in range(2, n + 1):
        fib_table[i] = fib_table[i - 1] + fib_table[i - 2]

    return fib_table[n]

# Example usage
n = 10
print(f"Fibonacci({n}) =", fibonacci_bottom_up(n))
```

The execution of the program output is demonstrated below for $n = 10$:

```
Fibonacci(10) = 55
```

The $\text{fibonacci\_bottom\_up}$ function begins by checking for the base cases of $n = 0$ and $n = 1$. For $n = 0$, the function directly returns $0$, and for $n = 1$, it returns $1$. For any other value of $n$, the function initializes an array $\text{fib\_table}$ of size $n+1$ to store the intermediate results. The array is then populated iteratively, starting from the base cases $\text{fib\_table}[0]$ and $\text{fib\_table}[1]$. Finally, the array is filled up to $\text{fib\_table}[n]$, which contains the $n$-th Fibonacci number.

The bottom-up approach ensures that each subproblem is solved only once, and the solution to each larger problem is built directly from the solutions to smaller subproblems. This approach avoids the overhead of function calls and recursion inherent in the top-down approach.

The efficacy of the bottom-up approach becomes even more pronounced when solving problems with overlapping subproblems and optimal substructure. Consider the problem of computing the minimum cost path in a grid where each cell contains a cost and we can only move right or down. The goal is to find the minimum cost path from the top-left to the bottom-right corner.

Let the grid be represented by a 2-dimensional array $\text{cost}$ where $\text{cost}[i][j]$ is the cost of moving through cell $(i, j)$. Define $\text{min\_cost}[i][j]$ as the minimum cost to reach cell $(i, j)$ from the top-left corner $(0, 0)$.

The dynamic programming recurrence relation is:

$$\text{min\_cost}[i][j] = \text{cost}[i][j] + \text{min}\begin{cases} \text{min\_cost}[i-1][j] & \text{if moving down from } (i-1, j) \\ \text{min\_cost}[i][j-1] & \text{if moving right from } (i, j-1) \end{cases}$$

The base case is initialized as:

$$\text{min\_cost}[0][0] = \text{cost}[0][0]$$

We then fill the table $\text{min\_cost}$ iteratively:

Here is the Python implementation:

```
def min_cost_path(cost):
    rows = len(cost)
    cols = len(cost[0])

    min_cost = [[0 for _ in range(cols)] for _ in range(rows)]
    min_cost[0][0] = cost[0][0]

    for i in range(1, rows):
        min_cost[i][0] = min_cost[i - 1][0] + cost[i][0]

    for j in range(1, cols):
        min_cost[0][j] = min_cost[0][j - 1] + cost[0][j]

    for i in range(1, rows):
        for j in range(1, cols):
            min_cost[i][j] = cost[i][j] + min(min_cost[i-1][j], min_cost[i][j-1])

    return min_cost[rows-1][cols-1]

# Example usage
cost = [
    [1, 2, 3],
    [4, 8, 2],
    [1, 5, 3]
]
print("Minimum cost path =", min_cost_path(cost))
```

The execution of the program output is demonstrated below:

```
Minimum cost path = 8
```

In the $\text{min\_cost\_path}$ function, we initialize the table $\text{min\_cost}$ with the same dimensions as the input $\text{cost}$ grid. The cell $\text{min\_cost}[0][0]$ is initialized to $\text{cost}[0][0]$. Then, we fill the first row and first column of $\text{min\_cost}$ since there are only single paths to these cells. For the remaining cells, the minimum cost to reach each cell is computed based on the minimum cost edges leading to that cell.

Both examples illustrate the significant advantage of the bottom-up approach in terms of time complexity, which is typically $O(n)$ for one-dimensional problems and $O(m \cdot n)$ for two-dimensional problems, where $m$ and $n$ represent the dimensions of the problem space (e.g., the grid dimensions).

Overall, the bottom-up approach to dynamic programming provides an iterative and efficient way to solve complex problems by breaking them down into smaller subproblems and systematically building the solution.

## 4.4 Comparing Top-Down and Bottom-Up

When analyzing dynamic programming (DP) approaches, it is crucial to understand the fundamental distinctions between the top-down and bottom-up methodologies. Both strategies aim to solve complex problems by breaking them down into simpler subproblems, however, they do so in different manners. This section will delve into these differences, highlighting the core principles, performance considerations, and practical applications of each approach.

The top-down approach, often referred to as memoization, works by recursively breaking down a problem into smaller subproblems. It starts solving the given problem directly and solves each subproblem as encountered, storing the results of subproblems to avoid redundant computations. It can be implemented efficiently using a recursive function combined with a data structure to store intermediate results, typically a dictionary in Python.

```
def fibonacci_top_down(n, memo={}):
    if n in memo:
        return memo[n]
    if n <= 1:
        return n
    memo[n] = fibonacci_top_down(n-1, memo) + fibonacci_top_down(n-2, memo)
    return memo[n]

print(fibonacci_top_down(10))
```

```
Output:
55
```

The bottom-up approach, also referred to as tabulation, starts by solving the smallest subproblems and uses their solutions to build up the solution to the original problem. This method typically involves iterative constructs and systematically solves all possible subproblems, storing their results in a tabular form.

```
def fibonacci_bottom_up(n):
    if n <= 1:
        return n
    fib_table = [0] * (n + 1)
    fib_table[1] = 1
```

```
    for i in range(2, n + 1):
        fib_table[i] = fib_table[i-1] + fib_table[i-2]
    return fib_table[n]

print(fibonacci_bottom_up(10))
```

Output:
55

Examining the two examples above reveals the primary difference in methodology. The top-down version begins the computation at 'n' and proceeds recursively downward, storing computations to avoid redundancy. The bottom-up version begins at the base cases and iteratively computes up to 'n', systematically filling a table.

Performance-wise, the top-down approach can have high memory usage due to the recursive call stack, especially in languages that do not optimize tail recursion. It also carries the risk of stack overflow for deep recursions. However, it is often more intuitive and easier to implement when the problem is more naturally described recursively.

Conversely, the bottom-up approach uses constant auxiliary stack space, thus avoiding the pitfalls of recursion. Additionally, in some cases, it can be more efficient due to better locality of reference, as it often accesses elements of an array sequentially. However, it may require predefining the size of the table and can be harder to construct correctly due to the need to establish the correct order of computations.

A quantitative comparison is also valuable. Consider the space complexity: for the Fibonacci example, the top-down approach with memoization will use $O(n)$ space for the memoization table plus maximum recursion stack depth (which is $O(n)$) if not optimized, leading to a total of $O(n)$ space. On the other hand, the bottom-up method uses $O(n)$ space for the table and $O(1)$ additional space for loop variables.

In practice, the choice between these approaches may depend on the specific problem context:

- Use the top-down approach when the problem has overlapping subproblems and can be described naturally in a recursive manner.
- Use the bottom-up approach for problems where determining the order of subproblem computation is straightforward, and there is a need to optimize space usage by avoiding recursion overhead.

Both methodologies exemplify the underlying essence of dynamic programming: solving complex problems by combining solutions of overlapping subproblems. Each has its own benefits and suitable use cases, and understanding their distinctions ensures more effective problem-solving strategies in varied scenarios.

## 4.5 Pros and Cons of Each Approach

The choice between top-down and bottom-up approaches in dynamic programming (DP) is pivotal in determining both the efficiency and readability of the solution. Each approach has distinctive strengths and weaknesses, which can influence their suitability depending on the specific problem and computational constraints.

The **top-down approach** primarily relies on recursive function calls paired with memoization to store the results of subproblems. This approach is often intuitive for problems that can naturally be broken down into smaller subproblems, especially when designing a solution from a high-level perspective.

- **Pros**:
  - **Ease of Implementation**: Often, the top-down approach allows for a more straightforward and intuitive implementation. Recursive functions closely align with the mathematical formulation of many problems, making the transition from problem statement to code seamless.
  - **Reduced Code Complexity**: By leveraging recursion, top-down DP tends to be more concise. Developers can focus on defining the base cases and recursive calls without worrying about iterating over all subproblem combinations explicitly.
  - **On-Demand Computation**: Memoization ensures that subproblems are only solved when needed. This can lead to savings in computation for problems where not all subproblems are required to reach the solution.
- **Cons**:
  - **Stack Overflow Risk**: Recursive calls introduce the risk of stack overflow, particularly if the recursion depth exceeds the system's call stack limit. This is a common issue for deeply nested recursive problems.

  - **Overhead of Function Calls**: Each recursive function call incurs overhead in terms of memory and time. The cumulative effect of these calls can make the top-down approach less efficient compared to its bottom-up counterpart, especially for large subproblems.
  - **Complexity in Handling Large Inputs**: For problems involving very large datasets or deep levels of recursion, maintaining and managing memoization tables (often implemented as dictionaries in Python) can become cumbersome.

The **bottom-up approach**, also known as tabulation, involves explicitly solving all subproblems in a systematic and incremental manner, storing the results in a tabular form (usually an array or matrix). This method is iterative and ensures that each subproblem is computed only once.

- **Pros**:
  - **Guaranteed Iterative Solution**: The bottom-up approach removes the risk of stack overflow by avoiding recursion altogether. This guarantees a solution for problems where the depth of recursion could be problematic.
  - **Improved Performance**: By iteratively filling up the table and avoiding function call overheads, bottom-up DP often executes faster than the top-down equivalent. This performance boost can be significant for computationally intensive problems.
  - **Clarity in Space-Time Trade-offs**: Explicitly constructing the table allows developers to clearly see and optimize space-time trade-offs. For instance, space optimization techniques such as reducing a 2D DP table to a 1D array can be easily implemented.
- **Cons**:
  - **Initialization Overhead**: Constructing and initializing the entire table or array upfront may introduce unnecessary overhead, particularly in cases where only a subset of subproblems is needed for the final solution.
  - **Loss of Intuitiveness**: The iterative nature of the bottom-up approach may obscure the relationship between the

problem's mathematical formulation and its implementation. While the same result is achieved, the process can be less intuitive and harder to understand.

- **Rigid Structure**: Bottom-up DP requires a rigid tabulation order. If the order of subproblem resolution is not followed correctly, it can lead to incorrect results. Adjusting this order for optimization purposes can add an additional layer of complexity.

To illustrate these concepts with examples, consider the classic *Fibonacci sequence* problem. Below is the Python implementation using the top-down approach with memoization:

```
def fibonacci_top_down(n, memo={}):
    if n <= 1:
        return n
    if n not in memo:
        memo[n] = fibonacci_top_down(n-1, memo) + fibonacci_top_down(n-2, memo)
    return memo[n]

result = fibonacci_top_down(10)
print(result)
```

The execution of this code yields:

```
55
```

This example highlights the simplicity of the recursive definition. By contrast, the bottom-up tabulation approach determines the same Fibonacci number iteratively:

```
def fibonacci_bottom_up(n):
    if n <= 1:
        return n
    fib = [0] * (n + 1)
    fib[1] = 1
    for i in range(2, n + 1):
        fib[i] = fib[i-1] + fib[i-2]
    return fib[n]

result = fibonacci_bottom_up(10)
print(result)
```

The execution of this code yields:

```
55
```

Both implementations compute the 10th Fibonacci number, yet demonstrate the distinct nature of each approach. Understanding these differences ensures that practitioners can select the most efficient and clear method tailored to their specific problem constraints.

## 4.6 When to Use Top-Down Approach

The top-down approach, also known as memoization, leverages recursion and the principle of solving subproblems to make the larger problem manageable. This technique is particularly effective in specific scenarios which we will delineate in this section, ensuring a comprehensive understanding of when this approach is most advantageous.

The top-down approach is most beneficial when the problem exhibits overlapping subproblems and optimal substructure. Overlapping subproblems imply that the same subproblems are solved multiple times, and optimal substructure means that the optimal solution of the problem can be obtained by combining optimal solutions of its subproblems. Many combinatorial optimization problems fall into this category, such as the computation of Fibonacci numbers, the Knapsack problem, and certain graph-related problems like shortest paths.

One clear indicator that a top-down approach may be appropriate is when the problem has a recursive solution but suffers from recomputation of the same values multiple times. For instance, consider the classic example of Fibonacci numbers, where the $n$-th Fibonacci number is the sum of the $(n-1)$-th and $(n-2)$-th Fibonacci numbers. This recursive definition naturally leads to an exponential number of recomputations without memoization.

```
def fibonacci_memo(n, memo={}):
    if n in memo:
        return memo[n]
    if n <= 2:
        return 1
    memo[n] = fibonacci_memo(n-1, memo) + fibonacci_memo(n-2, memo)
    return memo[n]

print(fibonacci_memo(10))
```

```
55
```

In the provided function fibonacci_memo, memoization ensures that each Fibonacci number is computed once by storing computed results in a dictionary, thus transforming an exponential time complexity to linear time complexity.

Another situation where the top-down approach is useful is when the problem involves decision making and branching, such as in the context of combinatorial problems where multiple choices need to be evaluated in a recursive manner. Memoization helps in efficiently pruning the recursion tree by storing results of previously computed states.

Consider the case of the Knapsack problem, where given weights and values of $n$ items, the goal is to put these items in a knapsack of capacity $W$ to get the maximum total value in the knapsack. A recursive solution needs to decide for each item whether to include it in the knapsack or not, leading to a branching factor of 2 per item.

```
def knapsack_memo(W, wt, val, n, memo={}):
    if (n, W) in memo:
        return memo[(n, W)]
    if n == 0 or W == 0:
        return 0
    if wt[n-1] > W:
        memo[(n, W)] = knapsack_memo(W, wt, val, n-1, memo)
    else:
        memo[(n, W)] = max(val[n-1] + knapsack_memo(W-wt[n-1], wt, val, n-1, memo
            ),
                           knapsack_memo(W, wt, val, n-1, memo))
    return memo[(n, W)]

val = [60, 100, 120]
wt = [10, 20, 30]
W = 50
n = len(val)
print(knapsack_memo(W, wt, val, n))
```

220

The above example of knapsack_memo demonstrates how the top-down approach efficiently solves the problem by avoiding redundant calculations through memoization.

When the problem has a depth-heavy recursion tree, meaning it is characterized by a recursive call depth that is manageable in size, the top-down approach may also be preferable. This is because each recursive call's state is stored on the stack, and memoization reduces unnecessary recursive calls, thus optimizing both time and space usage.

Furthermore, dynamic programming problems that can be naturally expressed in recursive form are often easier and more intuitive to implement using a top-down approach. This is particularly true for individuals more comfortable with recursion than iteration, as memoization seamlessly fits into a recursive structure.

In complex problems where establishing the relationship between subproblems and deriving iterative solutions from scratch can be challenging, starting with a top-down approach allows for an easier transition towards a solution. Once the recursive solution with memoization is fully understood, it can sometimes be converted to a bottom-up approach for potential optimizations.

Typically, a top-down approach is chosen for problems entailing significant state spaces where only a small subset of states is needed to compute the final result. This sparsity is due to the fact that not all recursive paths are traversed, making memoization particularly resource-efficient. This characteristic is advantageous in problems like computing the edit distance in text, where only certain pairs of substrings are evaluated.

The top-down approach provides a clear, structured method for solving complex problems by breaking them down recursively and leveraging memoization to avoid recomputation, ensuring efficient use of computational resources. By carefully analyzing the problem's properties and leveraging these principles, utilizing the top-down approach can lead to significant improvements in performance and clarity of the solution.

## 4.7 When to Use Bottom-Up Approach

The bottom-up approach in dynamic programming involves solving smaller subtasks first and using their results to build up the solution to the main problem. This method typically uses a tabulation technique, where an iterative process fills out a table (or array) with solutions to subproblems, eventually arriving at the final solution. Understanding when to use the bottom-up approach is crucial for optimizing performance and resource utilization. Below are key scenarios where the bottom-up approach proves advantageous:

**1. Predictable Subproblem Dependencies:**

When the subproblems' dependencies are well-defined and predictable, the bottom-up approach is highly efficient. By structuring the algorithm to start with the smallest subproblems and iteratively solve larger ones, we ensure that all necessary data for any subproblem is available when needed.

**2. Avoiding Recursive Call Overheads:**

In comparison to the top-down approach, which can suffer from substantial recursive call overheads and potential stack overflow, the bottom-up method avoids these concerns by relying on iterative loops. This is particularly beneficial in environments with limited stack space or where stack overflow could be an issue.

**3. Improved Space Complexity:**

The bottom-up approach sometimes allows for reduced space complexity. For instance, if we only need the last few computed values (as seen in the Fibonacci sequence problem), we can overwrite the array rather than storing all intermediate results. This optimization can lead to significant space savings.

**4. Uniform Subproblem Sizes:**

When subproblems are of equal size and computational effort, the bottom-up approach can streamline the process. Each subproblem gets solved in a straightforward, linear pass through the table or array, ensuring uniform progress toward the final solution.

**5. Iterative Constructs Preference:**

For programmers who strongly prefer or are required to use iterative constructs over recursion due to language constraints, execution environment limitations, or personal coding style, the bottom-up approach aligns with an iterative mindset.

**6. Enhancing Parallelism:**

In certain cases, the bottom-up approach can be more easily adapted to parallel computing environments. By breaking the problem into independently solvable subproblems that can be computed concurrently, and then combined, the bottom-up method can leverage multi-core processing power efficiently.

**7. Efficient Memory Access Patterns:**

When implemented carefully, the bottom-up approach tends to have beneficial memory access patterns due to its iterative nature. It typically involves contiguous memory access, as opposed to potentially scattered access patterns in a top-down recursive solution. This improves cache performance and, consequently, execution speed.

**Example of Bottom-Up Approach: The Fibonacci Sequence**

To illustrate the practical application of the bottom-up approach, consider the classic problem of computing the Fibonacci sequence. The goal is to compute $F(n)$ where the base cases are $F(0) = 0$ and $F(1) = 1$, and the recurrence relation is $F(n) = F(n-1) + F(n-2)$ for $n > 1$. A bottom-up approach uses an iterative method and tabulation to avoid redundant calculations:

```
def fibonacci_bottom_up(n):
    if n == 0:
        return 0
    elif n == 1:
        return 1
```

```
    # Initialize base values.
    prev2 = 0
    prev1 = 1

    # Iterate to compute each Fibonacci number using the previous two values.
    for i in range(2, n + 1):
        current = prev1 + prev2
        prev2 = prev1
        prev1 = current

    return prev1
```

This code iteratively computes the $n$-th Fibonacci number. The calculation of each Fibonacci number depends only on the last two computed values, allowing us to update in constant space.

```
>>> fibonacci_bottom_up(10)
55
```

**Execution Flow:**

The code starts by initializing the base values for $F(0)$ and $F(1)$. It then iterates from $2$ to $n$, at each step computing the next Fibonacci number by summing the last two computed values. This approach avoids the overhead of recursive calls, reducing the risk of stack overflow and improving execution speed.

By recognizing these specific scenarios and advantages, one can effectively determine when to employ the bottom-up approach, thereby optimizing the performance and efficiency of dynamic programming solutions.

## 4.8 Memoization in Top-Down Approach

Memoization is a technique used to optimize the top-down approach in dynamic programming by storing the results of expensive function calls and reusing these results when the same inputs occur again. It derives its name from "memorandum," indicating something that should be remembered. The primary goal of memoization is to reduce the number of recursive calls, which can significantly improve the performance of algorithms with overlapping subproblems.

Consider a naive recursive function to compute the $n$-th Fibonacci number. The naive implementation has an exponential time complexity due to the large number of redundant calculations.

```
def naive_fibonacci(n):
    if n <= 1:
        return n
```

```
    else:
        return naive_fibonacci(n-1) + naive_fibonacci(n-2)

print(naive_fibonacci(10))
```

55

In the above code, naive_fibonacci computes the Fibonacci number using a straightforward recursive approach. For $n = 10$, the function repeatedly recalculates Fibonacci numbers for smaller values, leading to redundant computations.

Memoization solves this inefficiency by storing previously computed results in a data structure—typically a dictionary in Python. Below is an optimized version of the Fibonacci function using memoization.

```
def memoized_fibonacci(n, memo={}):
    if n in memo:
        return memo[n]
    if n <= 1:
        return n
    memo[n] = memoized_fibonacci(n-1, memo) + memoized_fibonacci(n-2, memo)
    return memo[n]

print(memoized_fibonacci(10))
```

55

In this revised implementation, the memoized_fibonacci function checks if the result is already available in the memo dictionary before proceeding with the recursive computation. This simple change alters the time complexity from exponential $O(2^n)$ to linear $O(n)$.

The advantages of memoization extend beyond the Fibonacci sequence. Any recursive algorithm with overlapping subproblems can be optimized using this technique. Let's consider another classical dynamic programming problem: the calculation of binomial coefficients.

### Example: Binomial Coefficients

The binomial coefficient $\binom{n}{k}$ is defined as the number of ways to choose $k$ elements from a set of $n$ elements, and it can be computed using the following recursive formula:

$$\binom{n}{k} = \binom{n-1}{k-1} + \binom{n-1}{k}$$

with the base cases:

$$\binom{n}{0} = \binom{n}{n} = 1$$

A naive recursive implementation incurs redundant calculations:

```
def naive_binomial_coefficient(n, k):
    if k == 0 or k == n:
        return 1
    return naive_binomial_coefficient(n-1, k-1) + naive_binomial_coefficient(n-1, k)

print(naive_binomial_coefficient(5, 2))
```

```
10
```

Using memoization, we can optimize the binomial coefficient calculation:

```
def memoized_binomial_coefficient(n, k, memo={}):
    if (n, k) in memo:
        return memo[(n, k)]
    if k == 0 or k == n:
        return 1
    memo[(n, k)] = memoized_binomial_coefficient(n-1, k-1, memo) +
        memoized_binomial_coefficient(n-1, k, memo)
    return memo[(n, k)]

print(memoized_binomial_coefficient(5, 2))
```

```
10
```

This version demonstrates how memoization stores results of previously computed binomial coefficients in a dictionary, thereby avoiding redundant calculations.

### Evaluating Memoization

Memoization is particularly useful when the number of distinct subproblems is relatively small compared to the total number of recursive calls in a naive implementation. By storing the results of these subproblems, it effectively trades additional space for a substantial reduction in computation time.

A note of caution: although memoization can drastically reduce the time complexity, it increases the space complexity, as it requires storage for the results of subproblems. The space complexity of a memoized solution generally depends on the number of unique subproblems.

- For the Fibonacci sequence, the memoized solution uses $O(n)$ extra space.
- For the binomial coefficient computation, the space complexity is $O(n \times k)$, where $n$ and $k$ are the dimensions of the stored results.

Understanding and implementing memoization prepares one to tackle a wide range of dynamic programming problems with optimizations that are both efficient and easy to comprehend. In complex applications, proper utilization of memoization within a top-down approach can lead to significant performance improvements, enabling solutions to problems that would otherwise be computationally infeasible.

## 4.9 Tabulation in Bottom-Up Approach

Tabulation is a technique used in the bottom-up approach of dynamic programming. It involves filling up a table based on previously computed values, usually starting from the base cases and iterating towards the desired solution. This method ensures that all subproblems are solved iteratively and no subproblem is solved more than once, thus preventing redundant calculations.

To elucidate how tabulation works, consider a table, typically represented as a multidimensional array, where entries are systematically computed and stored. The general strategy involves defining the problem in terms of its smaller subproblems and iteratively computing and storing results in a table until the solution to the original problem is obtained.

Fundamental Steps in Tabulation

- **Define the Problem**: Determine the dimensions and state space of the problem. Identify the range of the indices and what each index represents.
- **Initialize the Base Cases**: Initialize the values of the base cases in the table. These are the simplest subproblems that can be solved trivially.
- **Iterate Towards the Solution**: Use nested loops to iterate through the table, filling entries based on the relations defined by the recurrence of the problem.
- **Extract the Result**: The final entry or entries of the table will contain the solution to the original problem.

Example: Fibonacci Series

A classic example to illustrate tabulation is the Fibonacci series, where each number is the sum of the two preceding ones. The goal is to find the $n^{\text{th}}$ Fibonacci number.

Given the recurrence relation:

$$F(n) = F(n-1) + F(n-2)$$

Where $F(0) = 0$ and $F(1) = 1$, we can use the tabulation approach as follows:

```
def fibonacci_tabulation(n):
    # Step 2: Initialize the base cases
    fib_table = [0] * (n + 1)
    fib_table[1] = 1

    # Step 3: Iterate towards the solution
    for i in range(2, n + 1):
        fib_table[i] = fib_table[i-1] + fib_table[i-2]

    # Step 4: Extract the result
    return fib_table[n]

# Test the function
print(fibonacci_tabulation(10))
```

When executed, the output is:

```
55
```

In this approach, we start by defining a table $\text{fib\_table}$ of size $n+1$ and initializing the base cases $F(0) = 0$ and $F(1) = 1$. We then iteratively fill the table for all indices from 2 to $n$ using the recurrence relation. The final result, $F(n)$, is stored in $\text{fib\_table[n]}$.

Solving the Coin Change Problem

To further understand tabulation, consider the coin change problem. The problem is to determine the minimum number of coins required to make up a given amount, given a set of denominations.

Given:

- Coin denominations: $\{d_1, d_2, \ldots, d_k\}$
- Target amount: $A$

We aim to fill a table $\text{min\_coins}$ such that $\text{min\_coins[i]}$ holds the minimum number of coins to make amount $i$.

```
def coin_change(coins, amount):
    # Initialize the table with infinity indicating unreachable amounts
    min_coins = [float('inf')] * (amount + 1)
    min_coins[0] = 0 # Base case
```

```
    # Iterate over all amounts from 1 to amount
    for i in range(1, amount + 1):
        # Check each coin denomination
        for coin in coins:
            if i - coin >= 0:
                min_coins[i] = min(min_coins[i], min_coins[i - coin] + 1)

    # If min_coins[amount] is still infinity, the amount is not reachable
    return min_coins[amount] if min_coins[amount] != float('inf') else -1

# Test the function
print(coin_change([1, 2, 5], 11))
```

When executed, the output is:

```
3
```

Here, $\text{min\_coins}[\text{i}] = \text{inf}$ indicates that the amount $i$ is initially assumed to be unreachable. We then iterate over all possible amounts and update the table based on previously computed values. For each coin denomination, if $i - coin \geq 0$, it implies that the amount $i$ can be reached from the amount $i - coin$ by adding one more coin. The final solution for the given amount is found in $\text{min\_coins}[\text{amount}]$.

Tabulation in the bottom-up approach brings out several benefits, such as ensuring subproblems are solved no more than once and eliminating the risk of excessive stack memory usage that is often associated with recursive approaches. This makes it particularly useful for problems where optimal substructure and overlapping subproblems are inherent.

## 4.10 Case Studies on Top-Down Approach

The top-down approach, also referred to as the memoization approach, is a popular method to solve dynamic programming problems. Below, we will delve into three intricate case studies to elucidate this approach, showcasing different problem types and their solutions using Python. Each case study will demonstrate the elegance and efficiency of the top-down method.

**Case Study 1: Fibonacci Sequence**

The Fibonacci sequence problem is a classic example used to illustrate the principles of dynamic programming. In this problem, we aim to compute the $n$-th Fibonacci number, where each number is the sum of the two preceding ones, starting from 0 and 1.

```
def fibonacci(n, memo={}):
    if n in memo:
        return memo[n]
    if n <= 1:
        return n
    memo[n] = fibonacci(n-1, memo) + fibonacci(n-2, memo)
    return memo[n]

# Computation example:
result = fibonacci(10)
print(result) # Output: 55
```

Here, we use a dictionary memo to store the results of previous computations. This dictionary is checked before making a recursive call, preventing the exponential growth in runtime typical of the naive recursive solution.

**Case Study 2: Edit Distance**

The Edit Distance problem, also known as the Levenshtein distance, is a measure of the minimum number of operations required to convert one string into another. The permissible operations are insertion, deletion, and substitution of a character.

```
def edit_distance(s1, s2, m, n, memo={}):
    if (m, n) in memo:
        return memo[(m, n)]
    if m == 0:
        return n
    if n == 0:
        return m
    if s1[m-1] == s2[n-1]:
        memo[(m, n)] = edit_distance(s1, s2, m-1, n-1, memo)
    else:
        insert_op = edit_distance(s1, s2, m, n-1, memo)
        delete_op = edit_distance(s1, s2, m-1, n, memo)
        replace_op = edit_distance(s1, s2, m-1, n-1, memo)
        memo[(m, n)] = 1 + min(insert_op, delete_op, replace_op)
    return memo[(m, n)]

# Computation example:
s1 = "intention"
s2 = "execution"
result = edit_distance(s1, s2, len(s1), len(s2))
print(result) # Output: 5
```

In this example, the memo dictionary stores the computed edit distances for pairs of substring lengths, thereby avoiding redundant calculations.

**Case Study 3: Longest Increasing Subsequence (LIS)**

The Longest Increasing Subsequence problem requires finding the length of the longest subsequence in a given array such that all elements of the subsequence are sorted in increasing order.

```
def LIS(arr, n, memo={}):
    if n == 1:
        return 1
    if n in memo:
        return memo[n]

    max_ending_here = 1
    for i in range(1, n):
        res = LIS(arr, i, memo)
        if arr[i-1] < arr[n-1]:
            max_ending_here = max(max_ending_here, res + 1)

    memo[n] = max_ending_here
    return memo[n]

def max_LIS(arr):
    n = len(arr)
    memo = {}
    max_len = 1
    for i in range(1, n + 1):
        max_len = max(max_len, LIS(arr, i, memo))
    return max_len

# Computation example:
arr = [10, 22, 9, 33, 21, 50, 41, 60, 80]
result = max_LIS(arr)
print(result) # Output: 6
```

In the LIS function, we utilize the memo dictionary to store the length of the LIS ending at each element. By iterating through the array and computing the LIS for each subset, we collectively find the maximum value, representing the length of the overall LIS.

Through these case studies, the power and efficiency of the top-down approach in solving dynamic programming problems are evident. Reuse of previously computed results ensures that the algorithm runs in polynomial time, making it suitable for a variety of real-world applications.

## 4.11 Case Studies on Bottom-Up Approach

In this section, we shall explore several case studies that exemplify the bottom-up approach to solving dynamic programming problems. Through these detailed examples, readers will gain a comprehensive understanding of how to systematically build up solutions from smaller subproblems and ultimately derive the solution to the entire problem.

**Case Study 1: Fibonacci Sequence**

The Fibonacci sequence is a textbook example used to illustrate dynamic programming concepts. Given the recurrence relation $F(n) = F(n-1)+F(n-2)$ with base cases $F(0) = 0$ and $F(1) = 1$, the bottom-up approach builds from the base cases up to the desired $F(n)$.

```
def fibonacci_bottom_up(n):
    if n == 0:
        return 0
    elif n == 1:
        return 1

    # Initialize base cases
    dp = [0] * (n + 1)
    dp[0] = 0
    dp[1] = 1

    # Build the dp array from the bottom up
    for i in range(2, n + 1):
        dp[i] = dp[i - 1] + dp[i - 2]

    return dp[n]

# Example usage
print(fibonacci_bottom_up(10)) # Outputs 55
```

In the above Python function, we create an array dp of size $n+1$ to store the Fibonacci numbers. Starting from the base cases, we iteratively fill in the array using the given recurrence relation. This method ensures that each subproblem is solved before it is used in the next computation, efficiently producing the desired result.

55

### Case Study 2: Knapsack Problem

The 0/1 knapsack problem is a classic optimization problem. Given weights and values of $n$ items, and a knapsack with capacity $W$, the objective is to maximize the total value that can be accommodated without exceeding the capacity. Using the bottom-up approach, we construct a 2D array where each entry $dp[i][w]$ represents the maximum value achievable with the first $i$ items and a knapsack capacity of $w$.

```
def knapsack_bottom_up(weights, values, W):
    n = len(weights)
    dp = [[0] * (W + 1) for _ in range(n + 1)]

    # Build the dp table from the bottom up
    for i in range(1, n + 1):
        for w in range(W + 1):
            if weights[i - 1] <= w:
                dp[i][w] = max(dp[i - 1][w],
                               dp[i - 1][w - weights[i - 1]] + values[i - 1])
            else:
                dp[i][w] = dp[i - 1][w]
```

```
    return dp[n][W]

# Example usage
weights = [1, 3, 4, 5]
values = [1, 4, 5, 7]
capacity = 7
print(knapsack_bottom_up(weights, values, capacity)) # Outputs 9
```

The above algorithm initializes a 2D $\mathrm{dp}$ table populated with zeros. The nested loops fill in the table by deciding whether to include the $i$-th item. If including the item offers a better value without exceeding capacity, it updates the cell with this new value. Otherwise, it carries forward the value from the previous item set.

9

### Case Study 3: Longest Common Subsequence

The longest common subsequence (LCS) problem involves finding the longest sequence present in both of two given strings. Using a bottom-up dynamic programming technique, we define $dp[i][j]$ as the length of LCS of sub-strings $X[0..i-1]$ and $Y[0..j-1]$.

```
def longest_common_subsequence(X, Y):
    m = len(X)
    n = len(Y)
    dp = [[0] * (n + 1) for _ in range(m + 1)]

    # Build the dp table from the bottom up
    for i in range(1, m + 1):
        for j in range(1, n + 1):
            if X[i - 1] == Y[j - 1]:
                dp[i][j] = dp[i - 1][j - 1] + 1
            else:
                dp[i][j] = max(dp[i - 1][j], dp[i][j - 1])

    return dp[m][n]

# Example usage
X = "AGGTAB"
Y = "GXTXAYB"
print(longest_common_subsequence(X, Y)) # Outputs 4
```

This algorithm constructs a matrix where rows represent characters of string $X$ and columns represent characters of string $Y$. If characters from both strings match, the cell value increments the diagonal value by one. If they do not match, the cell takes the maximum value from adjacent cells. Finally, the bottom-right cell of the matrix contains the length of the LCS.

4

These case studies elucidate the application of the bottom-up approach across various problem domains. By meticulously breaking down problems into smaller subproblems and iteratively solving them, we effectively build up optimal solutions. The bottom-up methodology not only enhances computational efficiency but also provides a structured and clear roadmap to dynamic programming problem-solving.

## 4.12 Converting Between Approaches

Dynamic programming problems can often be solved using either the top-down or bottom-up approach. Understanding how to convert solutions between these two methods is crucial for mastering dynamic programming. Converting a top-down dynamic programming solution (also known as memoization) to a bottom-up solution (also known as tabulation) and vice versa requires a clear comprehension of their respective mechanisms.

Consider a common dynamic programming problem: computing the $n$-th Fibonacci number. A top-down approach, which utilizes recursive function calls and memoization to store intermediate results, can be converted to a bottom-up approach, which iteratively computes results and stores them in a table.

We begin with the top-down approach for the Fibonacci problem:

```
def fibonacci_memo(n, memo={}):
    if n in memo:
        return memo[n]
    if n <= 1:
        return n
    memo[n] = fibonacci_memo(n-1, memo) + fibonacci_memo(n-2, memo)
    return memo[n]
```

In this top-down approach, we use a dictionary $memo$ to store the results of previously computed Fibonacci numbers, preventing redundant calculations and thus enhancing efficiency. The function checks if the result for $n$ is already in $memo$. If not, it recursively computes the result, stores it in $memo$, and then returns it.

To convert this into a bottom-up approach, we eliminate recursion and instead use a loop to fill a table:

```
def fibonacci_tab(n):
    if n <= 1:
        return n
    table = [0] * (n + 1)
    table[1] = 1
    for i in range(2, n + 1):
        table[i] = table[i-1] + table[i-2]
```

```
    return table[n]
```

In the bottom-up approach, an array $table$ is used to store Fibonacci numbers starting from $0$ up to $n$. Initially, $table[0]$ is set to $0$ and $table[1]$ to $1$. The loop iterates from $2$ through $n$, each time calculating $table[i]$ as the sum of $table[i-1]$ and $table[i-2]$. Finally, the function returns $table[n]$.

Key observations when converting from top-down to bottom-up are:

- Identify the base cases: In both approaches, the base cases (e.g., $n \leq 1$) need to be clearly defined.
- Memoization becomes tabulation: The $memo$ dictionary in the top-down approach transforms into an array $table$ in the bottom-up approach.
- Recursive calls transform into iterative steps: Recursion is replaced by a for-loop that iteratively computes the values.

Conversely, converting a bottom-up solution back to a top-down approach involves:

- Define a recursive function with base conditions: Translate loops into recursive function calls.
- Use a memoization technique (e.g., a dictionary) to store results of subproblems to avoid redundant computations.

Let us consider another dynamic programming problem: the Longest Common Subsequence (LCS).

A bottom-up approach for LCS is as follows:

```
def lcs_bottom_up(X, Y):
    m = len(X)
    n = len(Y)
    table = [[0] * (n + 1) for _ in range(m + 1)]
    for i in range(1, m + 1):
        for j in range(1, n + 1):
            if X[i-1] == Y[j-1]:
                table[i][j] = table[i-1][j-1] + 1
            else:
                table[i][j] = max(table[i-1][j], table[i][j-1])
    return table[m][n]
```

Here, a 2D table is filled iteratively based on comparisons between characters of the two input strings $X$ and $Y$. The bottom-up solution iteratively builds the solution by filling the table entries from smallest subproblems (individual characters) to the entire problem (the complete strings).

Converting this to a top-down approach with memoization looks like this:

```
def lcs_memo(X, Y, m, n, memo):
    if m == 0 or n == 0:
        return 0
    if memo[m][n] != -1:
        return memo[m][n]
    if X[m-1] == Y[n-1]:
        memo[m][n] = 1 + lcs_memo(X, Y, m-1, n-1, memo)
    else:
        memo[m][n] = max(lcs_memo(X, Y, m, n-1, memo), lcs_memo(X, Y, m-1, n,
            memo))
    return memo[m][n]

def lcs_top_down(X, Y):
    m = len(X)
    n = len(Y)
    memo = [[-1] * (n + 1) for _ in range(m + 1)]
    return lcs_memo(X, Y, m, n, memo)
```

In this conversion, the recursive function $lcs\_memo$ mirrors the structure of the loops in the bottom-up approach. The base case checks if either string has length zero, returning 0. The memoization table $memo$ is used to store intermediate results, initialized to $-1$ to indicate uncomputed entries.

Understanding these transformations allows for flexibility in choosing the most suitable approach based on the problem's context and constraints. This skill enriches the dynamic programming toolkit and underscores the interchangeability between top-down and bottom-up techniques.

# Chapter 5

# Implementing DP Solutions in Python

**This chapter focuses on the practical implementation of dynamic programming solutions in Python. It covers basic DP patterns, the use of lists and dictionaries for storing subproblem solutions, handling multiple states, and leveraging multidimensional arrays. Readers will learn space optimization techniques and how to write efficient DP code in Jupyter Notebooks. Profiling and optimizing Python code, alongside numerous real-world examples and case studies, are also included to provide a comprehensive understanding of effective DP implementation in Python programming.**

## 5.1 Introduction to Implementing DP Solutions in Python

Dynamic Programming (DP) is a method for solving complex problems by breaking them down into simpler subproblems. It is widely used in computer science for optimization problems where the problem can be divided into overlapping subproblems that can be solved independently. DP solutions are characterized by their use of recursive relations and optimal substructure. When implementing DP solutions in Python, it is crucial to understand both the theoretical aspects and the practical aspects of Python programming to effectively solve these problems.

Python, with its simple syntax and powerful libraries, provides an excellent platform for implementing DP solutions. The ability to use lists, dictionaries, and other data structures efficiently makes Python suitable for handling the various needs of a DP solution. In this section, we will explore the fundamental concepts of implementing DP solutions in Python, starting from basic principles, followed by practical strategies for effective coding.

First, it is important to understand the two key approaches in DP: the top-down approach (also known as memoization) and the bottom-up approach (also known as tabulation). Both approaches aim to solve the same problem but differ in their method of computation and storage of intermediate results.

The top-down approach involves solving the problem recursively and storing the results of subproblems to avoid redundant computations. This can be achieved using Python's in-built dictionary data structure to store solutions to subproblems. Consider the following simple example of computing the Fibonacci sequence using the top-down approach:

```
def fibonacci_memo(n, memo={}):
    if n in memo:
        return memo[n]
    if n <= 1:
        return n
    memo[n] = fibonacci_memo(n-1, memo) + fibonacci_memo(n-2, memo)
    return memo[n]

# To compute the 10th Fibonacci number
print(fibonacci_memo(10))
```

Here, we have used a dictionary memo to store the results of subproblems, avoiding redundant calculations by checking if the value is already computed before performing the recursive calls.

The bottom-up approach, in contrast, iteratively solves each subproblem starting from the smallest, storing results in a tabulated form (typically a list or array). This method helps in converting the recursive solution into an iterative one, often reducing the space complexity. Here is an example of computing the Fibonacci sequence using the bottom-up approach:

```
def fibonacci_tab(n):
    if n <= 1:
        return n
    fib = [0] * (n + 1)
    fib[1] = 1
    for i in range(2, n + 1):
        fib[i] = fib[i - 1] + fib[i - 2]
    return fib[n]
```

```
# To compute the 10th Fibonacci number
print(fibonacci_tab(10))
```

In this example, the list fib stores the Fibonacci numbers up to n, and each value is computed iteratively, ensuring that no redundant computations are performed.

Choosing between the top-down and bottom-up approach depends on the specific problem and constraints such as time complexity, space complexity, and readability of the code. Generally, the top-down approach is easier to implement and understand due to its recursive nature, while the bottom-up approach can be more efficient as it avoids the overhead of recursive function calls.

In Python, it is also essential to handle edge cases and input constraints effectively. Many DP problems have constraints that require careful consideration to prevent the program from running into recursion limits or excessive memory usage. Python's flexibility allows for custom-preprocessing of inputs and use of efficient data structures to handle such constraints.

One common Python feature that aids in implementing DP solutions is default arguments in function definitions. This can be particularly useful in passing the memoization dictionary in recursive functions without explicitly passing it every time. However, care should be taken to ensure that mutable default arguments do not lead to undesirable side effects.

DP solutions often involve nested loops or recursive calls, making Python's comprehensive error handling capabilities helpful. Using try-except blocks can help manage edge cases and errors that may arise during execution. For example:

```
def fibonacci_memo_safe(n, memo=None):
    if memo is None:
        memo = {}
    try:
        if n in memo:
            return memo[n]
        if n <= 1:
            return n
        memo[n] = fibonacci_memo_safe(n-1, memo) + fibonacci_memo_safe(n-2,
            memo)
        return memo[n]
    except RecursionError:
        raise ValueError('Input is too large, causing a recursion error.')

# To compute the 10th Fibonacci number
print(fibonacci_memo_safe(10))
```

In this example, we use try-except to handle potential recursion errors gracefully, providing a meaningful message to the user.

To sum up, implementing DP solutions in Python requires an understanding of both the theoretical aspects of dynamic programming and the practical features of Python. By leveraging Python's data structures, recursive functions, and error handling, one can efficiently solve a wide range of optimization problems. In the subsequent sections of this chapter, we will delve deeper into specific DP patterns, advanced techniques, and real-world examples, building on the foundational concepts introduced here.

## 5.2 Basic DP Patterns in Python

Dynamic programming (DP) is a powerful technique for solving problems with overlapping subproblems and optimal substructure. In this section, we will illustrate a few basic dynamic programming patterns in Python, namely the Fibonacci sequence, the 0/1 Knapsack problem, the Longest Common Subsequence (LCS), and the Coin Change problem. These patterns serve as a foundation for understanding more complex dynamic programming problems.

### Fibonacci Sequence

The Fibonacci sequence is a classic example to demonstrate the power of dynamic programming in reducing the time complexity of recursive solutions. Each term in the Fibonacci sequence is the sum of the two preceding terms. A naive recursive approach will lead to exponential time complexity due to the recomputation of the same subproblems. We can optimize this using DP as shown below.

```
def fibonacci(n):
    if n <= 0:
        return 0
    if n == 1:
        return 1

    fib = [0] * (n + 1)
    fib[1] = 1

    for i in range(2, n + 1):
        fib[i] = fib[i - 1] + fib[i - 2]

    return fib[n]

print(fibonacci(10))
```

### 0/1 Knapsack Problem

The 0/1 Knapsack problem is a typical example of combinatorial optimization. Given a set of weights and values of $n$ items, and a knapsack with capacity $W$, choose a subset of items such that the total weight is less than or equal to $W$, and the total value is maximized. Using dynamic programming, we can avoid recalculating already solved subproblems.

```
def knapsack(weights, values, W):
    n = len(weights)
    dp = [[0 for x in range(W + 1)] for y in range(n + 1)]

    for i in range(n + 1):
        for w in range(W + 1):
            if i == 0 or w == 0:
                dp[i][w] = 0
            elif weights[i-1] <= w:
                dp[i][w] = max(values[i-1] + dp[i-1][w-weights[i-1]], dp[i-1][w])
            else:
                dp[i][w] = dp[i-1][w]

    return dp[n][W]

weights = [10, 20, 30]
values = [60, 100, 120]
W = 50

print(knapsack(weights, values, W))
```



### Longest Common Subsequence (LCS)

The Longest Common Subsequence problem deals with finding the longest subsequence that is present in two given sequences. Dynamic programming can be instrumental in solving this efficiently by storing the results of subproblems and constructing the solution incrementally.

```
def lcs(X, Y):
    m = len(X)
    n = len(Y)
    L = [[0]*(n + 1) for i in range(m + 1)]

    for i in range(m + 1):
        for j in range(n + 1):
            if i == 0 or j == 0:
                L[i][j] = 0
            elif X[i-1] == Y[j-1]:
                L[i][j] = L[i-1][j-1] + 1
            else:
                L[i][j] = max(L[i-1][j], L[i][j-1])

    return L[m][n]

X = "AGGTAB"
Y = "GXTXAYB"
```

```
print(lcs(X, Y))
```

4

### Coin Change Problem

Given a target amount and an array of coin denominations, the goal is to determine the minimum number of coins required to make the target amount. Dynamic programming can optimize this problem by breaking it down into smaller subproblems and storing their results.

```
def coinChange(coins, amount):
    dp = [float('inf')] * (amount + 1)
    dp[0] = 0

    for coin in coins:
        for x in range(coin, amount + 1):
            dp[x] = min(dp[x], dp[x - coin] + 1)

    return dp[amount] if dp[amount] != float('inf') else -1

coins = [1, 2, 5]
amount = 11

print(coinChange(coins, amount))
```

3

These examples illustrate the power and flexibility of dynamic programming for solving a variety of problems. By identifying subproblems and leveraging the power of memoization or tabulation, dynamic programming can significantly improve the efficiency of your algorithms.

## 5.3 Top-Down Approach with Memoization

The top-down approach with memoization, often referred to as the memoized recursive approach, is a fundamental technique in dynamic programming. This method emphasizes solving a problem by recursively breaking it down into subproblems and storing the results of these subproblems to avoid redundant computations. The primary advantage of this approach is its ability to significantly reduce computation time by caching previously computed results.

Consider a classical example, the Fibonacci sequence, which is a simple yet effective illustration of the top-down approach with memoization.

The Fibonacci sequence is defined as follows:

$$F(n) = \begin{cases} 0 & \text{if } n = 0 \\ 1 & \text{if } n = 1 \\ F(n-1) + F(n-2) & \text{if } n > 1 \end{cases}$$

A naive recursive implementation of this definition will have an exponential time complexity of $O(2^n)$ due to repeated calculations of the same subproblems. By employing memoization, we store the results of these subproblems to improve the time complexity to linear, $O(n)$.

The following Python code demonstrates the use of memoization in calculating the Fibonacci sequence:

```
def fibonacci_memo(n, memo={}):
    if n in memo:
        return memo[n]
    if n <= 1:
        return n
    memo[n] = fibonacci_memo(n-1, memo) + fibonacci_memo(n-2, memo)
    return memo[n]
```

In this implementation, the memo dictionary serves as a cache to store the results of intermediate Fibonacci computations. This ensures each subproblem is solved only once, thus optimizing the overall computation.

Another critical application of the top-down approach with memoization is in solving the problem of finding the minimum cost path in a grid. The problem can be stated as follows: Given a grid where each cell has a certain cost, compute the minimum cost to reach the bottom-right cell from the top-left cell, moving only down or right.

For a grid cost$[m][n]$, the recursive relation to find the minimum cost to reach $(i, j)$ is:

$$\text{minCost}(i, j) = \text{cost}[i][j] + \min(\text{minCost}(i + 1, j), \text{minCost}(i, j + 1))$$

The Python implementation using memoization is given below:

```
def min_cost(grid, i, j, memo={}):
    if i >= len(grid) or j >= len(grid[0]):
        return float('inf')
    if (i, j) in memo:
        return memo[(i, j)]
    if i == len(grid) - 1 and j == len(grid[0]) - 1:
        return grid[i][j]
    memo[(i, j)] = grid[i][j] + min(min_cost(grid, i+1, j, memo), min_cost(grid, i, j+1,
        memo))
    return memo[(i, j)]
```

This implementation defines a function $\mathrm{min\_cost}$ which takes the grid, current indices $i$ and $j$, and a $\mathrm{memo}$ dictionary as arguments. If the indices are out of bounds of the grid, it returns infinity to signify an invalid path. The base case occurs when the function reaches the bottom-right cell, returning its cost. The recursive call updates the $\mathrm{memo}$ dictionary with the computed cost for each cell.

It is essential to understand that memoization can be applied to a variety of dynamic programming problems. The key steps to implement the top-down approach with memoization are: 1. Define the base cases clearly to handle the simplest instances of the problem. 2. Use a cache data structure to store intermediate results. In Python, this is typically done using a dictionary. 3. Recursively solve the problem, ensuring that results of subproblems are stored in and retrieved from the cache whenever required.

One frequent challenge in dynamic programming is handling problems with multiple parameters or states. The top-down approach with memoization seamlessly extends to such problems. Consider the problem of finding the longest common subsequence (LCS) between two strings $X$ and $Y$. The recursive relation for LCS is:

$$\text{LCS}(i,j) = \begin{cases} 0 & \text{if } i = 0 \text{ or } j = 0 \\ \text{LCS}(i-1, j-1) + 1 & \text{if } X[i-1] = Y[j-1] \\ \max(\text{LCS}(i-1, j), \text{LCS}(i, j-1)) & \text{if } X[i-1] \neq Y[j-1] \end{cases}$$

The following code demonstrates the memoized approach to solve LCS:

```
def lcs(X, Y, i, j, memo={}):
    if i == 0 or j == 0:
        return 0
    if (i, j) in memo:
        return memo[(i, j)]
    if X[i-1] == Y[j-1]:
        memo[(i, j)] = lcs(X, Y, i-1, j-1, memo) + 1
    else:
        memo[(i, j)] = max(lcs(X, Y, i-1, j, memo), lcs(X, Y, i, j-1, memo))
    return memo[(i, j)]
```

In this implementation, the $\mathrm{lcs}$ function computes the longest common subsequence length by recursively comparing the characters of the strings $X$ and $Y$. The results of subproblems are stored in the $\mathrm{memo}$ dictionary, allowing for efficient computation.

The top-down approach with memoization is a powerful strategy in dynamic programming. It allows the solution space to be explored elegantly via recursive decomposition while leveraging previously computed results for efficiency. This method is particularly useful in problems where the recurrence relations are straightforward, and the overlap of subproblems is significant, making memoization an indispensable tool for optimization.

## 5.4 Bottom-Up Approach with Tabulation

The bottom-up approach with tabulation, often referred to simply as tabulation, is a strategy in dynamic programming that iteratively solves smaller subproblems and uses their solutions to build up the solution to the original problem. Instead of using recursion and memoization, tabulation fills up a table based on the results of previously solved subproblems. This method typically leads to more efficient memory usage and avoids the stack overflow issues that can arise with deep recursion.

In a tabulation approach, we construct a table (often a list or a multidimensional array) where each entry represents the solution to a subproblem. The entries are filled in a specific order, such that each entry only depends on the previously computed entries. This ensures that when we attempt to solve a subproblem, all the necessary information is already available.

Consider the classic problem of computing the Fibonacci sequence:

$$F(n) = \begin{cases} 0 & \text{if } n = 0 \\ 1 & \text{if } n = 1 \\ F(n-1) + F(n-2) & \text{if } n > 1 \end{cases}$$

The tabulation approach involves creating an array $\mathrm{dp}$ where $\mathrm{dp[i]}$ will store the value of the Fibonacci number $F(i)$. We will build this array iteratively from the base cases up to the desired value of $n$.

Here is the implementation of the Fibonacci sequence using the bottom-up approach:

```
def fib(n: int) -> int:
    if n == 0:
        return 0
    elif n == 1:
        return 1

    dp = [0] * (n + 1)
    dp[0] = 0
```

```
    dp[1] = 1

    for i in range(2, n + 1):
        dp[i] = dp[i - 1] + dp[i - 2]

    return dp[n]
```

Here, the array dp is initialized to have $n+1$ elements, and it is specifically set to handle the base cases. The for loop iterates from 2 to $n$, filling each entry in the dp array based on the previous two entries. Finally, the value of dp[n] is returned, giving the $n$-th Fibonacci number.

A significant advantage of the bottom-up approach is its broad applicability to various dynamic programming problems. For instance, consider the problem of finding the minimum number of coins that make a given value. Given a set of coins of different denominations and a total amount, the objective is to compute the fewest number of coins needed to achieve that amount.

To solve the coin change problem using the bottom-up approach, we define dp[i] to be the minimum number of coins required to make the amount $i$. We initialize dp[0] to 0 because no coins are needed to make the amount 0. For other amounts, we initialize dp[i] to a large number (representing infinity).

The recursive relation is:

$$dp[i] = \min(dp[i], 1 + dp[i - coin]) \quad \text{for each coin in the given set}$$

The full implementation is as follows:

```
def coinChange(coins: List[int], amount: int) -> int:
    dp = [float('inf')] * (amount + 1)
    dp[0] = 0

    for coin in coins:
        for i in range(coin, amount + 1):
            dp[i] = min(dp[i], dp[i - coin] + 1)

    return dp[amount] if dp[amount] != float('inf') else -1
```

Here, the dp array is initialized with float('inf') to represent that initially, the minimum number of coins for any amount is unknown. Starting at each coin's value and up to the desired amount, we update dp[i] by computing the minimum number of coins needed. Finally, the function returns either the minimum number of coins (if the amount is achievable) or -1 (if the amount cannot be formed with the given denominations).

Tabulation provides an efficient and intuitive solution mechanism without the overhead of function calls characteristic of top-down recursion. Importantly, the bottom-up approach highlights dependencies between subproblems clearly, allowing other optimization techniques to be applied more readily.

## 5.5 Using Arrays for DP

Dynamic programming (DP) often relies on data structures that can efficiently store computed values for subproblems. Arrays are a fundamental data structure suitable for this purpose due to their indexed accessibility and fixed size, which allow constant time operations. In this section, we will explore the use of arrays for implementing dynamic programming algorithms in Python, analyzing their application to various classic DP problems.

When using arrays in DP, each element of the array typically corresponds to the solution of a subproblem. Depending on the problem, the dimensionality of the array can vary. One-dimensional arrays are used for simpler problems, while two-dimensional or even higher-dimensional arrays might be needed for more complex scenarios.

**One-Dimensional Arrays**

One-dimensional arrays are commonly used when the problem involves a single parameter that varies, and the subproblems' solutions depend linearly on this parameter. Consider the classic problem of computing the $n$-th Fibonacci number, where:

$$F(n) = F(n-1) + F(n-2)$$

with initial conditions $F(0) = 0$ and $F(1) = 1$. Using a one-dimensional array to store the Fibonacci numbers up to $n$, we have the following Python implementation:

```
def fibonacci(n):
    if n <= 1:
        return n
    fib = [0] * (n + 1)
    fib[1] = 1
    for i in range(2, n + 1):
        fib[i] = fib[i - 1] + fib[i - 2]
    return fib[n]
```

Here, the array fib captures the value of each Fibonacci number up to $F(n)$. The iterative update ensures that each Fibonacci number is computed based on previously computed values, demonstrating an optimal substructure in DP.

### Two-Dimensional Arrays

Two-dimensional arrays are applicable when the problem involves two parameters, and the state of each subproblem depends on these parameters. Consider the Longest Common Subsequence (LCS) problem, where we seek the length of the longest subsequence present in both strings $X$ and $Y$:

$$LCS[i,j] = \begin{cases} 0, & \text{if } i = 0 \text{ or } j = 0 \\ LCS[i-1, j-1] + 1, & \text{if } X[i-1] = Y[j-1] \\ \text{max}(LCS[i-1, j], LCS[i, j-1]), & \text{if } X[i-1] \neq Y[j-1] \end{cases}$$

Below is the implementation using a two-dimensional array:

```
def lcs(X, Y):
    m, n = len(X), len(Y)
    L = [[0] * (n + 1) for _ in range(m + 1)]
    for i in range(1, m + 1):
        for j in range(1, n + 1):
            if X[i - 1] == Y[j - 1]:
                L[i][j] = L[i - 1][j - 1] + 1
            else:
                L[i][j] = max(L[i - 1][j], L[i][j - 1])
    return L[m][n]
```

The array `L` is a two-dimensional list that records the length of the LCS for substrings of $X$ and $Y$. The nested loops populate this array based on the state transition rules of the LCS problem.

### Higher-Dimensional Arrays

Higher-dimensional arrays are used for problems where the state of subproblems depends on three or more parameters. For example, the 0/1 Knapsack problem can be extended to consider multiple capacity constraints or additional dimensions in each item, necessitating higher-dimensional DP arrays.

Consider the variation where an additional volume constraint must be met, leading to a three-dimensional array. The state transition would be defined as follows:

$$DP[i][w][v] = \text{max} \begin{cases} DP[i-1][w][v], \\ DP[i-1][w][v], DP[i-1][w - weight[i]][v - volume[i]] + \end{cases}$$

The implementation is not provided here but follows the same logic as previous examples, extending to three-dimensional arrays and considering two capacity constraints.

Arrays provide an efficient means of storing subproblem solutions due to their simple and direct index-based access. The primary advantage lies in the constant-time complexity for retrieval and update operations, which is critical for the efficiency of dynamic programming algorithms. By understanding the application of arrays in DP, one can effectively formulate and implement a wide range of DP solutions in Python, optimizing both computation time and storage.

## 5.6 Using Dictionaries for DP

Dynamic Programming (DP) solutions often require storing intermediate results to avoid redundant computations. While lists are commonly used for this purpose due to their efficient index-based operations, dictionaries provide a highly flexible alternative, especially useful in cases where the space of subproblems is sparse or not well-defined at the outset. Python's dictionary, implemented using hash tables, provides average-case constant time complexity for insertion, deletion, and lookup operations, making it a robust choice for many DP problems.

Consider the classic example of computing Fibonacci numbers. The recursive definition of the Fibonacci sequence is:

$$F(n) = \begin{cases} n & \text{if } n \leq 1 \\ F(n-1) + F(n-2) & \text{if } n > 1 \end{cases}$$

Without memoization, this recursive approach exhibits exponential time complexity due to repeated calculations of the same subproblems. By using a dictionary to store the computed values, we can reduce the time complexity to linear.

```
def fibonacci(n, memo={}):
    if n in memo:
        return memo[n]
    if n <= 1:
        return n
    memo[n] = fibonacci(n-1, memo) + fibonacci(n-2, memo)
    return memo[n]
```

In this implementation, memo is a dictionary where the keys are the arguments to the function and the values are the computed results. When the function is called, it first checks whether the result for the given $n$ is already in the dictionary. If it is, it returns the stored result, thereby avoiding redundant calculations.

Dictionaries also facilitate handling problems with more complex state representations. Consider the problem of finding the number of distinct ways to climb a staircase, where at each step you can take either one or two steps. The state can be represented by the current step number, and we can store the number of ways to reach each step in a dictionary.

```
def climb_stairs(n, memo={}):
    if n in memo:
        return memo[n]
    if n <= 1:
        return 1
    memo[n] = climb_stairs(n-1, memo) + climb_stairs(n-2, memo)
    return memo[n]
```

In problems where subproblem states depend on multiple parameters, dictionaries can easily accommodate tuples as keys. Suppose we need to compute the number of ways to form a given sum $k$ using a set of coins with given denominations. The state can be represented by a tuple $(sum, index)$, where $\mathrm{sum}$ is the remaining sum to be formed, and $\mathrm{index}$ represents the current position in the list of denominations.

```
def coin_change_ways(amount, coins, index, memo={}):
    if (amount, index) in memo:
        return memo[(amount, index)]
    if amount == 0:
        return 1
    if amount < 0 or index == len(coins):
        return 0

    # Calculate the two possibilities:
    # 1. include the coin at the current index
    # 2. exclude the coin at the current index
    include_coin = coin_change_ways(amount - coins[index], coins, index, memo)
    exclude_coin = coin_change_ways(amount, coins, index + 1, memo)

    memo[(amount, index)] = include_coin + exclude_coin
    return memo[(amount, index)]
```

In this example, $\mathrm{memo}$ is a dictionary keyed by tuples, allowing us to efficiently store and retrieve results for states defined by multiple variables. This technique generalizes readily to more complex DP problems, such as those involving grids, sequences, or multiple dimensions.

The power of dictionaries lies in their flexibility and ease of use. They can handle varying numbers of state dimensions and non-integer keys, which makes them ideal for problems where the problem space is not straightforwardly indexed, or when working with algorithms that require more sophisticated state representations.

When profiling and optimizing DP code, it is important to ensure that the use of dictionaries does not lead to excessive memory consumption. Python dictionaries, while efficient in terms of lookup and insertion times, can consume substantial memory if the number of stored keys becomes large. Strategies such as limiting the recursion depth, periodically clearing unneeded entries, or switching to more space-efficient data structures might be necessary in such cases.

Dictionaries also facilitate dynamic state space exploration, making them particularly useful for problems involving decision trees, graphs with variable structures, and scenarios where the problem space must be explored adaptively. This adaptability, combined with Python's inherent flexibility and expressive syntax, enhances the overall robustness and versatility of dynamic programming solutions implemented in Python.

## 5.7 Handling Multiple States

Dynamic programming (DP) problems often involve handling multiple states, which necessitates an adept management of multiple variables and dimensions. Handling these states efficiently in Python is key to crafting optimal solutions.

Consider the classic problem of the **Knapsack**, wherein each item has a weight and a value, and the challenge is to maximize the total value of items without exceeding a given weight limit. This problem can be described by two states: the remaining capacity of the knapsack and the index of the current item being considered.

**Example: 0/1 Knapsack Problem**

Given a list of items, each with a weight and a value, and a total weight capacity W, the task is to maximize the value within the weight limit.

The state can be defined with an array $dp[i][w]$, where $i$ denotes the number of items considered, and $w$ denotes the remaining weight capacity. The value at each state represents the maximum value achievable with the first $i$ items and weight capacity $w$.

```
def knapsack(weights, values, W):
    n = len(values)
    dp = [[0 for _ in range(W + 1)] for _ in range(n + 1)]

    for i in range(1, n + 1):
        for w in range(W + 1):
            if weights[i-1] <= w:
                dp[i][w] = max(dp[i-1][w], dp[i-1][w-weights[i-1]] + values[i-1])
            else:
```

```
                dp[i][w] = dp[i-1][w]

    return dp[n][W]

weights = [2, 3, 4, 5]
values = [3, 4, 5, 6]
W = 5
print(knapsack(weights, values, W))
```

7

The above code demonstrates the tabulation approach, handling two states: the item index 'i' and the remaining weight 'w'. The decision at each state depends on whether to include the current item or exclude it, and the resulting value is stored in the 'dp' table for future reference.

### Multiple State Variables in DP

Consider a scenario where the DP problem is characterized by more than two state variables. For illustrative purposes, let's explore a **3-dimensional DP problem**.

### Example: Minimum Cost Path in a Grid with Obstacles

Given a grid layout where each cell has a cost and obstacles, the task is to find the minimum cost path from the top-left corner to the bottom-right corner of the grid. Here, the states can be described by three variables: the current cell's row, column, and direction moved (up, down, left, right).

To handle this, a 3D DP array can be utilized where each dimension represents the row, column, and direction respectively.

```
def minCostPath(grid):
    rows, cols = len(grid), len(grid[0])
    directions = [(0,1), (1,0), (0,-1), (-1,0)]
    dp = [[[float('inf')] * len(directions) for _ in range(cols)] for _ in range(rows)]

    dp[0][0] = [grid[0][0]] * len(directions)

    for r in range(rows):
        for c in range(cols):
            for k, (dr, dc) in enumerate(directions):
                nr, nc = r + dr, c + dc
                if 0 <= nr < rows and 0 <= nc < cols:
                    dp[nr][nc][k] = min(dp[nr][nc][k], dp[r][c][k] + grid[nr][nc])

    return min(dp[-1][-1])

grid = [
    [1, 2, 3],
    [4, 8, 2],
    [1, 5, 3]
]
print(minCostPath(grid))
```

8

This 3D DP array 'dp' is used to track the minimum cost to reach each cell '(r, c)' from four possible directions. 'directions' lists the possible moves, and 'dp[r][c][k]' keeps the minimum cost to cell '(r, c)' coming from direction 'k'.

### Handling Multiple States with Dictionaries

For more complex state representations and better readability, Python dictionaries can be employed over arrays. This can be particularly useful when the state space is sparse or less regularly structured.

### Example: Fibonacci Sequence with Multiple Modulo Constraints

Consider finding Fibonacci numbers with an additional state constraint such as specific modulo conditions. In this case, a dictionary is used where keys represent tuples of the state variables.

```
def fibonacci_modified(n, mod1, mod2):
    memo = {}

    def dp(i, m1, m2):
        if i == 0: return 0
        if i == 1: return 1
        if (i, m1, m2) in memo: return memo[(i, m1, m2)]

        memo[(i, m1, m2)] = (dp(i-1, m2, m1) + dp(i-2, m1, m2)) % m1
        return memo[(i, m1, m2)]

    return dp(n, mod1, mod2)

n = 10
mod1, mod2 = 100, 50
print(fibonacci_modified(n, mod1, mod2))
```

55

In this example, the recursive function 'dp(i, m1, m2)' calculates the Fibonacci number for index 'i' under the constraints of modulo values 'm1' and 'm2'. State keys are represented as tuples '(i, m1, m2)' for memoization, ensuring efficient lookup and storage of subproblems.

Handling multiple states in dynamic programming requires a granular understanding of the problem's structure and careful management of state variables. By employing multidimensional arrays or dictionaries, complex problems with varied constraints can be tackled effectively in Python.

## 5.8 DP with Multidimensional Arrays

Dynamic programming often involves scenarios where multiple parameters or states must be optimized together. In such cases, multidimensional arrays can be a powerful tool to systematically store and access precomputed subproblem solutions. An understanding of leveraging these arrays is crucial for handling more complex DP problems efficiently.

Consider a practical example: the Longest Common Subsequence (LCS) problem. Given two sequences, the goal is to find the length of their longest subsequence present in both. This problem requires a two-dimensional DP array since it involves two indices, one for each sequence.

We define $dp[i][j]$ to represent the length of the LCS of the prefixes $X[0:i]$ and $Y[0:j]$. The DP table is initialized such that $dp[0][j]=0$ for all $j$, and $dp[i][0]=0$ for all $i$, because the LCS of any sequence with an empty sequence is 0.

The recursive relation for the LCS problem is defined as follows:

$$dp[i][j] = \begin{cases} 0 & \text{if } i=0 \text{ or } j=0 \\ dp[i-1][j-1]+1 & \text{if } X[i-1]=Y[j-1] \\ \max(dp[i-1][j], dp[i][j-1]) & \text{otherwise} \end{cases}$$

This relation ensures that the DP table is filled by aligning the characters of both sequences and iteratively building up to the solution.

Let's implement the LCS problem in Python using a two-dimensional array:

```
def longest_common_subsequence(X, Y):
    m = len(X)
    n = len(Y)

    # Create a 2D array to store lengths of LCS
    dp = [[0] * (n + 1) for _ in range(m + 1)]

    # Build the dp array from bottom up
    for i in range(1, m + 1):
        for j in range(1, n + 1):
            if X[i - 1] == Y[j - 1]:
                dp[i][j] = dp[i - 1][j - 1] + 1
            else:
                dp[i][j] = max(dp[i - 1][j], dp[i][j - 1])

    return dp[m][n]
```

```
# Example usage
X = "AGGTAB"
Y = "GXTXAYB"
print(f"Length of LCS is {longest_common_subsequence(X, Y)}")
```

```
Length of LCS is 4
```

In this example, the multidimensional array $dp$ of size $(m+1) \times (n+1)$ allows us to systematically fill values based on previously computed subproblem solutions.

For problems involving more complex states, higher-dimensional arrays can be applied. For instance, consider the problem where we need to find the minimum path sum in a 3D grid. Here, a three-dimensional DP table can be employed. The principles of defining the state space and transitioning between states remain the same, just extended to an additional dimension.

Let's conceptualize a DP solution for a 3D grid path problem. Suppose we have a grid $\mathrm{grid[x][y][z]}$ representing costs, and we need to find the minimum cost path from $(0,0,0)$ to $(X,Y,Z)$.

We define $dp[i][j][k]$ as the minimum cost to reach cell $(i,j,k)$. The base case is $dp[0][0][0] = grid[0][0][0]$, and the transition relation considers the minimum cost from three possible preceding cells:

$$dp[i][j][k] = grid[i][j][k] + \min(dp[i-1][j][k], dp[i][j-1][k], dp[i][j][k-1])$$

Here, we have translated the problem into three dimensions, accounting for 3D space traversal.

Below is a Python implementation using a three-dimensional DP array:

```
def min_path_sum_3d(grid):
    X = len(grid)
    Y = len(grid[0])
    Z = len(grid[0][0])

    # Create a 3D array to store minimum path sums
    dp = [[[0] * Z for _ in range(Y)] for _ in range(X)]

    dp[0][0][0] = grid[0][0][0]

    # Initialize first plane
    for i in range(1, X):
        dp[i][0][0] = dp[i-1][0][0] + grid[i][0][0]
    for j in range(1, Y):
        dp[0][j][0] = dp[0][j-1][0] + grid[0][j][0]
    for k in range(1, Z):
        dp[0][0][k] = dp[0][0][k-1] + grid[0][0][k]
```

```
    # Fill the rest of the dp array
    for i in range(1, X):
        for j in range(1, Y):
            for k in range(1, Z):
                dp[i][j][k] = grid[i][j][k] + min(dp[i-1][j][k], dp[i][j-1][k], dp[i][j][k-1])

    return dp[X-1][Y-1][Z-1]

# Example usage
grid = [[[1, 2, 3], [4, 5, 6]], [[7, 8, 9], [10, 11, 12]]]
print(f"Minimum path sum is {min_path_sum_3d(grid)}")
```

```
Minimum path sum is 28
```

The example provided illustrates the method to handle DP problems requiring multidimensional state tracking. By formulating a precise state transition and judiciously initializing the DP table, one can tackle a wide array of complex optimization problems.

## 5.9 Space Optimization Techniques

When implementing dynamic programming (DP) solutions, especially for problems involving large datasets or complex state spaces, one of the crucial considerations is the space complexity of the solution. Efficiently managing memory usage is paramount to handle larger inputs and improve the performance of our algorithms. This section delves into various space optimization techniques that can be employed in Python implementations of dynamic programming.

Traditionally, DP solutions involve maintaining a table (or array) to store the results of subproblems, leveraging them to build up to the solution of the original problem. While this method is straightforward, it can often result in high memory usage. Space optimization aims to reduce this memory footprint without compromising the correctness or efficiency of the algorithm.

**1. Reducing Dimensions in DP Tables**

Consider a typical DP problem such as the Fibonacci sequence, where we store intermediate results in an array. The naive DP approach uses an array of size $n$, where $n$ is the target Fibonacci number index. However, note that to compute any Fibonacci number $F(n)$, only the previous two Fibonacci numbers $F(n-1)$ and $F(n-2)$ are required. Therefore, keeping the entire array is redundant. Instead, we can optimize the space by maintaining only the last two calculated values.

The following code snippet demonstrates this optimization:

```
def fibonacci_optimized(n):
    if n <= 1:
        return n
    a, b = 0, 1
    for _ in range(2, n + 1):
        a, b = b, a + b
    return b

# Example Usage
print(fibonacci_optimized(10))
```

Output: 55

In this optimized version, we've reduced the space complexity from $O(n)$ to $O(1)$.

**2. Overlapping Subproblems and Reusing Memory**

In some problems, such as the Knapsack problem, the DP table can be constructed in a way that allows reusing memory from previous computations. Consider the 0/1 Knapsack problem, where we need to decide whether to include an item in the knapsack based on its value and weight.

The canonical DP solution uses a 2D table where each entry 'dp[i][w]' represents the maximum value achievable with the first $i$ items and a knapsack capacity $w$. To optimize space, observe that the current state only depends on the previous state, allowing us to use a sliding window approach with a 1D array.

Here's the optimized implementation:

```
def knapsack_optimized(weights, values, capacity):
    n = len(values)
    dp = [0] * (capacity + 1)
    for i in range(n):
        for w in range(capacity, weights[i] - 1, -1):
            dp[w] = max(dp[w], dp[w - weights[i]] + values[i])
    return dp[capacity]

# Example Usage
weights = [1, 3, 4, 5]
values = [1, 4, 5, 7]
capacity = 7
print(knapsack_optimized(weights, values, capacity))
```

Output: 9

This optimized approach reduces the space complexity from $O(n \cdot W)$ to $O(W)$, where $W$ is the capacity of the knapsack.

**3. Eliminating Redundant States**

Some problems exhibit redundant states, where certain entries in the DP table are either never accessed or do not contribute to the final result. Identifying and eliminating such states can considerably reduce the memory footprint.

Consider the Longest Common Subsequence (LCS) problem. A naive 2D implementation storing results for all substrings has a space complexity of $O(m \cdot n)$, where $m$ and $n$ are the lengths of the two sequences. By narrowing down to only the relevant states and using previous results, we can optimize the space.

Below is the optimized LCS implementation:

```
def lcs_optimized(X, Y):
    m, n = len(X), len(Y)
    prev = [0] * (n + 1)
    for i in range(1, m + 1):
        current = [0] * (n + 1)
        for j in range(1, n + 1):
            if X[i - 1] == Y[j - 1]:
                current[j] = prev[j - 1] + 1
            else:
                current[j] = max(prev[j], current[j - 1])
        prev = current
    return prev[n]

# Example Usage
X = "AGGTAB"
Y = "GXTXAYB"
print(lcs_optimized(X, Y))
```

```
Output: 4
```

This LCS solution uses two 1D arrays, reducing space complexity from $O(m \cdot n)$ to $O(n)$.

**4. iterator in Functional Programming**

Python's functional programming capabilities can also be leveraged for space optimization. The itertools module offers memory-efficient tools for handling iterables, which can be particularly useful in generating DP states on-the-fly without storing entire sequences in memory.

Consider the problem of generating the first $n$ rows of Pascal's triangle. Instead of storing all rows, we can generate each row using iterators:

```
import itertools

def pascal_triangle(n):
    row = [1]
    for _ in range(n):
        yield row
        row = list(itertools.accumulate([0] + row, lambda x, y: x + y))

# Example Usage
```

```
for row in pascal_triangle(5):
    print(row)
```

Output:
[1]
[1, 1]
[1, 2, 1]
[1, 3, 3, 1]
[1, 4, 6, 4, 1]

Using iterators helps conserve memory, especially for sequences that can be computed incrementally.

**5. Sparse Dynamic Programming Tables**

When dealing with sparse DP tables, where most of the entries are zero or do not need to be computed, we can employ data structures like dictionaries to store only the non-zero or relevant entries.

This technique is particularly advantageous for problems like counting paths on a grid with obstacles. Instead of maintaining a full grid, we use a dictionary to keep track of reachable positions.

Here is a Python code that demonstrates this approach:

```
def count_paths_with_obstacles(grid):
    rows, cols = len(grid), len(grid[0])
    dp = {}
    dp[(0, 0)] = 1 if grid[0][0] == 0 else 0
    for r in range(rows):
        for c in range(cols):
            if grid[r][c] == 1:
                dp[(r, c)] = 0
            else:
                if (r - 1, c) in dp:
                    dp[(r, c)] = dp.get((r, c), 0) + dp[(r - 1, c)]
                if (r, c - 1) in dp:
                    dp[(r, c)] = dp.get((r, c), 0) + dp[(r, c - 1)]
    return dp.get((rows - 1, cols - 1), 0)

# Example Usage
grid = [
    [0, 0, 0],
    [0, 1, 0],
    [0, 0, 0]
]
print(count_paths_with_obstacles(grid))
```

Output: 2

This dictionary-based approach ensures that only relevant cell states are stored, leading to efficient memory usage.

These space optimization techniques exemplify practical methods for reducing memory consumption in dynamic programming solutions, making them scalable and efficient for larger inputs and complex problems.

## 5.10 Dynamic Programming in Jupyter Notebooks

Jupyter Notebooks have become an indispensable tool in modern data science and scientific computing, providing an interactive environment for code, equations, visualizations, and narrative text. Implementing dynamic programming (DP) solutions within such notebooks is particularly advantageous for a multitude of reasons, including ease of experimentation, visualization of results, and the ability to document the thought process alongside code. This section elucidates how to effectively write and execute dynamic programming algorithms in Jupyter Notebooks, offering practical examples and best practices to leverage this powerful tool efficiently.

**Setting Up a Jupyter Notebook Environment**

To begin with, ensure that Jupyter Notebook is installed on your system. You can install it using pip:

```
pip install notebook
```

After installation, start the Jupyter Notebook server by executing:

```
jupyter notebook
```

This command will open a new tab in your web browser where you can create and manage notebooks. Create a new Python notebook to start implementing your dynamic programming solutions.

**Coding and Documentation**

Jupyter Notebooks offer a blend of markdown cells and code cells for documentation and execution, respectively. You can explain your dynamic programming approach using markdown cells and subsequently provide the code in code cells. For instance, consider a simple problem such as computing the $n$th Fibonacci number using dynamic programming. You first introduce the problem in a markdown cell:

```
# Fibonacci Number Calculation using Dynamic Programming

The Fibonacci sequence is defined as follows:
- F(0) = 0
- F(1) = 1
- F(n) = F(n-1) + F(n-2) for n >= 2
```

We will use a bottom-up dynamic programming approach to compute the nth Fibonacci number.

Next, you provide the implementation in a code cell:

```
def fibonacci(n):
    if n <= 1:
        return n
    dp = [0] * (n + 1)
    dp[1] = 1
    for i in range(2, n + 1):
        dp[i] = dp[i - 1] + dp[i - 2]
    return dp[n]

# Example
n = 10
print(f"The {n}th Fibonacci number is {fibonacci(n)}.")
```

Executing this cell yields:

```
The 10th Fibonacci number is 55.
```

### Visualization

One of the strengths of Jupyter Notebooks is the ability to visualize data using libraries like Matplotlib and Seaborn. Visualizing the results of a dynamic programming algorithm often helps in understanding its behavior and performance. For example, you can visualize the Fibonacci sequence up to the $n$th term as follows:

```
import matplotlib.pyplot as plt

def fibonacci_sequence(n):
    dp = [0] * (n + 1)
    if n >= 1:
        dp[1] = 1
    for i in range(2, n + 1):
        dp[i] = dp[i - 1] + dp[i - 2]
    return dp

fib_seq = fibonacci_sequence(n)

plt.plot(range(n + 1), fib_seq, marker='o', linestyle='--')
plt.title(f"Fibonacci Sequence up to {n}th Term")
plt.xlabel("Term")
plt.ylabel("Fibonacci Number")
plt.grid(True)
plt.show()
```

Executing this code cell will generate a visual plot of the Fibonacci sequence:

### Experimentation with Different Algorithms

Jupyter Notebooks facilitate the comparison of different algorithms by allowing you to write and execute multiple solutions within the same notebook. For instance, to compare the bottom-up and top-down approaches for the Fibonacci sequence, you could structure the notebook as follows:

# Top-Down Approach with Memoization

We will use a top-down dynamic programming approach (memoization) to compute the nth Fibonacci nu

```
def fibonacci_memo(n, memo=None):
    if memo is None:
        memo = {}
    if n in memo:
        return memo[n]
    if n <= 1:
        result = n
    else:
        result = fibonacci_memo(n - 1, memo) + fibonacci_memo(n - 2, memo)
    memo[n] = result
    return result

# Example
print(f"The {n}th Fibonacci number (memoized) is {fibonacci_memo(n)}.")
```

Executing this code cell yields:

The 10th Fibonacci number (memoized) is 55.

### Profiling and Performance Analysis

Jupyter Notebooks also support profiling and performance analysis, helping you optimize your dynamic programming solutions. Use the %timeit magic function to measure the execution time of code snippets:

# Comparing Performance

Let's compare the performance of the bottom-up and top-down approaches using the %timeit magic.

```
%timeit fibonacci(30)
%timeit fibonacci_memo(30)
```

Running these cells will output the time taken by each approach, aiding in the comparison and selection of the most efficient solution for the problem at hand.

### Sharing and Collaboration

Another notable feature of Jupyter Notebooks is their integrative capability with version control systems like Git and platforms such as GitHub. By pushing your notebooks to a GitHub repository, you can share them with collaborators or a broader audience. This practice not only facilitates collaborative work but also ensures that your dynamic programming solutions are well-documented and reproducible.

Moreover, Jupyter Notebooks can be exported to various formats, including HTML and PDF, making it easy to share your work in presentations or publications. To export a notebook, navigate to the File menu and select the desired export format.

**Using Magic Commands and Extensions**

Finally, Jupyter Notebooks support numerous magic commands and extensions that enhance functionality. For instance, the %matplotlib inline magic command ensures that Matplotlib plots are displayed inline within the notebook rather than in a separate window:

```
%matplotlib inline
```

Leverage these commands and extensions to streamline your workflow and optimize the usability of your dynamic programming notebooks.

The combination of code execution, visualization, documentation, and performance analysis within a single framework makes Jupyter Notebooks an ideal tool for implementing dynamic programming solutions. Efficiently utilizing these features will enhance your productivity and enable you to solve complex problems with clarity and precision.

## 5.11 Profiling and Optimizing DP Code

Profiling and optimizing code is crucial to ensure your dynamic programming (DP) solutions are efficient and can handle large inputs within a reasonable time frame. Profiling involves measuring the performance of your code to identify bottlenecks, while optimization focuses on improving these identified bottlenecks. Here we will discuss various tools and techniques available in Python for profiling and optimizing DP code.

To start with, Python's cProfile module provides a robust profiling utility. It can be used to gather statistics about how often and for how long various parts of your program execute.

```
import cProfile

def fibonacci(n, memo={}):
    if n in memo:
        return memo[n]
    if n <= 2:
        return 1
```

```
    memo[n] = fibonacci(n-1, memo) + fibonacci(n-2, memo)
    return memo[n]

def main():
    print(fibonacci(30))

cProfile.run('main()')
```

The above script uses a top-down dynamic programming approach with memoization to compute the 30th Fibonacci number. The cProfile.run function profiles the main() function and outputs detailed statistics including the time spent in each function call.

Using the output, you can identify which part of the program consumes most of the execution time and requires optimization. Suppose the memoization is not implemented efficiently, such profiling can guide you to optimize the hash table operations or consider alternative data structures.

Another powerful tool is the line_profiler module which provides a more granular profiling approach, measuring the time spent on each line of code. You can get precise, line-by-line performance data by decorating the function you want to profile.

```
from line_profiler import LineProfiler

def fibonacci(n, memo={}):
    if n in memo:
        return memo[n]
    if n <= 2:
        return 1
    memo[n] = fibonacci(n-1, memo) + fibonacci(n-2, memo)
    return memo[n]

def main():
    print(fibonacci(30))

profiler = LineProfiler()
profiler.add_function(fibonacci)
profiler.run('main()')
profiler.print_stats()
```

The LineProfiler output shows the time spent on each line in the fibonacci function, allowing you to pinpoint inefficient sections down to individual lines of code.

Once profiling identifies the bottlenecks in your DP solution, the next step is optimization. A common optimization technique is reducing the space complexity by implementing iterative (bottom-up) solutions where possible. For instance, instead of using a dictionary for memoization, a list or array can be used when the problem constraints are within a manageable range.

Additionally, another technique for space optimization in dynamic programming is state reduction. For example, in Fibonacci sequence computation, instead of storing all previous values, you only need to store the last two computed values.

```
def optimized_fibonacci(n):
    if n <= 2:
        return 1
    previous, current = 1, 1
    for _ in range(3, n + 1):
        previous, current = current, previous + current
    return current

def main():
    print(optimized_fibonacci(30))

cProfile.run('main()')
```

In the above code for the Fibonacci function, we only maintain the last two values calculated using two variables, reducing space complexity from O(n) to O(1).

To further optimize your code, consider the nature of operations. Using built-in functions and libraries optimized in C can significantly enhance performance over Python loops and operations. Libraries such as Numpy offer highly optimized functions for numerical computations that can be utilized in DP solutions.

```
import numpy as np

def fibonacci_matrix(n):
    F = np.matrix([[1, 1], [1, 0]])
    if n == 0:
        return 0
    return (np.linalg.matrix_power(F, n-1) * np.matrix([[1], [0]]))[0, 0]

def main():
    print(fibonacci_matrix(30))

cProfile.run('main()')
```

This approach uses matrix exponentiation to compute Fibonacci numbers efficiently. The numpy.linalg.matrix_power method computes the nth power of a matrix, optimizing the recursive nature of the DP problem.

Finally, consider algorithmic improvements such as pruning or using more complex data structures like segment trees or Fenwick trees when appropriate. These structures and techniques can make a significant difference in performance, particularly for certain classes of DP problems.

By using profiling to guide optimization, combining different techniques, and leveraging Python's powerful libraries, you can ensure your dynamic programming solutions are not only correct but also highly efficient.

## 5.12 Real-World Examples and Case Studies

The practical applicability of dynamic programming (DP) extends across various domains such as computational biology, operations research, finance, and artificial intelligence. In this section, we explore several real-world examples and case studies where dynamic programming has been effectively utilized to solve complex problems. Each example is carefully selected to demonstrate the power and versatility of DP techniques in practical applications.

**1. Longest Common Subsequence in Bioinformatics**

The Longest Common Subsequence (LCS) problem is a classic example in bioinformatics, where it is used to measure the similarity between two DNA sequences. Given two sequences, the aim is to find the longest subsequence present in both sequences.

```
def lcs(X, Y):
    m = len(X)
    n = len(Y)

    # Creating the DP table
    L = [[0] * (n + 1) for _ in range(m + 1)]

    for i in range(m + 1):
        for j in range(n + 1):
            if i == 0 or j == 0:
                L[i][j] = 0
            elif X[i - 1] == Y[j - 1]:
                L[i][j] = L[i - 1][j - 1] + 1
            else:
                L[i][j] = max(L[i - 1][j], L[i][j - 1])

    return L[m][n]

# Example usage
X = "AGGTAB"
Y = "GXTXAYB"
print("Length of LCS is", lcs(X, Y))
```

The output of the above code is:

```
Length of LCS is 4
```

The table 'L' stores the length of LCS of the substrings, and the solution is built in a bottom-up manner.

**2. Knapsack Problem in Operations Research**

The Knapsack Problem is pivotal in operations research for resource allocation under constraints. The task involves selecting items with given weights and values to maximize the total value without exceeding a weight limit.

```
def knapSack(W, wt, val, n):
    K = [[0 for x in range(W + 1)] for x in range(n + 1)]

    for i in range(n + 1):
        for w in range(W + 1):
            if i == 0 or w == 0:
                K[i][w] = 0
            elif wt[i - 1] <= w:
                K[i][w] = max(val[i - 1] + K[i - 1][w - wt[i - 1]], K[i - 1][w])
            else:
                K[i][w] = K[i - 1][w]

    return K[n][W]

# Example usage
val = [60, 100, 120]
wt = [10, 20, 30]
W = 50
n = len(val)
print("Maximum value in Knapsack =", knapSack(W, wt, val, n))
```

The output for the above code is:

```
Maximum value in Knapsack = 220
```

The DP table 'K' captures the maximum value obtainable with each item and weight limit combination, allowing for an optimal solution.

**3. Optimal Stock Trading Strategies in Finance**

In financial markets, dynamic programming aids in devising optimal stock trading strategies. The following problem involves determining the maximum profit that can be achieved with at most $k$ transactions.

```
def maxProfit(prices, k):
    if not prices:
        return 0

    n = len(prices)
    if k > n // 2:
        return sum(max(prices[i + 1] - prices[i], 0) for i in range(n - 1))

    dp = [[0] * n for _ in range(k + 1)]

    for i in range(1, k + 1):
        max_diff = -prices[0]
        for j in range(1, n):
            dp[i][j] = max(dp[i][j - 1], prices[j] + max_diff)
            max_diff = max(max_diff, dp[i - 1][j] - prices[j])
```

```
    return dp[k][n - 1]

# Example usage
prices = [3, 2, 6, 5, 0, 3]
k = 2
print("Maximum profit with at most", k, "transactions =", maxProfit(prices, k))
```

The output from the above code is:

```
Maximum profit with at most 2 transactions = 7
```

The table 'dp' stores the maximum profit achievable with up to $i$ transactions by day $j$.

**4. Sequence Alignment in Computational Biology**

Sequence alignment is essential for identifying regions of similarity that may indicate functional, structural, or evolutionary relationships between sequences. The Needleman-Wunsch algorithm, a common DP method, accomplishes this.

```
def needleman_wunsch(seq1, seq2, match=1, mismatch=-1, gap=-1):
    n, m = len(seq1), len(seq2)
    dp = [[0] * (m + 1) for _ in range(n + 1)]

    for i in range(1, n + 1):
        dp[i][0] = i * gap
    for j in range(1, m + 1):
        dp[0][j] = j * gap

    for i in range(1, n + 1):
        for j in range(1, m + 1):
            if seq1[i - 1] == seq2[j - 1]:
                score = match
            else:
                score = mismatch
            dp[i][j] = max(dp[i - 1][j - 1] + score,
                           dp[i - 1][j] + gap,
                           dp[i][j - 1] + gap)

    return dp[n][m]

# Example usage
seq1 = "GATTACA"
seq2 = "GCATGCU"
print("Alignment score:", needleman_wunsch(seq1, seq2))
```

The output of the above code is:

```
Alignment score: 0
```

The DP table 'dp' captures the optimal alignment score by comparing character matches, mismatches, and gaps.

**5. Interleaving Strings in Computational Theory**

Determining if a string is an interleaving of two other strings through dynamic programming demonstrates the computational theory's practical applications. The problem checks whether a target string is formed by interleaving characters of two input strings in a way that maintains their respective character order.

```
def isInterleave(s1, s2, s3):
    if len(s1) + len(s2) != len(s3):
        return False

    dp = [[False] * (len(s2) + 1) for _ in range(len(s1) + 1)]
    dp[0][0] = True

    for i in range(len(s1) + 1):
        for j in range(len(s2) + 1):
            if i > 0 and s3[i + j - 1] == s1[i - 1]:
                dp[i][j] = dp[i][j] or dp[i - 1][j]
            if j > 0 and s3[i + j - 1] == s2[j - 1]:
                dp[i][j] = dp[i][j] or dp[i][j - 1]

    return dp[len(s1)][len(s2)]

# Example usage
s1 = "aabcc"
s2 = "dbbca"
s3 = "aadbbcbcac"
print("Is interleaving:", isInterleave(s1, s2, s3))
```

The output from the above code is:

```
Is interleaving: True
```

The DP table 'dp' determines the feasibility of interleaving based on progressive character matches from both strings.

These examples underscore dynamic programming's utility across diverse, real-world problem domains. They illustrate how optimized solutions are systematically derived using structured DP techniques in Python, providing robust frameworks for addressing complex challenges.

# Chapter 6

# Memoization Techniques

**This chapter delves into memoization, a technique used to optimize recursive algorithms by caching previously computed results to avoid redundant calculations. Readers will learn how memoization works, its implementation in Python using lists and dictionaries, and its application in recursive functions. The chapter discusses handling side effects, multi-argument functions, and space complexity considerations. Common pitfalls and scenarios where memoization is not appropriate are also covered, along with real-world examples to solidify understanding and practical application of memoization techniques.**

## 6.1 Introduction to Memoization

Memoization is a technique used in computer science to optimize programs by storing the results of expensive function calls and reusing the cached results when the same inputs occur again. This method significantly reduces the time complexity of recursive functions that might otherwise result in repetitive and redundant computations. Conceptually, memoization bridges the gap between naive recursive implementations and their iterative counterparts, combining the simplicity of recursion with the efficiency of iteration.

To better understand memoization, consider the computational complexity of a naive recursive function. Let us take the classic example of computing the Fibonacci sequence. The naive approach to compute the $n$th Fibonacci number can lead to an exponential time complexity of $O(2^n)$ due to the redundant recalculations of the same subproblems.

```
def naive_fibonacci(n):
    if n <= 1:
        return n
    else:
        return naive_fibonacci(n-1) + naive_fibonacci(n-2)
```

In the above code snippet, each call to naive_fibonacci for any $n \geq 2$ invokes two more calls to naive_fibonacci. Given that these calls are not identified and stored, they result in overlapping subproblem computations. For instance, computing naive_fibonacci(5) results in redundant calls to naive_fibonacci(3) and naive_fibonacci(2) multiple times.

Memoization circumvents this inefficiency by caching the results of these subproblems in a data structure such as a dictionary or list, from which the results can be retrieved in constant time. Thus, subsequent calls with the same arguments can return the previously computed result immediately.

In Python, a common way to implement memoization is via dictionaries, leveraging the language's dynamic nature to cache function results. Below is an example:

```
def memoized_fibonacci(n, cache={}):
    if n in cache:
        return cache[n]
    if n <= 1:
        result = n
    else:
        result = memoized_fibonacci(n-1, cache) + memoized_fibonacci(n-2, cache)
    cache[n] = result
    return result
```

In this implementation, the dictionary cache stores the results of the Fibonacci function for each value of $n$. When the function is called, it first checks if the result for the given $n$ is already present in the cache. If so, it returns the cached value, thereby avoiding redundant computations. If not, the function proceeds with the computation and stores the result in the cache before returning it. By doing so, the function's time complexity is optimized to $O(n)$.

Memoization is not confined to simple problems like the Fibonacci sequence. It can be applied to a wide range of problems, including but not limited to dynamic programming problems, where solutions can be broken into overlapping subproblems. Through intelligent caching, memoization transforms the time complexity of the problem, ensuring that each subproblem is solved only once.

While memoization significantly improves the efficiency of recursive functions, it is crucial to consider the memory overhead. As the results of subproblems are stored in a cache, the space complexity may rise to $O(n)$ or higher depending on the number of distinct subproblems involved. Thus, while memoization is a powerful optimization technique, its application must be judicious, considering both the problem size and the available system memory.

In summary, understanding and implementing memoization can greatly enhance the efficiency of recursive algorithms, transforming problems with impractical naive solutions into feasible computations suitable for real-world applications. The following sections will further detail the various strategies and paradigms for implementing memoization in Python, offering practical insights and advanced techniques to maximize the potential of this optimization method.

## 6.2 How Memoization Works

Memoization is an optimization technique used primarily to speed up computer programs by caching the results of expensive function calls and reusing those cached results when the same inputs occur again. The fundamental idea is to store the results of expensive function calls and reuse these results the next time the function is invoked with the same arguments, avoiding redundant calculations.

When a function is called with a particular set of parameters, memoization ensures that the result is stored and indexed with those parameters. When the same function is invoked with identical parameters, instead of recalculating the result, the function retrieves and returns the stored result. This drastically reduces computational overhead in problems with overlapping subproblems, such as those encountered in dynamic programming.

The conceptual workflow of memoization involves the following operations:

- **Checking the Cache:** Before performing computations, the function checks whether the result for the given parameters is already stored in the cache.
- **Cache Hit:** If the result is found in the cache, the function immediately returns the cached result.

- **Cache Miss:** If the result is not found, the function computes the result, stores it in the cache, and then returns the result.

This process can be illustrated through the Fibonacci sequence. The Fibonacci sequence is defined as:

$$F(n) = \begin{cases} 0 & \text{if } n = 0 \\ 1 & \text{if } n = 1 \\ F(n-1) + F(n-2) & \text{if } n > 1 \end{cases}$$

A naive recursive implementation of the Fibonacci sequence involves significant repetitive calculations, particularly for larger values of $n$. This can be optimized using memoization:

```
def fib(n, memo={}):
    if n in memo:
        return memo[n]
    if n <= 1:
        return n
    memo[n] = fib(n-1, memo) + fib(n-2, memo)
    return memo[n]
```

In this example, the memo dictionary caches the results of previously computed Fibonacci numbers. Before performing recursive computations, the function first checks if the result is already in the memo dictionary. If it is, that result is returned directly. If not, the function computes the result, stores it in memo, and then returns the result.

The benefits of this approach are substantial as can be observed by comparing the time complexity. The time complexity of the naive recursive approach to compute $F(n)$ is $O(2^n)$, whereas with memoization, it is reduced to $O(n)$.

Another intricacy of memoization is its application in multi-argument functions. Consider the problem of computing the edit distance (also known as Levenshtein distance) between two strings. The edit distance is defined as follows:

Let dist$(i, j)$ be the edit distance between the first $i$ characters of string $A$ and the first $j$ characters of string $B$.

$$\text{dist}(i, j) = \begin{cases} \max(i, j) & \text{if } \min(i, j) = 0 \\ \text{dist}(i-1, j-1) & \text{if } A[i-1] = B[j-1] \\ 1 + \min(\text{dist}(i-1, j), \text{dist}(i, j-1), & \\ \text{dist}(i-1, j-1)) & \text{otherwise} \end{cases}$$

A memoized version of this function in Python can be implemented as:

```
def edit_distance(A, B, i=None, j=None, memo=None):
    if memo is None:
        memo = {}
    if i is None and j is None:
        i, j = len(A), len(B)
    if (i, j) in memo:
        return memo[(i, j)]
    if i == 0:
        return j
    if j == 0:
        return i
    if A[i-1] == B[j-1]:
        memo[(i,j)] = edit_distance(A, B, i-1, j-1, memo)
    else:
        memo[(i,j)] = 1 + min(
            edit_distance(A, B, i-1, j, memo),
            edit_distance(A, B, i, j-1, memo),
            edit_distance(A, B, i-1, j-1, memo)
        )
    return memo[(i, j)]
```

In this example, the memo dictionary has tuples of the form $(i, j)$ as keys, representing the state of computation for subproblems defined by the edit distances between prefixes of lengths $i$ and $j$. By storing intermediary results and reusing them, the memoized approach significantly decreases the computational effort required compared to the naive recursive implementation.

Memoization can also be implemented through decorators in Python. A decorator is a higher-order function that takes a function as input and returns a new function that augments the original function with additional behavior—memoization, in this case. The following example demonstrates a simple memoization decorator:

```
def memoize(f):
    cache = {}
    def wrapped(*args):
        if args in cache:
            return cache[args]
        result = f(*args)
        cache[args] = result
        return result
    return wrapped

@memoize
def fib(n):
    if n <= 1:
        return n
    return fib(n-1) + fib(n-2)

print(fib(10))
```

The memoize function creates an internal cache and returns a wrapped function that first checks the cache before invoking the original function

$f$. This way of incorporating memoization is syntactically elegant and reusable for any function, enhancing modularity and reducing redundancy in code.

Outputs for these implementations, given certain inputs, demonstrate their efficiency:

```
>>> fib(10)
55

>>> edit_distance("kitten", "sitting")
3
```

The theoretical and practical aspects of memoization underscore its utility in reducing the time complexity of recursive algorithms by effectively managing previously computed subproblem results.

## 6.3 Implementing Memoization in Python

Implementing memoization in Python involves storing the results of expensive function calls and reusing these results when the same inputs occur again. This technique can be implemented in several ways, using different data structures such as lists and dictionaries, each offering distinct advantages depending on the use case.

A common scenario where memoization is highly effective is in the computation of Fibonacci numbers with recursive algorithms. Without memoization, the naive recursive approach would result in an exponential time complexity due to repeated calculations. By caching the results of function calls, we can reduce this time complexity significantly.

To implement memoization, we can either use manual memoization techniques or leverage Python's built-in caching decorators such as functools.lru_cache. We will start by exploring manual methods, which provide a deeper understanding of the mechanics underlying memoization, followed by the usage of built-in decorators.

The following example illustrates a simple recursive function to compute Fibonacci numbers without memoization:

```
def fibonacci(n):
    if n <= 0:
        return 0
    elif n == 1:
        return 1
    else:
        return fibonacci(n-1) + fibonacci(n-2)
```

In this implementation, the function fibonacci is called recursively without storing intermediate results, leading to redundant computations. For instance, fibonacci(5) would call fibonacci(4) and fibonacci(3), while fibonacci(4) would again call fibonacci(3) and fibonacci(2), causing fibonacci(3) to be computed multiple times.

By employing memoization, we can optimize this function. First, we will use a dictionary to store results of the function calls:

```
def fibonacci_memo(n, memo={}):
    if n in memo:
        return memo[n]
    if n <= 0:
        result = 0
    elif n == 1:
        result = 1
    else:
        result = fibonacci_memo(n-1, memo) + fibonacci_memo(n-2, memo)

    memo[n] = result
    return result
```

In this improved version, the memo dictionary caches the results of the Fibonacci computations. Before computing fibonacci_memo(n), the function checks if the result is already stored in memo. If it is, the cached result is returned immediately, avoiding redundant calculations.

Using lists for memoization is another effective method, particularly useful for sequences that involve indices directly, such as Fibonacci numbers. Here's how it can be done with a list:

```
def fibonacci_list(n):
    memo = [0] * (n + 1)
    if n > 0:
        memo[1] = 1
    for i in range(2, n + 1):
        memo[i] = memo[i-1] + memo[i-2]
    return memo[n]
```

This implementation initializes a list memo of size $n + 1$, with the first two Fibonacci numbers predefined. Then, it iterates from 2 to n, computing each Fibonacci number iteratively and storing each result in the list. The final result is memo[n].

An alternative, more advanced approach, leverages Python's functools.lru_cache decorator to memoize the function automatically:

```
from functools import lru_cache

@lru_cache(maxsize=None)
def fibonacci_lru(n):
    if n <= 0:
        return 0
    elif n == 1:
        return 1
```

```
    else:
        return fibonacci_lru(n-1) + fibonacci_lru(n-2)
```

The lru_cache decorator transforms the function into one that records the results of function calls in a Least Recently Used (LRU) cache, making the function both concise and efficient. The maxsize parameter indicates the number of results to store before discarding the least recently used results.

Here's an example demonstrating the execution and performance of memoized versus non-memoized Fibonacci functions:

```
import time

# Non-memoized
start = time.time()
print(fibonacci(30))
end = time.time()
print("Non-memoized time:", end - start)

# Memoized with dictionary
start = time.time()
print(fibonacci_memo(30))
end = time.time()
print("Memoized with dictionary time:", end - start)

# Memoized with lru_cache
start = time.time()
print(fibonacci_lru(30))
end = time.time()
print("Memoized with lru_cache time:", end - start)
```

The expected outputs are:

```
832040
Non-memoized time: 1.2 (varies with system speed)
832040
Memoized with dictionary time: 0.0001 (varies with system speed)
832040
Memoized with lru_cache time: 0.0001 (varies with system speed)
```

When running these implementations, you'll observe a significant performance difference between the non-memoized and memoized versions. The memoized functions bypass redundant calculations by reusing previously computed results, illustrating the profound efficiency memoization brings to recursive algorithms.

Memoization is a versatile optimization technique that significantly improves the performance of recursive functions with overlapping subproblems. The choice of data structure for memoization—whether dictionaries, lists, or built-in caching mechanisms—should be guided by the specific requirements and context of the problem at hand.

## 6.4 Using Lists for Memoization

When implementing memoization in Python, one common approach is to use lists to store previously computed results. This method is generally suitable for problems where the range of possible inputs is known and can be bounded effectively. Lists, being ordered collections, provide efficient indexing, making them a straightforward choice for this purpose.

Consider the classical example of computing Fibonacci numbers. In a typical recursive implementation, the computational complexity can grow exponentially due to repeated calculations. Memoization, however, optimizes this process significantly.

To use lists for memoization in the Fibonacci sequence, we initialize a list with a size equal to the upper limit of the Fibonacci numbers we wish to compute. This list will store computed Fibonacci values, enabling us to access them in constant time, leading to substantial performance improvement.

```
def fibonacci(n, memo=None):
    if memo is None:
        memo = [-1] * (n + 1)

    if memo[n] != -1:
        return memo[n]

    if n <= 1:
        memo[n] = n
    else:
        memo[n] = fibonacci(n - 1, memo) + fibonacci(n - 2, memo)

    return memo[n]

# Example usage
result = fibonacci(10)
print(result) # Output: 55
```

In this implementation:

- The ‘memo‘ list is initialized to a size of $n+1$, where $n$ is the integer for which the Fibonacci number is to be computed. - Initially, all elements of ‘memo‘ are set to $-1$, indicating uncomputed states. - Upon calling the function with a value $n$, the function checks if the value is already computed by inspecting ‘memo[n]‘. If not, the recursive call proceeds. - The computed Fibonacci number is stored in ‘memo[n]‘, and subsequent calls with the same $n$ will retrieve the value in $O(1)$ time.

Using lists for memoization yields a significant reduction in the time complexity from $O(2^n)$ in the naive recursive approach to $O(n)$, where

$n$ is the term number in the Fibonacci sequence.

Instead of Fibonacci, let us consider another example: computing the number of ways to climb stairs if you can take 1 or 2 steps at a time. This problem also benefits greatly from memoization.

```
def climb_stairs(n, memo=None):
    if memo is None:
        memo = [-1] * (n + 1)

    if n <= 1:
        return 1

    if memo[n] != -1:
        return memo[n]

    memo[n] = climb_stairs(n - 1, memo) + climb_stairs(n - 2, memo)
    return memo[n]

# Example usage
result = climb_stairs(5)
print(result) # Output: 8
```

Here:

- The 'memo' list is once again initialized to $n+1$. - For cases where the input $n \leq 1$, the function returns 1 directly since there's only one way to climb a staircase with 0 or 1 step. - The results are stored in 'memo' and fetched quickly if the same sub-problem is encountered again.

Using lists for memoization is particularly efficient when:

1. Inputs are small integers within a known range. 2. The maximum input size can be predetermined. 3. The function is likely to encounter the same sub-problems multiple times.

This method, however, is less suitable for problems where the input domain is vast or cannot be bounded easily, as it may lead to excessive memory consumption. Under such circumstances, dictionaries (discussed in the next section) might be a more appropriate choice due to their dynamic and flexible nature.

## 6.5 Using Dictionaries for Memoization

Dictionaries in Python provide an efficient way to implement memoization due to their $O(1)$ average-time complexity for lookups, insertions, and deletions. This section will explore the systematic implementation of memoization using dictionaries, highlighting their advantages and practical applications.

When implementing recursive functions, redundant calculations can significantly hinder performance, especially in problems exhibiting overlapping subproblems. Dictionaries can be utilized as a lookup table where previously computed results are stored with the subproblem's parameters as the key.

Consider the naive implementation of the Fibonacci sequence:

```
def fibonacci(n):
    if n <= 1:
        return n
    return fibonacci(n-1) + fibonacci(n-2)
```

This function exhibits an exponential time complexity $O(2^n)$ because it performs redundant calculations. By leveraging dictionaries for memoization, we can optimize this function.

First, we initialize an empty dictionary to store the results of subproblems:

```
fibonacci_cache = {}
```

Next, we modify the function to check the dictionary before performing recursive calls. If the result for a given $n$ is already in the dictionary, the function returns the cached value. Otherwise, it computes the value and stores it in the dictionary.

The optimized Fibonacci function with dictionary-based memoization is as follows:

```
def fibonacci(n):
    # Check if the value is in the cache
    if n in fibonacci_cache:
        return fibonacci_cache[n]

    # Compute the nth Fibonacci number
    if n <= 1:
        value = n
    else:
        value = fibonacci(n-1) + fibonacci(n-2)

    # Cache the computed value
    fibonacci_cache[n] = value
    return value
```

The implementation above ensures that each value of $n$ is only computed once, reducing the time complexity to $O(n)$. The insertion and lookup operations in the dictionary are average $O(1)$ time complexity, making this approach highly efficient.

To further illustrate the extensibility of this approach, consider memoizing a function with multiple arguments. Here is an example involving the binomial coefficient calculation, commonly known as n choose k:

```
binomial_cache = {}

def binomial_coefficient(n, k):
    # Ensure valid input
    if k > n:
        return 0
    if k == 0 or k == n:
        return 1

    # Check if the value is in the cache
    if (n, k) in binomial_cache:
        return binomial_cache[(n, k)]

    # Compute the binomial coefficient
    result = binomial_coefficient(n-1, k-1) + binomial_coefficient(n-1, k)

    # Cache the computed value
    binomial_cache[(n, k)] = result
    return result
```

In this function, the cache key is a tuple $(n, k)$, which uniquely identifies each subproblem. The rest of the implementation follows the same principles as the Fibonacci function, ensuring that previously computed results are reused, thus improving performance.

The use of dictionaries for memoization can extend beyond simple recursive problems. They are particularly useful in dynamic programming approaches where the state space can be efficiently managed with dictionary structures. Here is an example involving the Longest Common Subsequence (LCS) problem:

```
lcs_cache = {}

def lcs(X, Y, m, n):
    # Base case: If either string is empty
    if m == 0 or n == 0:
        return 0

    # Check if the value is in the cache
    if (m, n) in lcs_cache:
        return lcs_cache[(m, n)]

    # If last characters of both sequences match
    if X[m-1] == Y[n-1]:
        result = 1 + lcs(X, Y, m-1, n-1)
    else:
        result = max(lcs(X, Y, m, n-1), lcs(X, Y, m-1, n))

    # Cache the computed value
    lcs_cache[(m, n)] = result
    return result
```

In this LCS example, we recursively solve overlapping subproblems and store their solutions in a dictionary. Each call is characterized by the remaining lengths $m$ and $n$ of the strings X and Y. By using the dictionary, we avoid the exponential time complexity inherent in the naive recursive approach.

When implementing these optimized functions, it is essential to consider the space complexity implications. Using dictionaries for memoization requires additional space to store the cached results. The space complexity is usually dependent on the number and size of unique subproblems. In the Fibonacci and binomial coefficient examples, the space complexity is $O(n)$, while in the LCS problem, it is $O(m \times n)$, where $m$ and $n$ are the lengths of the input strings.

While dictionaries provide a robust mechanism for memoization, it is crucial to be mindful of the trade-offs between time and space. Efficient use of dictionaries enhances performance by reducing computational costs, making them a valuable tool in dynamic programming and recursive problem-solving.

```
$ python lcs.py
Length of LCS is 4
```

## 6.6 Memoization in Recursive Functions

Memoization is especially powerful when applied to recursive functions, as it can dramatically reduce the time complexity of algorithms that would otherwise have exponential running times. In a recursive function, the same subproblem may be solved multiple times, leading to inefficiencies. Memoization mitigates this by storing the results of these subproblems the first time they are computed and reusing them in subsequent recursive calls.

Consider the classic example of computing the $n$-th Fibonacci number. The naive recursive solution has a time complexity of $O(2^n)$ due to the redundant calculations of the same subproblems. By memoizing these results, we can reduce the time complexity to $O(n)$.

The naive recursive implementation is straightforward:

```
def fibonacci(n):
    if n <= 0:
        return 0
    elif n == 1:
        return 1
    else:
        return fibonacci(n-1) + fibonacci(n-2)
```

Although this function is elegant and concise, it performs redundant calculations. To illustrate, computing $fibonacci(5)$ involves recomputing $fibonacci(3)$ and $fibonacci(2)$ multiple times. By adding memoization, we store results of each Fibonacci calculation in a dictionary and retrieve them when needed.

Here is the optimized, memoized version using a dictionary:

```
def fibonacci_memoized(n, memo=dict()):
    if n in memo:
        return memo[n]
    if n <= 0:
        return 0
    elif n == 1:
        return 1
    else:
        memo[n] = fibonacci_memoized(n-1, memo) + fibonacci_memoized(n-2, memo)
        return memo[n]
```

In this version, the dictionary 'memo' is used to store previously computed values. The first condition checks if the result for the current value of $n$ is already in the dictionary. If it is, the function returns the stored result, thus avoiding redundant computations. If the result is not in the dictionary, the function computes it and stores it in the dictionary before returning it.

Another common problem that benefits from memoization in a recursive function is the computation of binomial coefficients. Consider the recursive definition of the binomial coefficient $\binom{n}{k}$:

$$\binom{n}{k} = \begin{cases} 1 & \text{if } k = 0 \text{ or } k = n \\ \binom{n-1}{k-1} + \binom{n-1}{k} & \text{otherwise} \end{cases}$$

The non-memoized version of this computation would involve redundant calculations similar to those in the Fibonacci example. The implementation can be as follows:

```
def binomial_coefficient(n, k):
    if k == 0 or k == n:
        return 1
    return binomial_coefficient(n-1, k-1) + binomial_coefficient(n-1, k)
```

By implementing memoization, we can significantly improve the performance of this function:

```
def binomial_coefficient_memoized(n, k, memo=dict()):
    if k == 0 or k == n:
        return 1
    if (n, k) in memo:
        return memo[(n, k)]
    memo[(n, k)] = binomial_coefficient_memoized(n-1, k-1, memo) +
        binomial_coefficient_memoized(n-1, k, memo)
```

```
    return memo[(n, k)]
```

The 'memo' dictionary here uses tuples as keys to store the results of subproblems characterized by both $n$ and $k$. This ensures that each unique subproblem is computed only once.

Memoization can also extend beyond single-argument functions. For multi-argument functions, it is crucial to carefully track multiple parameters. Here's how the same memoization technique can enhance the generalized recursive functions.

Consider a problem of computing the maximum value of items that can be put in a knapsack of capacity $W$ given $n$ items with specific weights and values. This classic problem can be solved using recursion but benefits greatly from memoization to optimize performance.

The naive recursive function looks like this:

```
def knapsack(w, weights, values, n):
    if n == 0 or w == 0:
        return 0
    if weights[n-1] > w:
        return knapsack(w, weights, values, n-1)
    else:
        return max(values[n-1] + knapsack(w-weights[n-1], weights, values, n-1),
                knapsack(w, weights, values, n-1))
```

Applying memoization would involve storing results of subproblems in a dictionary with keys representing both the current weight capacity and the number of items considered:

```
def knapsack_memoized(w, weights, values, n, memo=dict()):
    if n == 0 or w == 0:
        return 0
    if (w, n) in memo:
        return memo[(w, n)]
    if weights[n-1] > w:
        memo[(w, n)] = knapsack_memoized(w, weights, values, n-1, memo)
    else:
        memo[(w, n)] = max(values[n-1] + knapsack_memoized(w-weights[n-1], weights,
              values, n-1, memo),
                           knapsack_memoized(w, weights, values, n-1, memo))
    return memo[(w, n)]
```

In this implementation, the tuple $(w, n)$ functions as the key for caching the result of each subproblem. Memoization ensures that each unique configuration of the knapsack's remaining capacity and the subset of items considered is computed just once, considerably speeding up the function.

By leveraging memoization in recursive functions, complex problems—amortized over multiple identical subproblems—can be solved efficiently. This technique is fundamental in transforming exponential-time algorithms into linear or polynomial-time algorithms, making it indispensable for a wide range of applications in computer science, from dynamic programming to graph theory and beyond.

## 6.7 Handling Side-effects in Memoized Functions

In computational processes, side effects refer to any state changes that occur outside the returning values of a function. These include modifying variables, input/output operations, and interacting with other parts of the system. When integrating memoization into functions, it is crucial to account for these side effects to maintain program correctness and predictability. This section discusses strategies for handling side effects through careful design and proper encapsulation within memoized functions.

Consider a function that performs an external operation, such as printing to the console or modifying a global variable. Memoization caches the results based on input arguments; if side effects are involved, the cached results may not reflect the true state changes intended by the function. To illustrate, let's examine a simple function that modifies a global counter and returns its value:

```
counter = 0

def modify_counter(x):
    global counter
    counter += x
    return counter
```

If we attempt to memoize this function, the cached results will not account for the increments to the global counter, leading to incorrect behavior:

```
from functools import lru_cache

@lru_cache(maxsize=None)
def memoized_modify_counter(x):
    global counter
    counter += x
    return counter
```

Invocation of memoized_modify_counter(2) multiple times will yield the same cached result, ignoring the intended accumulation in the counter variable. To handle such side effects, the function's design must be adjusted to ensure that the side effect's state management is coherent with memoization.

### Strategies to Manage Side Effects

Several strategies can effectively manage functions with side effects in the context of memoization:

- **Encapsulating State within Objects:** Refactor the function to encapsulate state within an object, making the side effects part of the object's internal state. This approach uses object-oriented principles to abstract and manage state changes.
- **Separating Pure and Impure Functions:** Distinguish between the pure computational aspect of the function and the side effects. Memoize only the pure function and handle side effects separately.
- **Using Immutable Data Structures:** Where feasible, utilize immutable data structures to manage state, ensuring that side effects do not inadvertently alter cached results.

### Encapsulating State within Objects

Encapsulating state within objects leverages object-oriented design principles to manage side effects. Consider the following refactored example, where the counter state is encapsulated within a class:

```
class Counter:
    def __init__(self):
        self.counter = 0

    def modify(self, x):
        self.counter += x
        return self.counter

from functools import lru_cache

class MemoizedCounter(Counter):

    @lru_cache(maxsize=None)
    def memoized_modify(self, x):
        return self.modify(x)

# Usage
counter_instance = MemoizedCounter()
print(counter_instance.memoized_modify(2)) # Outputs: 2
print(counter_instance.memoized_modify(3)) # Outputs: 5
```

### Separating Pure and Impure Functions

Separate the side effects from the pure logic of the function, memoizing only the pure part. Below is an example demonstrating this technique:

```
# Pure function
def pure_modify(x, counter):
    return counter + x

# Impure function handling side effect and memoization separately
class SideEffectManager:
    def __init__(self):
        self.counter = 0

    @lru_cache(maxsize=None)
    def memoized_pure_modify(self, x):
        return pure_modify(x, self.counter)

    def perform_operation(self, x):
        result = self.memoized_pure_modify(x)
        self.counter += x
        return result

# Usage
sem = SideEffectManager()
print(sem.perform_operation(2)) # Outputs: 2
print(sem.perform_operation(3)) # Outputs: 5
```

### Using Immutable Data Structures

Immutable data structures help ensure that the state changes do not affect the side effects unpredictably. Here is an example using immutable tuples to manage state:

```
from functools import lru_cache

@lru_cache(maxsize=None)
def memoized_addition(x, counter):
    return counter + x

# Handling immutable state
counter = 0
new_counter = memoized_addition(2, counter)
print(new_counter) # Outputs: 2

new_counter = memoized_addition(3, counter)
print(new_counter) # Outputs: 3 since the input state hasn't altered.
```

These strategies collectively address the conundrums posed by side effects within memoized functions, promoting predictable and correct program behavior. Adopting methods such as encapsulating state, separating pure and impure operations, and using immutable data structures ensures that memoization optimizes recursive calls without compromising the integrity of state changes.

## 6.8 Common Pitfalls in Memoization

Despite its many benefits, memoization is not without its challenges. Misapplication or poor implementation can not only negate performance improvements but may also introduce bugs and inefficiencies. Understanding these common pitfalls will equip you to leverage memoization effectively while avoiding potential problems.

One frequent issue is failure to handle the cache properly. When using dictionaries or lists as caches, it is imperative to ensure that the keys used in the cache are hashable and immutable. For example, mutable types like lists cannot be reliably used as dictionary keys. The following example demonstrates an attempt to cache function results using a list, which will result in a TypeError:

```
def function_with_issue(arr):
    # Incorrectly trying to use a list as a dictionary key
    cache = {}
    if arr in cache:
        return cache[arr]
    result = complex_computation(arr)
    cache[arr] = result
    return result
```

Running this code snippet will throw the following error:

```
TypeError: unhashable type: 'list'
```

In contrast, using a tuple provides a correct and immutable alternative:

```
def function_corrected(arr):
    # Using a tuple as a dictionary key
    cache = {}
    arr_tuple = tuple(arr)
    if arr_tuple in cache:
        return cache[arr_tuple]
    result = complex_computation(arr)
    cache[arr_tuple] = result
    return result
```

Another common pitfall is failing to manage the size of the cache, which can lead to excessive memory consumption. If the domain of possible inputs is vast, the cache may grow unbounded, impacting both performance and resource utilization. Techniques such as limiting the cache size or periodically clearing the cache can mitigate this issue. For instance, using Python's functools.lru_cache allows you to specify a maximum size for the cache:

```
from functools import lru_cache

@lru_cache(maxsize=1000)
```

```
def cached_function(x):
    return complex_computation(x)
```

In this example, the cache is automatically cleared once it exceeds 1000 entries, which helps keep memory usage in check.

Another pitfall to consider is related to the memoization of functions with side effects. Functions that modify global states or have I/O operations should ideally not be memoized because memoization can obscure these side effects from manifesting as they should. For instance:

```
def function_with_side_effects(x):
    print("This should run each time.")
    return x * x

@lru_cache(maxsize=None)
def cached_function_with_side_effects(x):
    print("This should only run once per unique input.")
    return x * x

# Calling demonstrates side effect behavior
print(function_with_side_effects(3))
print(cached_function_with_side_effects(3))
print(cached_function_with_side_effects(3))
```

The output will be:

```
This should run each time.
9
This should only run once per unique input.
9
```

Note that print("This should only run once per unique input.") is displayed just once for the cached_function_with_side_effects, illustrating how the memoization impacts the visibility of side effects.

A critical pitfall is improper handling of multi-argument functions. When memoizing such functions, always consider the combined set of arguments as a single, hashable key. Failure to do so will result in incorrect caching behavior. Reviewing a function with multiple arguments, we should define:

```
def mult_arg_function(a, b):
    return complex_computation(a, b)

# Memoize using a dictionary
cache = {}
def memoized_mult_arg_function(a, b):
    if (a, b) in cache:
        return cache[(a, b)]
    result = mult_arg_function(a, b)
    cache[(a, b)] = result
    return result
```

Incorrectly treating each argument separately will fail to cache the combined effect of argument pairs.

Finally, consider the appropriateness of memoization for the problem at hand. Not all recursive functions benefit from memoization, particularly when dealing with overlapping subproblems. Functions that lack overlapping subproblems or exhibit significant differences in execution time for different inputs might not experience performance benefits from caching. The process of caching introduces its overhead, and in cases where redundant calculations are minimal, the overhead can outweigh the benefits. An empirical approach involving profiling and testing can help determine whether memoization will be beneficial for a specific function.

Implementing memoization thus requires careful attention to proper key selection, cache size management, side effect handling, and suitability for multi-argument functions. Thorough consideration of these factors ensures the effective and efficient application of memoization techniques.

## 6.9 Memoization in Multi-argument Functions

Memoization can be effectively applied to multi-argument functions, transforming potentially inefficient recursive solutions into highly optimized versions. When dealing with functions that accept multiple arguments, the primary challenge lies in appropriately storing and retrieving cached results. Python dictionaries, which allow keys to be tuples, are particularly suited to this task.

Consider a multi-argument function where memoization is necessary. For illustration, suppose we need to calculate the binomial coefficient $\binom{n}{k}$, defined as:

$$\binom{n}{k} = \frac{n!}{k!(n-k)!}$$

While the factorial-based formula is simple, it poses computational inefficiencies for large $n$. The recursive definition is:

$$\binom{n}{k} = \begin{cases} 1 & \text{if } k = 0 \text{ or } k = n \\ \binom{n-1}{k-1} + \binom{n-1}{k} & \text{otherwise} \end{cases}$$

We now implement memoization to optimize this recursive computation. Using a dictionary to store results, with tuple keys representing function arguments, the recursive function can be efficiently executed.

Below is the Python code implementing this approach:

```
def binomial_coefficient(n, k, memo={}):
    # Base cases
    if k == 0 or k == n:
        return 1

    # Check memo dictionary
    if (n, k) in memo:
        return memo[(n, k)]

    # Recursive calls with memoization
    result = binomial_coefficient(n-1, k-1, memo) + binomial_coefficient(n-1, k, memo)

    # Store the result in the memo dictionary
    memo[(n, k)] = result

    return result

# Example usage
print(binomial_coefficient(5, 2))
```

Executing the above code should produce:

```
10
```

### Explanation of the Code

- **Base Case Handling:** The function first addresses base cases where $k = 0$ or $k = n$, directly returning 1 as per the definition of binomial coefficients.
- **Memoization Condition:** Before proceeding with recursive calls, the function checks whether the result for the current arguments $(n, k)$ is already computed and stored in the $\text{memo}$ dictionary.
- **Recursive Calls:** If the result is not found in the $\text{memo}$, the function performs the recursive calls necessary to compute $\binom{n}{k}$. The computed result is then stored in the dictionary to avoid repeated calculations.
- **Storing Results:** After computing the result, it is saved in the $\text{memo}$ dictionary with $(n, k)$ as the key.

### Benefits of Using Tuple Keys in Dictionaries

Tuples provide an efficient solution for multi-argument memoization because:

- **Immutable Nature:** Tuples are immutable, meaning their hash values do not change, allowing them to serve reliably as dictionary keys.
- **Compactness:** Tuples compactly represent the series of arguments in a single, hashable entity.

### Handling Multi-Argument Recursive Functions

In practical applications, functions can take more than two arguments. Consider a function $f(a, b, c)$ representing a complex calculation requiring memoization. The general approach is similar, extending to handle any number of arguments by utilizing tuple keys.

```
def complex_function(a, b, c, memo={}):
    # Hypothetical base case
    if a == 0:
        return b + c
    if b == 0:
        return a + c

    # Check memo dictionary
    if (a, b, c) in memo:
        return memo[(a, b, c)]

    # Recursive calls with memoization
    result = complex_function(a-1, b, c, memo) + complex_function(a, b-1, c, memo)

    # Store the result in the memo dictionary
    memo[(a, b, c)] = result

    return result

# Example usage
print(complex_function(2, 2, 2))
```

Executing this code should produce the corresponding result based on the hypothetical base case and recursive logic.

18

Each function call explores decreasing values of $a$ and $b$, summing their values upon reaching the base case.

### Considerations for Argument Order

The order of function arguments influences the dictionary keys' structure. Consistency in argument order across recursive calls and dictionary access is crucial. Any discrepancy leads to errors or redundant calculations. This is particularly relevant when extending or modifying the function.

### Memory Overhead and Optimization

Caching results for multiple arguments introduces memory overhead. The storage grows with the number of distinct argument combinations. Efficient memory management necessitates:

- **Pruning Unnecessary Results:** Periodically removing entries unlikely to be reused.
- **Limiting Cache Size:** Employing strategies such as Least Recently Used (LRU) caching through decorator functions.

The functools.lru_cache decorator in Python provides a built-in mechanism to handle these concerns effectively.

```
from functools import lru_cache

@lru_cache(maxsize=None)
def binomial_coefficient_lru(n, k):
    # Base cases
    if k == 0 or k == n:
        return 1

    # Recursive calls with LRU caching
    return binomial_coefficient_lru(n-1, k-1) + binomial_coefficient_lru(n-1, k)

# Example usage
print(binomial_coefficient_lru(5, 2))
```

This method automatically manages the cache, allowing the focus to remain on logic implementation while benefiting from automatic cache eviction policies. Using decorators simplifies function memoization and allows fine-grained control over cache behavior.

## 6.10 Space Complexity Considerations

Space complexity is a crucial aspect to evaluate when implementing memoization techniques. Unlike time complexity, which focuses on the execution time of an algorithm, space complexity addresses the additional memory storage required due to memoization. Proper analysis allows for balancing the trade-offs between time saved and space consumed, which is central to optimizing algorithms in resource-constrained environments.

Memoization typically involves storing previously computed results to avoid redundant calculations. This storage incurs additional memory overhead, commonly in the form of lists or dictionaries. The space complexity, therefore, is directly associated with the size and structure of these storage mechanisms.

To formalize the space complexity of a memoized function, consider a recursive function with a single argument ranging from 1 to $n$. If we use a list to store the computed values, the space complexity is $O(n)$ because our list will potentially hold $n$ elements, each taking constant space. The following Python code uses a list for memoization:

```
def fib(n, memo=None):
    if memo is None:
        memo = [None] * (n + 1)
    if n <= 1:
        return n
    if memo[n] is not None:
        return memo[n]
    memo[n] = fib(n - 1, memo) + fib(n - 2, memo)
    return memo[n]
```

In this example, the list 'memo' is initialized with $n + 1$ slots. Thus, the space complexity is $O(n)$ due to the linear growth of the list in relation to the input size $n$.

Consider also the scenario of a multi-argument function requiring memoization using a dictionary. Suppose the function takes two arguments, $x$ and $y$, with values constrained by $m$ and $n$ respectively. In this case, memoization uses a dictionary to store results indexed by tuples. The space complexity in this scenario is $O(m \times n)$.

```
def compute(x, y, memo=None):
    if memo is None:
        memo = {}
    if (x, y) in memo:
        return memo[(x, y)]
    if x == 0 or y == 0:
        return 1
    result = compute(x - 1, y, memo) + compute(x, y - 1, memo)
    memo[(x, y)] = result
    return result
```

This function uses a dictionary, 'memo', indexing results based on the tuple $(x, y)$. The space complexity is $O(m \times n)$, originating from the Cartesian product of the input sizes.

Understanding the growth rate and memory overhead of memoization is critical. When memoizing functions with large input space, either due to immense ranges or multiple arguments, the memory footprint can become prohibitive.

Visualize the following scenario for clarity:

```
def complex_recursion(a, b, c, memo=None):
```

```
    if memo is None:
        memo = {}
    if (a, b, c) in memo:
        return memo[(a, b, c)]
    if a == 0 or b == 0 or c == 0:
        return 1
    result = complex_recursion(a - 1, b, c, memo) + complex_recursion(a, b - 1, c,
            memo) + complex_recursion(a, b, c - 1, memo)
    memo[(a, b, c)] = result
    return result
```

Here, the function takes three arguments, leading to an exponential growth in storage requirements. The space complexity in this case approaches $O(a \times b \times c)$, making it vital to consider such growth for larger values of $a, b$, and $c$.

Additionally, one must account for stack space consumed by recursive calls. Although memoization reduces the number of redundant calculations, the depth of the recursion stack is influenced by the structure of the recursion itself. For instance, a tail-recursive function typically has $O(n)$ stack space because of the depth-first traversal, whereas a more balanced recursion tree might reduce this.

In practical terms, developers should always profile their programs to observe real-world memory consumption. Here's a useful Python script snippet illustrating how to estimate memory usage dynamically:

```
import resource

def get_memory_usage_kb():
    return resource.getrusage(resource.RUSAGE_SELF).ru_maxrss

# Before computation
initial_memory = get_memory_usage_kb()

# Call memoized function
complex_recursion(10, 10, 10)

# After computation
final_memory = get_memory_usage_kb()

print(f"Memory usage increased by {final_memory - initial_memory} KB")
```

```
Memory usage increased by X KB
```

By carefully analyzing the trade-off between time efficiency and memory overhead, developers can implement memoization techniques that balance performance benefits while mitigating the risk of excessive memory consumption. Use of dynamic profiling and algorithmic optimizations is vital to manage and maintain manageable space complexity in practice.

## 6.11 When Not to Use Memoization

Memoization is a potent optimization strategy, but it is not universally applicable. Certain scenarios and types of problems render memoization inefficient or even counterproductive. Understanding when not to use memoization is crucial for applying it effectively and ensuring computational resources are utilized optimally.

**1. Problems with High Space Complexity:**

Memoization inherently involves storing results of function calls. If a problem has a vast number of unique subproblems, the memory requirements for storing these results can become prohibitive. Consider a scenario where a function depends on multiple parameters, each taking on a large number of distinct values. The resultant cache would grow exponentially, potentially exhausting system memory.

**2. Stateless Functions and Idempotent Operations:**

Some functions are stateless or involve operations that do not benefit from caching. For instance, consider functions that perform simple, deterministic arithmetic operations like addition or subtraction. Such functions execute very quickly, and the overhead of managing a cache may outweigh the benefits of memoization.

**3. Problems with Minimal Overlapping Subproblems:**

Memoization is most effective for problems exhibiting overlapping subproblems, where the same subproblem is solved multiple times. In cases where subproblems rarely repeat, such as certain divide-and-conquer algorithms including merge sort, there is little to gain from memoization. The unique nature of subproblems in these instances means the cache will rarely, if ever, be utilized.

**4. Non-deterministic Functions:**

If a function produces different outputs for the same inputs due to non-determinism—such as functions relying on random number generation or external data fetching—memoization can lead to incorrect results. Caching results based on input parameters under these circumstances can introduce errors and inconsistencies.

**5. Functions with Side Effects:**

Functions that modify states or produce side effects present challenges for memoization. Consider a function that updates a global variable or interacts with external systems. Caching the result of such a function call would bypass the side effects in subsequent executions, potentially leading to inconsistent states or missed side actions.

**6. Initialization and Overhead Cost:**

The initialization and maintenance of a memoization cache incur overhead. If the function being optimized is called infrequently relative to the setup and management cost of the cache, memoization may prove inefficacious. Additionally, for functions with trivial computational complexity, the overhead might negate any potential performance gains.

**7. Concurrency and Synchronization Issues:**

In multithreaded or concurrent environments, memoization requires careful synchronization to ensure thread safety. Uncoordinated access to the cache can lead to race conditions, data corruption, or inconsistent states. Implementing thread-safe memoization mechanisms, such as synchronized accesses or using thread-local storage, can introduce significant complexity and performance overhead.

**8. Problems with Dynamic Inputs and Invalidations:**

Problems requiring frequent updates or invalidations of the memoization cache are not ideal candidates for memoization. Consider algorithms where inputs evolve dynamically, and previously cached results become obsolete. Managing cache invalidation efficiently can be intricate and resource-intensive, leading to diminished returns from memoization.

**Example of Ineffective Memoization: Fibonacci Sequence with Large Parameters**

Suppose a memoization technique is employed to compute Fibonacci numbers. While this is often an effective use case, it can become impractical if the parameters grow excessively and the cache size becomes unmanageable.

```
def fibonacci_large(n, memo={}):
    if n in memo:
        return memo[n]
    if n <= 2:
        return 1
    memo[n] = fibonacci_large(n - 1, memo) + fibonacci_large(n - 2, memo)
    return memo[n]
```

For extremely large values of $n$, the dictionary used for memoization would grow significantly, consuming substantial memory. In practical applications where $n$ might exceed reasonable limits, such as $F(10^6)$ or higher, the overhead and space complexity render memoization impractical.

Memoization is invaluable when applied to appropriate problems, but it is critical to recognize its limitations and constraints. Evaluating the nature of the problem, the computational complexity, and resource implications will guide the decision on whether or not to employ memoization.

## 6.12 Real-World Examples of Memoization

Memoization plays a critical role in optimizing algorithms across various domains, ranging from dynamic programming problems to real-time data processing tasks. In this section, we will explore several practical examples that illustrate the application of memoization techniques in real-world scenarios. We will cover problems such as the Fibonacci sequence, solving the shortest path in a grid, and optimizing gameplay strategies. These examples will demonstrate the versatility and power of memoization in improving computational efficiency.

**Fibonacci Sequence**

The Fibonacci sequence is a classic example where memoization significantly reduces the time complexity of an otherwise exponential recursive solution. The naive recursive implementation of the Fibonacci sequence suffers from redundant calculations, leading to an exponential time complexity $\mathcal{O}(2^n)$.

Consider the following naive implementation of the Fibonacci sequence:

```
def fibonacci(n):
    if n <= 1:
        return n
    return fibonacci(n-1) + fibonacci(n-2)
```

This approach recalculates the same values multiple times. By incorporating memoization, we can optimize the function to run in linear time $\mathcal{O}(n)$.

```
def fibonacci_memo(n, memo={}):
    if n in memo:
        return memo[n]
    if n <= 1:
        return n
    memo[n] = fibonacci_memo(n-1, memo) + fibonacci_memo(n-2, memo)
    return memo[n]
```

In this example, the dictionary 'memo' is used to store previously computed values of the Fibonacci sequence. Each recursive call checks if the value is already in the memo dictionary to avoid redundant calculations.

### Shortest Path in a Grid

Another common problem where memoization is beneficial is finding the shortest path in a grid, where you can move either down or right. The objective is to find the minimal path sum from the top-left corner to the bottom-right corner of a given grid of non-negative integers.

Without memoization, a straightforward recursive approach would recompute the path sums for overlapping subproblems, resulting in a high time complexity.

Consider the naive recursive solution:

```
def min_path_sum(grid, i, j):
    if i == len(grid) or j == len(grid[0]):
        return float('inf')
    if i == len(grid) - 1 and j == len(grid[0]) - 1:
        return grid[i][j]
    return grid[i][j] + min(min_path_sum(grid, i+1, j), min_path_sum(grid, i, j+1))
```

By employing memoization, we enhance the efficiency:

```
def min_path_sum_memo(grid, i=0, j=0, memo={}):
    if (i, j) in memo:
        return memo[(i, j)]
    if i == len(grid) or j == len(grid[0]):
        return float('inf')
    if i == len(grid) - 1 and j == len(grid[0]) - 1:
        return grid[i][j]

    memo[(i, j)] = grid[i][j] + min(min_path_sum_memo(grid, i+1, j, memo),
          min_path_sum_memo(grid, i, j+1, memo))
    return memo[(i, j)]
```

In this version, the memo dictionary uses tuples of grid indices as keys, ensuring that each subproblem is computed only once.

### Optimizing Gameplay Strategies

Memoization is also extensively used in optimizing strategies for various board games, such as chess or tic-tac-toe. One such example is the minimax algorithm, which is used for decision-making in two-player games.

The minimax algorithm evaluates game positions to find the optimal move by simulating all possible move sequences. Without memoization, this approach can become computationally infeasible due to an exponential number of possible game states.

Consider the naive minimax algorithm:

```
def minimax(board, depth, is_maximizing):
    if is_winner(board):
        return score(board)
    if is_maximizing:
        best_score = float('-inf')
        for move in all_possible_moves(board):
            score = minimax(make_move(board, move), depth+1, False)
            best_score = max(best_score, score)
        return best_score
    else:
        best_score = float('inf')
        for move in all_possible_moves(board):
            score = minimax(make_move(board, move), depth+1, True)
            best_score = min(best_score, score)
        return best_score
```

By integrating memoization, we can store and reuse the results of previously evaluated game states:

```
def minimax_memo(board, depth, is_maximizing, memo={}):
    board_tuple = tuple(map(tuple, board))
    if board_tuple in memo:
        return memo[board_tuple]
    if is_winner(board):
        return score(board)
    if is_maximizing:
        best_score = float('-inf')
        for move in all_possible_moves(board):
            score = minimax_memo(make_move(board, move), depth+1, False, memo)
            best_score = max(best_score, score)
    else:
        best_score = float('inf')
        for move in all_possible_moves(board):
            score = minimax_memo(make_move(board, move), depth+1, True, memo)
            best_score = min(best_score, score)

    memo[board_tuple] = best_score
    return memo[board_tuple]
```

In this enhanced version, the board state is converted to a tuple and stored in the memo dictionary. This significantly reduces the number of evaluations required, making the algorithm feasible for practical use in real-time game decisions.

These examples illustrate how applying memoization can drastically enhance the performance of recursive algorithms, leading to efficient and feasible solutions for complex real-world problems. Through these practical applications, it is evident that memoization is a vital technique for optimizing recursive processes, enabling solutions to scale efficiently with input size.

# Chapter 7

# Tabulation Techniques

**This chapter provides an in-depth look at tabulation, a dynamic programming technique that builds solutions iteratively from the ground up. Readers will learn how tabulation works, how to implement it in Python using arrays and multi-dimensional arrays, and how to convert recursive solutions to tabulated formats. The chapter also covers handling edge cases, space optimization, and evaluating time complexity. Common mistakes in tabulation and practical real-world examples are discussed to ensure a thorough understanding of this bottom-up approach.**

## 7.1 Introduction to Tabulation

Tabulation, a core technique in dynamic programming, involves solving complex problems by iteratively building solutions from the smallest subproblems up to the desired problem size. This approach stands in contrast to memoization, which employs a top-down recursive methodology with caching. Tabulation adopts a bottom-up method, where solutions for smaller subproblems are combined systematically to arrive at the solution for larger problems.

The primary advantage of tabulation lies in its iterative nature, which often results in more straightforward and efficient implementations. By eliminating the function call overhead inherent in recursion, tabulation can lead to notable improvements in both space and time efficiency. This characteristic makes tabulation particularly well-suited for problems with a high degree of overlapping subproblems.

To illustrate the process, consider a generic problem with overlapping subproblems. Assume that our goal is to compute function $F(n)$ where the computation of $F$ can be broken down into smaller subproblems $F(0)$, $F(1)$, ..., $F(n-1)$. In a tabulated approach, these subproblems are first solved and their results stored in a table (usually an array or matrix). The final solution is then derived by combining these precomputed values according to the problem's recurrence relation.

A canonical example of this approach is the computation of the Fibonacci sequence. Here, the value of each Fibonacci number is the sum of the two preceding Fibonacci numbers. Using tabulation, we can compute the sequence iteratively as follows:

```
def fibonacci(n):
    if n <= 1:
        return n

    # Initialize a table to store Fibonacci numbers
    fib_table = [0] * (n + 1)
    fib_table[1] = 1

    # Fill the table iteratively
    for i in range(2, n + 1):
        fib_table[i] = fib_table[i - 1] + fib_table[i - 2]

    return fib_table[n]
```

Output from the above code when $n = 5$:

```
5
```

In this function, we initialize an array, fib_table, which stores computed Fibonacci numbers. Starting with base cases $F(0) = 0$ and $F(1) = 1$, we iteratively fill the table until we reach $F(n)$. This process ensures that each Fibonacci number is computed just once, rendering the solution efficient.

Moving beyond scalar problems like Fibonacci, tabulation can also be extended to more complex scenarios involving multi-dimensional arrays. Problems such as the shortest path in a grid or the knapsack problem can leverage tabulation by representing subproblems in a two-dimensional or higher-dimensional table, systematically solving from the ground up.

Consider the knapsack problem: given a set of items each with a weight and value, determine the maximum value that can be achieved within a given weight limit. For this problem, we define $DP[i][j]$ as the maximum value obtainable using the first $i$ items within a weight limit of $j$.

The solution can be obtained by filling up the $DP$ table iteratively as demonstrated below:

```
def knapsack(weights, values, W):
    n = len(weights)
    # Initialize DP table
    DP = [[0] * (W + 1) for _ in range(n + 1)]

    # Fill table iteratively
    for i in range(1, n + 1):
        for w in range(W + 1):
            if weights[i-1] <= w:
                DP[i][w] = max(DP[i-1][w], DP[i-1][w-weights[i-1]] + values[i-1])
            else:
                DP[i][w] = DP[i-1][w]

    return DP[n][W]
```

Output from the above code:

```
Assuming weights = [1, 2, 3] and values = [10, 20, 30] with W = 5:

60
```

In this implementation, $\mathrm{DP}$ is a two-dimensional table where each entry $\mathrm{DP[i][w]}$ represents the maximum value achievable with the first $i$ items within weight $w$. By filling this table iteratively and building on previously computed results, we efficiently find the optimal solution to the knapsack problem.

The benefits of tabulation are evident from these examples: space-efficient storage of subproblem results, elimination of recursive function call overhead, and straightforward numerical stability due to a deterministic iterative process. As we delve deeper into this chapter, we will explore various nuances and advanced aspects of tabulation, augmenting our capacity to solve even more intricate dynamic programming problems.

## 7.2 How Tabulation Works

At the core of tabulation is the concept of solving problems by building up solutions iteratively, leveraging previously computed results to avoid redundant calculations. This method contrasts with the top-down memoization technique, wherein the problem is broken down into subproblems recursively, with intermediate results stored for future use. Tabulation, by contrast, takes a bottom-up approach.

To understand how tabulation works, consider a problem that can be divided into smaller overlapping subproblems. By solving each of these subproblems sequentially, we store their results in a table, usually an array or a multi-dimensional array. These stored results are used to build the solution to the original problem.

**Example: Fibonacci Sequence**

The Fibonacci sequence, where each number is the sum of the two preceding ones, can be efficiently calculated using tabulation. The sequence, starting from $0$ and $1$, can be represented as follows:

$$F(n) = \begin{cases} 0 & \text{if } n = 0 \\ 1 & \text{if } n = 1 \\ F(n-1) + F(n-2) & \text{if } n > 1 \end{cases}$$

To illustrate the tabulation approach, consider the following Python implementation:

```
def fib_tabulation(n):
    # Initialize the base cases
    dp = [0] * (n + 1)
    dp[0] = 0
    if n > 0:
        dp[1] = 1

    # Build the table from the ground up
    for i in range(2, n + 1):
        dp[i] = dp[i - 1] + dp[i - 2]

    # The final element in the table is the result
    return dp[n]

# Example usage
print(fib_tabulation(10)) # Output: 55
```

Execution of the above code will produce:

```
55
```

In this example, we initialize an array $\mathrm{dp}$ of size $n+1$, where $n$ is the Fibonacci number we wish to compute. The first two elements, corresponding to $F(0)$ and $F(1)$, are set to $0$ and $1$, respectively. We then iteratively fill in the remaining elements of the array using the relation $F(i) = F(i-1) + F(i-2)$.

By iterating from the base case upwards, we ensure that each result is computed using previously stored values, making the algorithm both time and space efficient. This approach avoids the overhead associated with recursive calls in a memoization strategy.

**General Steps in Tabulation**

1. *Identify the subproblems:* Break down the primary problem into

smaller, overlapping subproblems. 2. *Determine the table structure:* Decide the appropriate data structure (e.g., array, multi-dimensional array) for storing intermediate results. 3. *Initialize base cases:* Set up the initial values required to start the iterative process. 4. *Iteratively solve subproblems:* Use a loop to fill in each entry in the table using the results of the previously computed subproblems. 5. *Extract the final result:* After the table is completely filled, the solution to the original problem is extracted from the last entry of the table.

**Properties of Tabulation**

- **Time complexity:** Generally depends on the number of subproblems and the time required to fill each table entry. For many problems, this results in a polynomial time complexity. - **Space complexity:** Depends on the size of the table used to store intermediate results. Optimization techniques, discussed in later sections, can sometimes reduce this. - **Deterministic behavior:** Unlike recursive backtracking, tabulation follows a predictable, sequential pattern, making it easier to analyze and debug.

**Advantages**

- It eliminates the overhead of recursive calls. - It implicitly handles overlapping subproblems by using a single table for storage. - It can be more intuitive to implement for problems with a clear iterative structure.

**Disadvantages**

- For problems without a clear iterative structure, it may be harder to set up. - It can consume more memory if the table becomes very large, although space optimization techniques can mitigate this.

The detailed understanding of these mechanics forms the foundation for effectively implementing dynamic programming solutions using tabulation. Each of the concepts introduced here will be elaborated and applied throughout this chapter, ensuring a comprehensive grasp of tabulation techniques in Python.

## 7.3 Implementing Tabulation in Python

To implement tabulation in Python, it is essential to understand the iterative, bottom-up approach central to this dynamic programming technique. Unlike memoization, which uses a top-down strategy, tabulation starts from the base cases and incrementally builds up solutions to larger subproblems. This is achieved by filling out a table, usually an array or multi-dimensional array, iteratively.

To begin, consider a simple problem often solved using dynamic programming: the Fibonacci sequence. The Fibonacci sequence forms where each number is the sum of the two preceding ones, typically starting with 0 and 1.

Here is a naive, recursive implementation of the Fibonacci sequence:

```
def fibonacci(n):
    if n <= 1:
        return n
    return fibonacci(n - 1) + fibonacci(n - 2)
```

While this function works, it is inefficient due to repeated calculations. Using tabulation, we can design a more efficient solution by storing the results of subproblems.

First, initialize an array to store the values of the Fibonacci sequence:

```
def fibonacci(n):
    if n <= 1:
        return n
    table = [0] * (n + 1)
    table[1] = 1
```

Next, iteratively fill the table based on the Fibonacci recurrence relation $F(n) = F(n-1) + F(n-2)$:

```
    for i in range(2, n + 1):
        table[i] = table[i - 1] + table[i - 2]
    return table[n]
```

Combining these parts, the complete tabulated implementation is:

```
def fibonacci(n):
    if n <= 1:
        return n
    table = [0] * (n + 1)
    table[1] = 1
    for i in range(2, n + 1):
        table[i] = table[i - 1] + table[i - 2]
    return table[n]
```

A notable advantage of this approach is its $O(n)$ time complexity compared to the exponential time complexity of the naive recursive implementation.

Let's extend our discussion to a more complex example: the Knapsack problem. In the 0/1 Knapsack problem, we are given weights and values of items, and a knapsack with a capacity. The goal is to determine the maximum value that we can obtain by selecting items such that their total weight does not exceed the capacity.

Given:

$$\text{weights} = [w_1, w_2, \ldots, w_n]$$

$$\text{values} = [v_1, v_2, \ldots, v_n]$$

$$\text{capacity} = C$$

We define a table dp where dp$[i][w]$ represents the maximum value attainable with the first $i$ items and knapsack capacity $w$.

The Python implementation is as follows:

```
def knapsack(weights, values, capacity):
    n = len(weights)
    dp = [[0 for _ in range(capacity + 1)] for _ in range(n + 1)]

    for i in range(1, n + 1):
        for w in range(1, capacity + 1):
            if weights[i - 1] <= w:
                dp[i][w] = max(dp[i - 1][w], values[i - 1] + dp[i - 1][w - weights[i - 1]])
            else:
                dp[i][w] = dp[i - 1][w]

    return dp[n][capacity]
```

In this implementation, the table dp is filled iteratively. Each cell dp$[i][w]$ compares the maximum value obtainable by either including or excluding the $i^{\text{th}}$ item. If the weight of the $i^{\text{th}}$ item is less than or equal to the current capacity $w$, we compute the maximum of the value by including $i$ or by excluding it.

The tabulation method ensures that we solve each subproblem only once. The time complexity of this approach is $O(n \times C)$, where $n$ is the number of items and $C$ is the capacity of the knapsack, making this approach more efficient for larger potential values of $n$ and $C$.

By focusing on a structured approach to filling the table iteratively and ensuring each subproblem is solved in sequence, we effectively demonstrate how tabulation allows for efficient computation and optimal solutions in dynamic programming problems. This method is crucial for handling large datasets and ensuring computational efficiency in applied problem-solving.

## 7.4 Using Arrays for Tabulation

When implementing the tabulation method in dynamic programming, the use of arrays is fundamental. Arrays are data structures that store elements of the same type in a contiguous memory block, allowing efficient indexing. In this section, we will explore how to use one-dimensional and multi-dimensional arrays to build iterative solutions for various dynamic programming problems.

A common problem type suited for single-dimensional arrays is the computation of the Fibonacci sequence. Here, the nth Fibonacci number is defined as the sum of the two preceding ones, starting from 0 and 1. To calculate the nth Fibonacci number using tabulation with a one-dimensional array, follow these steps:

1. Initialize an array $\text{fib}$ of size $n + 1$.
2. Set the first two elements, $\text{fib}[0]$ and $\text{fib}[1]$, to 0 and 1, respectively.
3. Iterate from 2 to $n$, filling each $\text{fib}[\text{i}]$ as the sum of $\text{fib}[\text{i-1}]$ and $\text{fib}[\text{i-2}]$.
4. The value $\text{fib}[\text{n}]$ will contain the desired nth Fibonacci number.

The corresponding Python implementation is as follows:

```
def fibonacci(n):
    fib = [0] * (n + 1)
    fib[1] = 1
    for i in range(2, n + 1):
        fib[i] = fib[i - 1] + fib[i - 2]
    return fib[n]

# Example usage
print(fibonacci(10))
```

```
Output:
55
```

For more complex problems, such as the Knapsack problem, a two-dimensional array can be utilized. The 0/1 Knapsack problem can be solved using a table where the rows represent the items and the columns represent the maximum weight capacity. The table entry at $\text{dp}[\text{i}][\text{w}]$ represents the maximum value that can be achieved with items up to the ith item and a total weight not exceeding $\text{w}$.

Steps to implement the 0/1 Knapsack problem with a two-dimensional array:

1. Initialize a 2D array dp with dimensions (n+1) x (W+1), where n is the number of items and W is the maximum weight capacity.
2. Set dp[0][w] to 0 for all w, as with zero items, the maximum value is zero.
3. Iterate through each item i from 1 to n.
4. For each weight capacity w from 0 to W, update dp[i][w] as the maximum of the value without the current item dp[i-1][w] and the value with the current item (value[i-1] + dp[i-1][w-weight[i-1]]) if the current item can fit into the weight capacity.
5. The value dp[n][W] will contain the maximum value achievable with n items and weight capacity W.

The following is a Python implementation for the 0/1 Knapsack problem:

```
def knapsack(values, weights, W):
    n = len(values)
    dp = [[0 for x in range(W + 1)] for x in range(n + 1)]

    for i in range(n + 1):
        for w in range(W + 1):
            if i == 0 or w == 0:
                dp[i][w] = 0
            elif weights[i - 1] <= w:
                dp[i][w] = max(values[i - 1] + dp[i - 1][w - weights[i - 1]], dp[i - 1][w])
            else:
                dp[i][w] = dp[i - 1][w]

    return dp[n][W]

# Example usage
values = [60, 100, 120]
weights = [10, 20, 30]
W = 50
print(knapsack(values, weights, W))
```

```
Output:
220
```

Understanding how to populate and manipulate these arrays is crucial. Use well-structured loops and conditions to ensure efficient filling of the tables. Tabulation inherently leads to iterative solutions, avoiding the pitfalls of stack overflows associated with deep recursion.

The selection between one-dimensional and multi-dimensional arrays should be driven by the problem's requirements. For problems like the Fibonacci sequence, where relationships are linear, one-dimensional arrays suffice. For more complex relationships, like combinations of items and capacities in the Knapsack problem, multi-dimensional arrays are necessary to capture the interdependent states effectively.

## 7.5 Using Multi-Dimensional Arrays

In dynamic programming, utilizing multi-dimensional arrays or tables can significantly enhance the capability to solve problems that have multiple indices or parameters involved in their state representation. This section delves into the details of implementing multi-dimensional arrays in the context of tabulation, demonstrating how to address complex problems using Python.

When dealing with problems that require tracking multiple dimensions of state, such as the 0/1 knapsack problem, edit distance, or problems on graphs, two-dimensional or higher-dimensional arrays become essential. The fundamental idea is to establish a table where each dimension represents a specific parameter of the problem. This approach enables a structured and systematic exploration of all subproblems, ensuring that each is computed only once and reused when necessary.

To begin, consider a simple yet illustrative example: the classic 0/1 Knapsack problem. Here, we have a set of items, each with a weight and a value, and a knapsack with a maximum capacity. The goal is to maximize the total value of items in the knapsack without exceeding the capacity.

We define a two-dimensional array $\mathrm{dp}$ where $\mathrm{dp[i][w]}$ represents the maximum value that can be attained with the first $i$ items and a knapsack capacity $w$. Here is how you can implement this in Python:

```
def knapsack(values, weights, capacity):
    n = len(values)
    dp = [[0 for _ in range(capacity + 1)] for _ in range(n + 1)]

    for i in range(1, n + 1):
        for w in range(1, capacity + 1):
            if weights[i-1] <= w:
                dp[i][w] = max(dp[i-1][w], dp[i-1][w-weights[i-1]] + values[i-1])
            else:
                dp[i][w] = dp[i-1][w]

    return dp[n][capacity]

values = [60, 100, 120]
weights = [10, 20, 30]
capacity = 50
print(knapsack(values, weights, capacity))
```

In this example, the $i$ dimension of the $\mathrm{dp}$ array traverses through the items, while the $w$ dimension traverses through the possible capacities from 0 to the given capacity. Each entry in this table is filled based on whether the current item is included or excluded, leveraging previously computed values to ensure optimal decisions.

Executing the above code yields the following output:

```
220
```

Another example worth considering is the problem of computing the edit distance between two strings. The edit distance, or Levenshtein distance, between two strings is the minimum number of operations required to transform one string into another, where operations can include insertions, deletions, or substitutions.

To solve this using tabulation with multi-dimensional arrays:

```
def edit_distance(str1, str2):
    m, n = len(str1), len(str2)
    dp = [[0 for _ in range(n + 1)] for _ in range(m + 1)]

    for i in range(m + 1):
        for j in range(n + 1):
            if i == 0:
                dp[i][j] = j
            elif j == 0:
                dp[i][j] = i
            elif str1[i-1] == str2[j-1]:
                dp[i][j] = dp[i-1][j-1]
            else:
                dp[i][j] = 1 + min(dp[i][j-1], # Insert
                                   dp[i-1][j], # Remove
                                   dp[i-1][j-1]) # Replace

    return dp[m][n]

str1 = "kitten"
str2 = "sitting"
print(edit_distance(str1, str2))
```

Here, $\mathrm{dp[i][j]}$ represents the edit distance between the first $i$ characters of $\mathrm{str1}$ and the first $j$ characters of $\mathrm{str2}$. This table is filled iteratively, with the edit distance for each subproblem being determined by the previously solved subproblems.

After executing the above code, the output is:

```
3
```

These examples highlight the strength of tabulation using multi-dimensional arrays. Each dimension in the array reflects a specific parameter or state of the problem, allowing for a comprehensive and non-redundant exploration of all possible subproblems. This structured approach guarantees optimal substructure and overlapping subproblems, key characteristics of dynamic programming.

When adapting recursive solutions to utilize tabulation with multi-dimensional arrays, the following steps are critical: 1. Identify the parameters that define the state of the problem. 2. Initialize a table with dimensions corresponding to these parameters. 3. Populate the base cases in the table. 4. Use nested loops to fill in the table based on the previously computed values, ensuring that each state is computed only once.

Carefully constructing and using multi-dimensional arrays provide a powerful methodology for solving complex problems efficiently, proving the versatility and robustness of tabulation in dynamic programming.

## 7.6 Converting Recursive Solutions to Tabulation

To effectively convert recursive solutions to tabulated forms, a systematic approach is required. The crux of this conversion lies in transforming a top-down recursive solution, which may involve significant redundancy and excessive function calls, into a bottom-up tabulated approach that iteratively builds the solution using a storage structure, such as an array or a table.

**Step-by-Step Conversion Process**

1. **Identify the Recursive Structure**: Begin by understanding the recursive function, specifically how the problem is broken down into smaller subproblems. This typically involves identifying the function's base cases and recursive cases.

2. **Define the State and State Transitions**: Identify the parameters that define the state of the problem. These parameters will determine the dimensions of the table used for tabulation. Establish the state transitions based on the recursive relations derived.

3. **Initialize the Table with Base Cases**: Construct a table with dimensions according to the state parameters. Initialize the table entries corresponding to the base cases of the recursive function.

4. **Iterate to Fill the Table**: Using iteration, fill in the table entries based on the state transitions and previously computed entries. This step simulates the recursive calls iteratively.

5. **Retrieve the Final Solution**: The final solution for the original problem can be found in a specific entry of the table, typically corresponding to the complete state of the problem.

Consider the classic example of computing Fibonacci numbers. The recursive approach is straightforward but inefficient due to overlapping subproblems.

```
def fibonacci(n):
    if n <= 1:
        return n
    return fibonacci(n-1) + fibonacci(n-2)
```

### Step 1: Identify the Recursive Structure The recursive structure involves computing Fibonacci of n as the sum of Fibonacci of $n-1$ and $n-2$. The base cases are ‘fibonacci(0)‘ and ‘fibonacci(1)‘.

### Step 2: Define the State and State Transitions For the Fibonacci problem, the state can be defined by the single parameter $n$. The state transition is as follows:

$$\text{fibonacci}(n) = \text{fibonacci}(n-1) + \text{fibonacci}(n-2)$$

### Step 3: Initialize the Table with Base Cases Create an array to store Fibonacci numbers and initialize the base cases.

```
fib = [0] * (n+1)
fib[0] = 0
fib[1] = 1
```

### Step 4: Iterate to Fill the Table Fill in the table using an iterative approach.

```
for i in range(2, n+1):
    fib[i] = fib[i-1] + fib[i-2]
```

### Step 5: Retrieve the Final Solution The nth Fibonacci number is stored in ‘fib[n]‘.

```
result = fib[n]
```

**Example: Converting Recursive Solution for Longest Common Subsequence (LCS)**

The LCS problem is more complex and involves a recursive structure with two state parameters. The recursive relation for LCS is:

```
def lcs(X, Y, m, n):
    if m == 0 or n == 0:
        return 0
    elif X[m-1] == Y[n-1]:
        return 1 + lcs(X, Y, m-1, n-1)
    else:
        return max(lcs(X, Y, m, n-1), lcs(X, Y, m-1, n))
```

### Step 1: Identify the Recursive Structure The base cases are when either sequence has length 0. The state transitions involve progressing through both sequences, comparing elements, and either including the matching elements or excluding them.

### Step 2: Define the State and State Transitions The states can be defined by the parameters $m$ and $n$, representing lengths of sequences $X$ and $Y$, respectively.

lcs$(X, Y, m, n)$ is the length of LCS of prefixes $X[0..m-1]$ and $Y[0..n-1]$

### Step 3: Initialize the Table with Base Cases Create a table L with dimensions $[m + 1][n + 1]$ and initialize base cases:

```
L = [[0] * (n + 1) for _ in range(m + 1)]
for i in range(m + 1):
    L[i][0] = 0
for j in range(n + 1):
    L[0][j] = 0
```

### Step 4: Iterate to Fill the Table Fill in the table using nested loops:

```
for i in range(1, m + 1):
    for j in range(1, n + 1):
        if X[i - 1] == Y[j - 1]:
            L[i][j] = L[i - 1][j - 1] + 1
        else:
            L[i][j] = max(L[i][j - 1], L[i - 1][j])
```

### Step 5: Retrieve the Final Solution The length of the LCS is stored in $L[m][n]$.

```
lcs_length = L[m][n]
```

The conversion of recursive solutions to tabulation can significantly enhance efficiency by eliminating redundant computations and leveraging iterative approaches to build solutions bottom-up. By systematically following the steps outlined, recursive algorithms can be transformed into robust tabulation-based implementations suitable for larger problem instances.

## 7.7 Tabulating Bottom-Up Solutions

The bottom-up approach in dynamic programming involves solving subproblems first and using their solutions to build solutions for larger subproblems. This method is in contrast to the top-down approach, where the problem is broken down into subproblems recursively. The bottom-up approach often provides a more efficient solution, both in terms of time and space complexity, due to its iterative nature.

To illustrate how to tabulate bottom-up solutions, we will revisit some classic dynamic programming problems, converting their recursive or memoization-based solutions into a bottom-up tabulated form.

**Example 1: Fibonacci Sequence**

Let's start with a simple example: computing the $n$-th Fibonacci number. In a recursive solution, we would define Fibonacci recursively as follows:

$$\text{Fib}(n) = \begin{cases} n & \text{if } n \leq 1 \\ \text{Fib}(n-1) + \text{Fib}(n-2) & \text{otherwise} \end{cases}$$

The recursive formula is intuitive but inefficient due to repeated evaluations of the same subproblems. The bottom-up approach avoids this inefficiency by storing the results of subproblems in a table.

Here is how you can implement the bottom-up tabulation for the Fibonacci sequence in Python:

```
def fibonacci(n):
    if n <= 1:
        return n
    fib = [0] * (n + 1)
    fib[1] = 1
    for i in range(2, n + 1):
        fib[i] = fib[i - 1] + fib[i - 2]
    return fib[n]
```

In this implementation:

- We initialize an array 'fib' of size $\mathrm{n}+1$ to store the Fibonacci numbers.
- We set the base cases: 'fib[0] = 0' and 'fib[1] = 1'.
- We iterate from 2 to 'n', filling each entry in the table by summing the previous two entries.
- Finally, we return 'fib[n]'.

**Example 2: 0/1 Knapsack Problem**

Next, consider a more complex problem—the 0/1 knapsack problem. Given 'n' items, each with a weight and a value, and a knapsack with a maximum weight capacity 'W', the goal is to determine the maximum value that can be obtained by selecting a subset of the items such that their total weight does not exceed the knapsack's capacity.

The recursive relation for this problem is:

$$K(n, w) = \begin{cases} 0 & \text{if } n = 0 \text{ or } w = 0 \\ K(n-1, w) & \text{if weight}[n-1] > w \\ \max(\text{value}[n-1] + K(n-1, w - \text{weight}[n-1]), K(n-1, w)) & \text{otherwise} \end{cases}$$

The bottom-up tabulated version builds a table where 'table[i][j]' represents the maximum value that can be obtained with the first 'i' items and maximum weight 'j'.

Here is the Python implementation:

```
def knapsack(weights, values, W):
    n = len(weights)
    table = [[0 for _ in range(W + 1)] for _ in range(n + 1)]

    for i in range(1, n + 1):
        for w in range(W + 1):
            if weights[i - 1] <= w:
                table[i][w] = max(values[i - 1] + table[i - 1][w - weights[i - 1]], table[i - 1][
                    w])
            else:
                table[i][w] = table[i - 1][w]

    return table[n][W]
```

In this implementation:

- We initialize a table with dimensions '(n+1) x (W+1)' to store maximum values for subproblems.
- We iterate over each item 'i' and each capacity 'w'.
- If the item's weight is less than or equal to the current capacity 'w', we decide whether to include the item in the knapsack or not by comparing the value of including the item with the value of excluding it.
- If the item's weight is greater than 'w', we inherit the value from the previous item.
- Finally, 'table[n][W]' contains the maximum value for the full problem.

**Example 3: Longest Common Subsequence (LCS)**

The LCS problem, which involves finding the longest subsequence common to two sequences, lends itself well to bottom-up tabulation as well. The recursive relation is:

$$LCS(X, Y, m, n) = \begin{cases} 0 & \text{if } m = 0 \text{ or } n = 0 \\ 1 + LCS(X, Y, m-1, n-1) & \text{if } X[m-1] = Y[n-1] \\ \max(LCS(X, Y, m-1, n), LCS(X, Y, m, n-1)) & \text{otherwise} \end{cases}$$

The tabulated version uses a 2D table, where 'table[i][j]' holds the length of the LCS of the first 'i' characters of 'X' and the first 'j' characters of 'Y'.

Here's the Python code:

```
def lcs(X, Y):
    m = len(X)
    n = len(Y)
    table = [[0] * (n + 1) for _ in range(m + 1)]

    for i in range(1, m + 1):
        for j in range(1, n + 1):
            if X[i - 1] == Y[j - 1]:
                table[i][j] = table[i - 1][j - 1] + 1
            else:
                table[i][j] = max(table[i - 1][j], table[i][j - 1])

    return table[m][n]
```

In this implementation:

- We create a table of dimensions '(m+1) x (n+1)' to store lengths of LCS for subproblems.
- We iterate over each character of 'X' and 'Y'.
- If the characters match, we increment the LCS length from the previous subproblem 'table[i-1][j-1]'.
- If the characters do not match, we take the maximum value of the two possible subproblems: excluding the current character from either 'X' or 'Y'.
- The final answer 'table[m][n]' represents the length of the LCS of 'X' and 'Y'.

The above examples show the shift from recursive thinking to iterative tabulation. This fundamental change results in improvements to the efficiency of solutions.

## 7.8 Handling Edge Cases in Tabulation

Edge cases represent scenarios where the input parameters are at their boundary limits or exhibit exceptional behavior. Properly managing edge cases is crucial in any algorithmic approach, especially in dynamic programming with tabulation, where overlooking such cases can lead to incorrect results or runtime errors. This section delves into various strategies for identifying and managing edge cases in tabulated solutions, ensuring robustness and correctness.

### Identifying Edge Cases

Identifying potential edge cases involves performing a thorough analysis of the problem constraints and understanding the input domain. Typical edge cases in dynamic programming often include:

- Minimum input sizes (e.g., an empty array, a single element).
- Maximum input sizes, often constrained by problem limits.
- Values at their extremities (e.g., smallest or largest possible values).
- Special parameter values, such as zeros or negative numbers, which might trigger unique computational paths.

### Example: Fibonacci Sequence

Consider the classic Fibonacci sequence problem, solved via tabulation. The edge cases here include the smallest possible inputs, specifically $n = 0$ and $n = 1$.

```
def fib(n):
    if n <= 0:
        return 0
    elif n == 1:
        return 1

    dp = [0] * (n + 1)
    dp[1] = 1

    for i in range(2, n + 1):
        dp[i] = dp[i - 1] + dp[i - 2]

    return dp[n]
```

For $n = 0$, the function should return 0, and for $n = 1$, it should return 1, which are both handled explicitly before constructing the tabulation array.

### Negative Inputs and Invalid Data

In many practical applications, input validation must be performed to handle cases where users might provide invalid data. While the Fibonacci example naturally disallows negative inputs by mathematical definition, other problems might need explicit checks.

Consider a more complex scenario where we tabulate the ways to partition a set into subsets with equal sum. Here, invalid inputs could include cases where the array cannot be partitioned due to insufficient elements or negative numbers that violate problem constraints.

```
def canPartition(nums):
    total = sum(nums)

    if total % 2 != 0:
        return False

    n = len(nums)
    target = total // 2

    dp = [[False] * (target + 1) for _ in range(n + 1)]
    for i in range(n + 1):
        dp[i][0] = True

    for i in range(1, n + 1):
        for j in range(1, target + 1):
            if j >= nums[i - 1]:
                dp[i][j] = dp[i - 1][j] or dp[i - 1][j - nums[i - 1]]
            else:
                dp[i][j] = dp[i - 1][j]

    return dp[n][target]
```

This code ensures the input list can indeed be partitioned by first verifying the sum is even. It also incorporates edge cases where the array might be too small to partition.

### Empty Arrays and Single Element Cases

Algorithms often face challenges handling arrays or lists that contain no elements or just one element. Edge conditions with empty arrays should typically return results directly or trigger specific branches of code to avoid indexing errors.

Observe the tabulated solution for finding the maximum subarray sum, which needs to handle both empty and singly-filled arrays efficiently.

```
def maxSubArray(nums):
    if not nums:
        return 0

    n = len(nums)
    dp = nums[0]
    max_sum = dp
```

```
    for i in range(1, n):
        dp = max(nums[i], dp + nums[i])
        max_sum = max(max_sum, dp)

    return max_sum
```

Here, an empty array directly returns 0, and the single-element case is automatically managed by the loop mechanism, ensuring robust handling.

**Boundary Conditions in Multidimensional Tabulation**

When managing multi-dimensional arrays, understanding and correctly handling boundary conditions is crucial. Consider the example of finding the longest increasing path in a matrix, which involves traversing each cell and making decisions based on adjacent cell values.

```
def longestIncreasingPath(matrix):
    if not matrix or not matrix[0]:
        return 0

    rows, cols = len(matrix), len(matrix[0])
    memo = [[-1] * cols for _ in range(rows)]

    def dfs(r, c, prevVal):
        if r < 0 or r >= rows or c < 0 or c >= cols or matrix[r][c] <= prevVal:
            return 0
        if memo[r][c] != -1:
            return memo[r][c]

        val = matrix[r][c]
        left = dfs(r, c - 1, val)
        right = dfs(r, c + 1, val)
        up = dfs(r - 1, c, val)
        down = dfs(r + 1, c, val)

        memo[r][c] = 1 + max(left, right, up, down)
        return memo[r][c]

    max_path = 0
    for i in range(rows):
        for j in range(cols):
            max_path = max(max_path, dfs(i, j, -1))

    return max_path
```

This solution properly handles edge cases by incorporating boundary checks within the depth-first search (DFS) routine to ensure the validity of cell indices and managing memoization effectively.

Ensuring that all boundary conditions and special cases are covered systematically prevents logical errors, leading to more reliable dynamic programming solutions through tabulation. Analyzing inputs thoroughly and testing against edge cases forms a core part of the rigorous development process in algorithm design.

## 7.9 Space Optimization with Tabulation

Space optimization is a crucial aspect of dynamic programming, particularly when dealing with problems where memory usage can become excessive. Tabulation inherently requires the storage of intermediate results in a table, which can sometimes be optimized to use less space without affecting the correctness of the solution. This section explores various strategies to achieve such space efficiencies.

Consider the classical Fibonacci sequence problem, where the objective is to find the $n$-th Fibonacci number. Using tabulation, one might typically construct an array of size $n+1$ to store the Fibonacci values from $F(0)$ to $F(n)$. While this method provides a clear and direct solution, it does not leverage potential space optimization techniques.

Here is the traditional approach using tabulation:

```
def fibonacci(n):
    if n <= 1:
        return n
    fib_table = [0] * (n + 1)
    fib_table[1] = 1
    for i in range(2, n + 1):
        fib_table[i] = fib_table[i - 1] + fib_table[i - 2]
    return fib_table[n]
```

In this implementation, an array of size $n+1$ is necessary to hold all intermediate Fibonacci values. The space complexity is $O(n)$.

To optimize space, observe that at any point $i$ in the calculation, only the last two Fibonacci numbers are needed: $F(i-1)$ and $F(i-2)$. Thus, the entire table is not required, and two variables can suffice.

Here is the space-optimized version of the Fibonacci sequence calculation:

```
def fibonacci_optimized(n):
    if n <= 1:
        return n
    previous, current = 0, 1
    for i in range(2, n + 1):
        next_fib = previous + current
        previous, current = current, next_fib
    return current
```

This optimized approach reduces the space complexity to $O(1)$ by using only two variables instead of an array.

Now, let's generalize this concept to more complex problems where multi-dimensional arrays are used. Consider the 0/1 Knapsack problem, where a table $dp$ is used for storing the maximum value achievable with given items and weight limits. The traditional implementation uses a 2-dimensional array:

```
def knapsack(weights, values, W):
    n = len(weights)
    dp = [[0 for _ in range(W + 1)] for _ in range(n + 1)]
    for i in range(1, n + 1):
        for w in range(1, W + 1):
            if weights[i-1] <= w:
                dp[i][w] = max(dp[i-1][w], values[i-1] + dp[i-1][w - weights[i-1]])
            else:
                dp[i][w] = dp[i-1][w]
    return dp[n][W]
```

Here, the space complexity is $O(nW)$, where $n$ is the number of items and $W$ is the maximum weight capacity of the knapsack. Similar to the Fibonacci sequence optimization, at any iteration, we only need the current row and the previous row of the DP table. Thus, we can optimize this to use only a 1-dimensional array:

```
def knapsack_optimized(weights, values, W):
    n = len(weights)
    dp = [0 for _ in range(W + 1)]
    for i in range(1, n + 1):
        for w in range(W, 0, -1):
            if weights[i-1] <= w:
                dp[w] = max(dp[w], values[i-1] + dp[w - weights[i-1]])
    return dp[W]
```

This optimization reduces the space complexity to $O(W)$ while maintaining the same time complexity $O(nW)$.

Beyond specific problems like Fibonacci or Knapsack, space optimization principles can be applied broadly:

- **Rolling Arrays:** For problems where only a fixed number of previous states are needed, maintain only those states in a smaller array.
- **In-Place Computation:** Modify the existing data structure if it can store results without the need for an auxiliary table.
- **Sparse Tables:** Use a hashmap or dictionary for sparse matrices where most values remain zero, conserving memory by storing only non-zero entries.

  Consider the Longest Common Subsequence (LCS) problem, often solved using a 2D array. The transformation principle here can reduce the space usage from $O(m \times n)$ to $O(min(m, n))$ by maintaining only the previous and current rows during the iteration. Thus, adaptive space optimization techniques enable efficient memory use without adversely affecting the computational integrity of dynamic programming solutions.

## 7.10 Time Complexity in Tabulation

Time complexity is a fundamental concept in computer science that quantitatively measures the amount of time taken by an algorithm to run as a function of the input size. In the context of dynamic programming and specifically tabulation, it is essential to understand how the iterative process impacts the overall performance of the algorithm.

Tabulation involves filling up a table (usually an array or multi-dimensional array) based on a bottom-up strategy, where each entry in the table corresponds to a subproblem that is solved iteratively. To analyze the time complexity, we focus on the following factors: the number of subproblems, the time required to solve each subproblem, and any additional overhead.

Consider the classic problem of computing the Fibonacci sequence using tabulation. The recursive relation for the Fibonacci sequence is given by $F(n) = F(n-1) + F(n-2)$ with the base cases $F(0) = 0$ and $F(1) = 1$. To implement this using tabulation:

```
def fibonacci_tab(n):
    if n <= 1:
        return n
    dp = [0] * (n + 1)
    dp[1] = 1
    for i in range(2, n + 1):
        dp[i] = dp[i - 1] + dp[i - 2]
    return dp[n]

print(fibonacci_tab(10))
```

55

In the above code, we create an array ‘dp‘ of size $n + 1$ and iteratively fill it based on the given recurrence relation. Let's break down the time complexity:

1. **Initialization**: The initialization step involves creating an array of size $n + 1$. This operation takes $O(n)$ time. 2. **Iteration**: There is a single loop that runs from 2 to $n$, performing a constant amount of work

(i.e., addition of two elements) in each iteration. Therefore, this loop runs $n-1$ times, with each iteration taking $O(1)$ time. Hence, the total time for this loop is $O(n)$.

Consequently, the overall time complexity of the Fibonacci tabulation algorithm is $O(n)+O(n)=O(n)$. This linear time complexity provides a significant improvement over the exponential time complexity of the naive recursive approach, which is $O(2^n)$.

Next, let us consider a more complex example such as the Longest Common Subsequence (LCS) problem, which determines the longest subsequence present in both given sequences. The LCS problem's tabulation approach relies on a 2D table where each entry $dp[i][j]$ denotes the LCS length of substrings $X[0:i]$ and $Y[0:j]$. Here is an implementation using tabulation:

```
def lcs_tab(X, Y):
    m = len(X)
    n = len(Y)
    dp = [[0] * (n + 1) for _ in range(m + 1)]
    for i in range(1, m + 1):
        for j in range(1, n + 1):
            if X[i - 1] == Y[j - 1]:
                dp[i][j] = dp[i - 1][j - 1] + 1
            else:
                dp[i][j] = max(dp[i - 1][j], dp[i][j - 1])
    return dp[m][n]

X = "AGGTAB"
Y = "GXTXAYB"
print(lcs_tab(X, Y))
```

4

For the LCS implementation, time complexity analysis is as follows:

1. **Initialization**: Creating a 2D array 'dp' of dimensions $(m+1)\times(n+1)$, where $m$ and $n$ are the lengths of sequences $X$ and $Y$, respectively. This initialization step takes $O(m\times n)$ time. 2. **Iteration**: The main part of the algorithm involves nested loops over the lengths of the two sequences. Specifically, both the outer and inner loops run from 1 to $m$ and 1 to $n$, respectively. Each iteration of the nested loops involves constant time operations, resulting in a total time of $O(m\times n)$.

Thus, the overall time complexity of the LCS tabulation algorithm is $O(m\times n)+O(m\times n)=O(m\times n)$. This quadratic time complexity is efficient given that LCS is a problem that inherently requires comparison across every character of the input strings.

It is essential to note that while tabulation often reduces the complexity from exponential to polynomial time, the exact time complexity depends on the specific problem and the recurrence relation being solved. In general, the time complexity of a tabulated dynamic programming algorithm can be expressed as $O(\text{number of subproblems} \times \text{time per subproblem})$. By carefully structuring the table and subproblems, we can ensure that the iterative computation is efficient and optimal.

## 7.11 Common Mistakes in Tabulation

Despite the power and efficiency of tabulation, there are several common pitfalls that learners and practitioners frequently encounter. Recognizing and understanding these mistakes will not only help avoid errors but also deepen one's comprehension of the dynamic programming paradigm.

**1. Incorrect Base Case Initialization**

One of the most prevalent mistakes involves improper initialization of the base cases. As tabulation is a bottom-up approach, the initial values of the table (often representing base cases) lay the groundwork for computing all subsequent values. Any oversight here can propagate through the entire table, leading to incorrect results.

Consider the classic example of computing the Fibonacci sequence using tabulation. The Fibonacci sequence is defined as:

$$F(0) = 0, \quad F(1) = 1, \quad F(n) = F(n-1) + F(n-2) \text{ for } n \geq 2$$

The Python implementation for this using tabulation could look like this:

```
def fibonacci(n):
    if n <= 0:
        return 0
    elif n == 1:
        return 1

    fib = [0] * (n + 1)
    fib[0] = 0
    fib[1] = 1

    for i in range(2, n + 1):
        fib[i] = fib[i-1] + fib[i-2]

    return fib[n]

print(fibonacci(10))
```

Output:

```
55
```

Missing or incorrectly setting $\text{fib}[0]$ and $\text{fib}[1]$ would result in a fundamentally flawed table. Ensure base cases are carefully initialized as per the problem's requirements.

**2. Incorrect Table Size**

Another frequent error occurs in defining the size of the table. An undersized table will lead to array out-of-bounds errors, while an oversized table can waste space and unnecessarily increase the algorithm's space complexity. Appropriately dimensioning the table requires a clear understanding of the problem constraints.

In multi-dimensional problems, such as those requiring $n \text{ x } m$ tables, this mistake becomes more pronounced. For instance, when solving the 0/1 Knapsack problem using tabulation:

```
def knapsack(values, weights, W):
    n = len(values)
    dp = [[0 for x in range(W + 1)] for x in range(n + 1)]

    for i in range(1, n + 1):
        for w in range(1, W + 1):
            if weights[i-1] <= w:
                dp[i][w] = max(dp[i-1][w], values[i-1] + dp[i-1][w - weights[i-1]])
            else:
                dp[i][w] = dp[i-1][w]

    return dp[n][W]

values = [60, 100, 120]
weights = [10, 20, 30]
W = 50
print(knapsack(values, weights, W))
```

Output:

```
220
```

Properly dimensioning $\text{dp}$ as $[W + 1]$ and $[n + 1]$ is crucial. Miscalculations here could lead to invalid table entries and incorrect results.

**3. Overlapping Subproblems Not Handled**

Tabulation implicitly assumes the problem can be decomposed into overlapping subproblems. Failing to recognize or handle this characteristic results in redundant calculations, negating the efficiency gains from dynamic programming.

For example, misunderstanding the bounded subproblems in a Longest

Common Subsequence (LCS) problem can lead to errors:

$$LCS(X,Y) = \begin{cases} 0 & \text{if } i = 0 \text{ or } j = 0 \\ LCS(X_{m-1}, Y_{n-1}) + 1 & \text{if } X_m = Y_n \\ \max(LCS(X_m, Y_{n-1}), LCS(X_{m-1}, Y_n)) & \text{if } X_m \neq Y_n \end{cases}$$

The corresponding tabulated solution:

```
def lcs(X, Y):
    m = len(X)
    n = len(Y)
    dp = [[0] * (n + 1) for _ in range(m + 1)]

    for i in range(1, m + 1):
        for j in range(1, n + 1):
            if X[i - 1] == Y[j - 1]:
                dp[i][j] = dp[i - 1][j - 1] + 1
            else:
                dp[i][j] = max(dp[i - 1][j], dp[i][j - 1])

    return dp[m][n]

print(lcs("ABCBDAB", "BDCAB"))
```

Output:

```
4
```

Recognizing overlapping subproblems ensures efficient use of table entries.

### 4. Mismanagement of Indices

Index mismanagement is a subtle yet common issue, particularly in nested loops or when transitioning between problem definitions and zero-based indexing in programming languages like Python.

```
def coinChange(coins, amount):
    dp = [float('inf')] * (amount + 1)
    dp[0] = 0

    for coin in coins:
        for x in range(coin, amount + 1):
            dp[x] = min(dp[x], dp[x - coin] + 1)

    return dp[amount] if dp[amount] != float('inf') else -1

coins = [1, 2, 5]
amount = 11
print(coinChange(coins, amount))
```

Output:

```
3
```

Correctly managing indices, especially in loops updating $\mathrm{dp}[\mathrm{x}]$, is essential for maintaining the integrity of the solution.

**5. Ignoring Space Optimization Possibilities**

While focusing on tabulation, one might overlook potential space optimizations. Many problems can reduce space complexity from $\mathcal{O}(n^2)$ to $\mathcal{O}(n)$ by only retaining necessary current and previous values.

For instance, optimizing the space for the Fibonacci sequence calculation:

```
def fibonacci_optimized(n):
    if n <= 0:
        return 0
    elif n == 1:
        return 1

    a, b = 0, 1
    for _ in range(2, n + 1):
        a, b = b, a + b

    return b

print(fibonacci_optimized(10))
```

Output:

```
55
```

Small but significant adjustments can greatly optimize space usage, particularly in resource-constrained environments.

Avoiding these common mistakes ensures the reliability and efficiency of tabulation, fostering better algorithmic solutions and a more detailed understanding of dynamic programming principles. Proper initialization, dimensioning, and handling of subproblems along with mindful indexing and optimization pave the path for precise and efficient tabulated solutions.

## 7.12 Real-World Examples of Tabulation

Real-world applications of tabulation highlight its power and versatility in solving complex computational problems efficiently. This section will examine several practical examples to illustrate how tabulation can be deployed to achieve optimal solutions. These examples will build on what has been introduced in previous sections.

**Example 1: Fibonacci Sequence**

The Fibonacci sequence is a classic example often used to introduce dynamic programming concepts. When implemented recursively, it exhibits exponential time complexity due to the numerous repeated calculations. Tabulation offers a more efficient approach.

```
def fibonacci(n):
    if n <= 1:
        return n

    # Create an array to store the Fibonacci numbers
    fib = [0] * (n + 1)
    fib[1] = 1

    for i in range(2, n + 1):
        fib[i] = fib[i - 1] + fib[i - 2]

    return fib[n]

# Example usage
print(fibonacci(10))
```

55

In this implementation, the function avoids repetitive calculations by storing intermediate results in an array, thus reducing the time complexity from $O(2^n)$ to $O(n)$.

**Example 2: Longest Common Subsequence (LCS)**

The LCS problem involves finding the longest subsequence present in both given sequences. This has applications in text comparison algorithms, DNA sequence alignment, and more.

```
def lcs(X, Y):
    m = len(X)
    y = len(Y)

    # Create a 2D table to store lengths of longest common subsequence
    L = [[0] * (n + 1) for _ in range(m + 1)]

    for i in range(m + 1):
        for j in range(n + 1):
            if i == 0 or j == 0:
                L[i][j] = 0
            elif X[i - 1] == Y[j - 1]:
                L[i][j] = L[i - 1][j - 1] + 1
            else:
                L[i][j] = max(L[i - 1][j], L[i][j - 1])

    # L[m][n] contains the length of LCS of X and Y
    return L[m][n]

# Example usage
X = "AGGTAB"
Y = "GXTXAYB"
print(lcs(X, Y))
```

4

The 2-dimensional table stores lengths of LCS for various substrings, allowing the solution to be built incrementally. The time and space complexity of this solution is $O(m \cdot n)$.

### Example 3: 0/1 Knapsack Problem

The knapsack problem is famous in combinatorial optimization, where one needs to maximize the total value in a knapsack without exceeding the weight limit. Tabulation provides an efficient way to approach this.

```
def knapsack(W, weights, values, n):
    # Create a 2D array to store the maximum value
    K = [[0 for w in range(W + 1)] for i in range(n + 1)]

    for i in range(n + 1):
        for w in range(W + 1):
            if i == 0 or w == 0:
                K[i][w] = 0
            elif weights[i - 1] <= w:
                K[i][w] = max(values[i - 1] + K[i - 1][w - weights[i - 1]], K[i - 1][w])
            else:
                K[i][w] = K[i - 1][w]

    return K[n][W]

# Example usage
values = [60, 100, 120]
weights = [10, 20, 30]
W = 50
n = len(values)
print(knapsack(W, weights, values, n))
```



Here, the 2D table ‘K‘ keeps the maximum values for subsets of items for each weight limit, resulting in a time complexity of $O(n \cdot W)$.

### Example 4: Edit Distance

Edit distance measures the minimum number of operations required to convert one string into another, commonly applied in spell checkers and computational biology.

```
def edit_distance(str1, str2):
    m = len(str1)
    n = len(str2)

    # Create a table to store the minimum edit distance
    dp = [[0 for x in range(n + 1)] for x in range(m + 1)]

    for i in range(m + 1):
        for j in range(n + 1):
            if i == 0:
                dp[i][j] = j # Min. operations = j (all insertions)
            elif j == 0:
                dp[i][j] = i # Min. operations = i (all deletions)
            elif str1[i - 1] == str2[j - 1]:
                dp[i][j] = dp[i - 1][j - 1]
```

```
            else:
                dp[i][j] = 1 + min(dp[i][j - 1], # Insert
                                   dp[i - 1][j], # Remove
                                   dp[i - 1][j - 1]) # Replace

    return dp[m][n]

# Example usage
str1 = "sunday"
str2 = "saturday"
print(edit_distance(str1, str2))
```

3

This solution employs a 2D table to store minimal edit distances for subsequences, achieving $O(m \cdot n)$ complexity.

**Example 5: Coin Change Problem**

The coin change problem involves finding the minimum number of coins required to make a given amount. This problem appears in finance and resource allocation.

```
def coin_change(coins, amount):
    dp = [float('inf')] * (amount + 1)
    dp[0] = 0

    for i in range(1, amount + 1):
        for coin in coins:
            if i - coin >= 0:
                dp[i] = min(dp[i], dp[i - coin] + 1)

    return dp[amount] if dp[amount] != float('inf') else -1

# Example usage
coins = [1, 2, 5]
amount = 11
print(coin_change(coins, amount))
```

3

The single-dimensional array 'dp' is used to store the minimum number of coins needed for each amount up to the target, leading to a time complexity of $O(n \cdot k)$, where $n$ is the amount and $k$ is the number of coin types.

These examples provide concrete illustrations of how tabulation can be applied to a variety of real-world problems, demonstrating its efficiency and effectiveness in implemented solutions. These approaches not only optimize computational performance but also provide clear, systematic ways to solve otherwise complex problems.

# Chapter 8

# Combinatorial Problems

**This chapter explores the application of dynamic programming to combinatorial problems. It begins with basic combinatorial concepts and progresses through various types of problems such as permutations, combinations, and subset sums. Key problems like the knapsack, partition, coin change, and rod cutting are examined in detail. The chapter also covers combinatorial optimization and more complex issues like the bin packing problem. Through these examples, readers will learn how to apply dynamic programming techniques to solve a range of combinatorial challenges effectively.**

## 8.1 Introduction to Combinatorial Problems

Combinatorial problems involve the arrangement, selection, and combination of items according to specific rules. These problems are significant in various fields, including computer science, operations research, and applied mathematics. Dynamic programming offers powerful techniques to address and solve combinatorial challenges efficiently by breaking them down into simpler subproblems.

Consider the fundamental components of combinatorial problems: permutations and combinations. Permutations refer to the arrangements of items where order matters, while combinations refer to selections of items where order does not matter.

To solve such problems, it is crucial to understand the underlying mathematical principles and leverage efficient algorithms to handle the computational complexity. Here, dynamic programming shines by utilizing overlapping subproblems and optimal substructure properties.

```
def permutations(arr):
    if len(arr) == 0:
        return []
    if len(arr) == 1:
        return [arr]
    perms = []
    for i in range(len(arr)):
        m = arr[i]
        rem_list = arr[:i] + arr[i+1:]
        for p in permutations(rem_list):
            perms.append([m] + p)
    return perms

# Example usage:
arr = [1, 2, 3]
print(permutations(arr))
```

```
[[1, 2, 3], [1, 3, 2], [2, 1, 3], [2, 3, 1], [3, 1, 2], [3, 2, 1]]
```

Understanding the basic dynamic programming approach is essential when dealing with combinatorial problems. The technique involves three primary steps:

- **Characterize the structure of an optimal solution.**
- **Formulate the problem as a recursive relation of subproblems.**
- **Compute the value of an optimal solution systematically from smaller subproblems.**

Applying these steps to combinatorial problems allows one to build solutions incrementally, ensuring that each step leans on already computed solutions of smaller subproblems.

The **Binomial Coefficient** $C(n, k)$, which calculates the number of ways to choose $k$ elements from $n$ elements without regard for the order, serves as a fundamental example of combinatorial computations easily managed by dynamic programming. The recursive relation for binomial coefficients can be expressed as:

$$C(n, k) = \begin{cases} 1 & \text{if } k = 0 \text{ or } k = n \\ C(n-1, k-1) + C(n-1, k) & \text{otherwise} \end{cases}$$

This recursive relationship is a blueprint for deriving a dynamic programming approach, wherein calculated values are stored to avoid redundant computations. The Python implementation of this recursive formula can be exhibited as follows:

```
def binomial_coefficient(n, k):
    dp = [[0 for _ in range(k+1)] for _ in range(n+1)]
    for i in range(n+1):
        for j in range(min(i, k)+1):
            if j == 0 or j == i:
                dp[i][j] = 1
            else:
                dp[i][j] = dp[i-1][j-1] + dp[i-1][j]
    return dp[n][k]

# Example usage:
n = 5
k = 2
print(binomial_coefficient(n, k))
```

```
10
```

Dynamic programming's aptitude for handling combinatorial problems extends beyond binomial coefficients. Consider subset sum problems wherein the objective is to determine if there exists a subset of given sets with a sum equal to a specified value. Utilizing dynamic programming in these scenarios ensures that partial results are reused, thereby optimizing the computation.

The following Python code illustrates how dynamic programming is applied to solve the subset sum problem:

```
def is_subset_sum(arr, sum_val):
    n = len(arr)
    dp = [[False for _ in range(sum_val + 1)] for _ in range(n + 1)]
    for i in range(n + 1):
        dp[i][0] = True
    for i in range(1, n + 1):
        for j in range(1, sum_val + 1):
            if j < arr[i-1]:
                dp[i][j] = dp[i-1][j]
            else:
                dp[i][j] = dp[i-1][j] or dp[i-1][j-arr[i-1]]
    return dp[n][sum_val]

# Example usage:
arr = [3, 34, 4, 12, 5, 2]
sum_val = 9
print(is_subset_sum(arr, sum_val))
```

```
True
```

The initial exploration of combinatorial problems sets the stage for more complex challenges and hybrid techniques. Through dynamic programming, not only do we optimize the computational efficiency, but we also gain a structured way to dissect and conquer intricate combinatorial puzzles.

Understanding and applying these foundational methods enable deeper insights and prepare us to tackle advanced combinatorial problems systematically and confidently.

## 8.2 Basic Combinatorial Concepts

Combinatorial problems form a foundational aspect of dynamic programming and computer science. The ability to systematically and efficiently search through possible configurations and count or optimize particular outcomes underlies many algorithms. In this section, we delve into basic combinatorial concepts that will serve as the building blocks for the more complex problems discussed later in the chapter.

Central to combinatorics is the concept of counting. Counting is the process of determining the number of ways certain arrangements can be made. These arrangements can be permutations, combinations, or more structured groupings like subsets.

**Permutations** are arrangements of elements where the order matters. For instance, if we have a set $S = \{a, b, c\}$, possible permutations of this set would be $abc$, $acb$, $bac$, $bca$, $cab$, and $cba$. The number of permutations of a set of $n$ elements is denoted by $n!$ (n factorial), where:

$$n! = n \times (n-1) \times (n-2) \times \ldots \times 1$$

For example, $3! = 3 \times 2 \times 1 = 6$, confirming our six permutations for the set $S$.

**Combinations** differ from permutations as the order does not matter. When selecting $k$ elements from a set of $n$ elements, combinations count how many ways we can choose these $k$ unordered elements. The formula for combinations is given by:

$$\binom{n}{k} = \frac{n!}{k!(n-k)!}$$

For example, with a set $S = \{a, b, c, d\}$ and selecting $k = 2$ elements, the combinations are $\{a, b\}$, $\{a, c\}$, $\{a, d\}$, $\{b, c\}$, $\{b, d\}$, and $\{c, d\}$. Calculating the number of these combinations gives:

$$\binom{4}{2} = \frac{4!}{2!(4-2)!} = \frac{24}{2 \times 2} = 6$$

Understanding how to systematically generate and count these permutations and combinations is crucial for tackling dynamic programming problems.

When addressing combinatorial problems, it is often necessary to develop a recursive approach. A classic example is the calculation of binomial coefficients, frequently implemented using Pascal's Triangle. The direct approach might use recursion:

```
def binomial_coefficient(n, k):
    if k == 0 or k == n:
        return 1
    return binomial_coefficient(n-1, k-1) + binomial_coefficient(n-1, k)
```

Executing the function binomial_coefficient$(4, 2)$ returns:

```
6
```

However, due to overlapping subproblems inherent in this recursive approach, it is more efficient to use dynamic programming. We can reformulate this calculation with a bottom-up approach, storing intermediate results:

```
def binomial_coefficient_dp(n, k):
    C = [[0 for x in range(k+1)] for x in range(n+1)]

    for i in range(n+1):
        for j in range(min(i, k)+1):
            if j == 0 or j == i:
                C[i][j] = 1
            else:
                C[i][j] = C[i-1][j-1] + C[i-1][j]

    return C[n][k]
```

Executing the function binomial_coefficient_dp$(4, 2)$ yields the same result:

```
6
```

This bottom-up dynamic programming approach efficiently reduces the exponential time complexity of the naive recursive solution to $O(n \times k)$ space and time complexity.

Another fundamental concept is the combinatorial structure known as the **subset**, where the power set of a set $S$ is the set of all subsets of $S$. If $S$ contains $n$ elements, its power set contains $2^n$ subsets. For example, if $S = \{1, 2, 3\}$, the power set is $\{\}, \{1\}, \{2\}, \{3\}, \{1, 2\}, \{1, 3\}, \{2, 3\}, \{1, 2, 3\}$.

To generate all subsets of a set programmatically, we can use a bit manipulation approach:

```
def generate_subsets(S):
    subsets = []
    n = len(S)
    for i in range(2**n):
        subset = []
        for j in range(n):
            if (i & (1 << j)) > 0:
                subset.append(S[j])
        subsets.append(subset)
    return subsets
```

Invoking generate_subsets([1, 2, 3]) produces:

```
[[], [1], [2], [1, 2], [3], [1, 3], [2, 3], [1, 2, 3]]
```

These concepts of permutations, combinations, and subsets not only build the foundation for more advanced combinatorial problems but are also crucial for designing efficient dynamic programming solutions that exploit overlapping subproblems and optimal substructure properties.

## 8.3 Permutation Problems

Permutation problems involve rearranging elements of a set into a sequence or ordering. Given a collection of distinct elements, permutations consider all possible sequences that can be formed. This section delves into the application of dynamic programming to solve several types of permutation problems.

Consider a set $S$ with $n$ elements. The number of permutations of this set is given by $n!$ (n factorial), which represents the product of all positive integers up to $n$. For instance, the number of permutations of a set {1, 2, 3} is $3! = 3 \times 2 \times 1 = 6$.

We start with a seemingly simple yet computationally intensive problem: determining whether a given permutation can be obtained by performing a series of valid swaps from another permutation, specifically addressing permutations that meet certain criteria given constraints.

**Example Problem: Count Permutations that Satisfy a Constraint**

Given an integer $n$, compute the number of permutations of the sequence $\{1, 2, \ldots, n\}$ such that for all $i$ (where $1 \leq i < n$), some property $P(i, a[i], a[i+1])$ holds for the permutation $a$.

This problem often requires constructing the permutation in a way that adheres to the constraint $P$ iteratively while leveraging dynamic programming to manage the complexity. We will examine the approach using a constraint typical in permutation problems: the number of inversions, where an inversion is a pair $(i, j)$ such that $i < j$ and $a[i] > a[j]$.

Let $dp[k][inv]$ represent the number of permutations of the first $k$ elements with exactly $inv$ inversions. Starting from the base case:

$$dp[0][0] = 1$$

For other states:

$$dp[k][inv] = \sum_{m=0}^{k-1} dp[k-1][inv-m]$$

This recurrence relationship can be interpreted as constructing a permutation of $k$ elements by inserting the $k$-th element into each possible position in the permutations of the first $k-1$ elements, calculating the impact on the number of inversions.

The implementation in Python can be accomplished as follows:

```
def count_permutations(n, k):
    # Initialize the DP table with zeros
    dp = [[0] * (n * (n - 1) // 2 + 1) for _ in range(n + 1)]
    dp[0][0] = 1

    for i in range(1, n + 1):
        for j in range(n * (n - 1) // 2 + 1):
            dp[i][j] = 0
            for m in range(min(j + 1, i)):
                dp[i][j] += dp[i - 1][j - m]

    return dp[n][k]

n = 5
k = 3
print(count_permutations(n, k))
```

```
Output:
10
```

**Explanation:** In this scenario, count_permutations(n, k) calculates the number of permutations of the first $n$ numbers $\{1, 2, \ldots, 5\}$ with exactly $k = 3$ inversions. The table dp is initialized for $n+1$ rows and $\frac{n(n-1)}{2}+1$ columns to store intermediate results.

The nested loops iterate over possible counts of elements $i$ and inversion values $j$, populating the DP table by summing up the values from previous states that contribute to the inversion count increment. The innermost loop iterates over possible positions $m$ where the new element can be placed, adjusting the inversion count accordingly.

Towards solving more complex permutation problems, dynamic programming can be further extended and combined with other techniques such as memoization or bit masking. Each permutation problem may have unique constraints and characteristics requiring tailored optimization strategies. For example:

- Counting permutations such that no element appears in its original position (derangements).
- Generating all k-th lexicographical permutations.
- Finding permutations with specific properties and constraints on adjacency or relative positioning.

Solutions to these problems typically involve careful consideration of the problem constraints and developing efficient recursive formulation and state transition representation. Properly designed dynamic programming solutions, often combined with pre-computation and space optimization, can efficiently handle a broad class of permutation challenges.

## 8.4 Combination Problems

Combination problems involve selecting subsets of a given set where the order of elements does not matter. These problems often require considering different possible groupings or selections of a set of items. They are essential in fields such as operations research, algorithm design, and statistics.

Dynamic programming is an effective approach to address combination problems, particularly when the problem exhibits optimal substructure and overlapping subproblems. In dynamic programming solutions, we often use a table or memoization to store intermediate results and avoid redundant computations.

Consider the problem of computing the binomial coefficient, commonly known as "n choose k" and denoted as $\binom{n}{k}$. This coefficient represents the number of ways to choose $k$ elements from a set of $n$ elements. The recursive definition of the binomial coefficient is:

$$\binom{n}{k} = \begin{cases} 1 & \text{if } k = 0 \text{ or } k = n \\ \binom{n-1}{k-1} + \binom{n-1}{k} & \text{otherwise} \end{cases}$$

Using dynamic programming, we can compute $\binom{n}{k}$ efficiently by filling a table 'C[][]' where 'C[i][j]' contains $\binom{i}{j}$:

```
def binomial_coefficient(n, k):
    # Initialize a (n+1) x (k+1) table with 0s
    C = [[0 for _ in range(k + 1)] for _ in range(n + 1)]

    # Fill the table according to the recursive definition
    for i in range(n + 1):
        for j in range(min(i, k) + 1):
            # Base cases: C[i][0] = C[i][i] = 1
            if j == 0 or j == i:
                C[i][j] = 1
            else:
                C[i][j] = C[i - 1][j - 1] + C[i - 1][j]

    return C[n][k]

# Example usage
n = 5
k = 2
print(f"Binomial Coefficient C({n}, {k}) = {binomial_coefficient(n, k)}")
```

The output of the above code will be:

```
Binomial Coefficient C(5, 2) = 10
```

This approach has a time complexity of $O(nk)$ and a space complexity of $O(nk)$. For large values of 'n' and 'k', space optimization can be achieved by storing only the current and previous rows of the table, reducing the space complexity to $O(k)$.

Another classic combination problem is the subset sum problem. Given a set of integers and a target sum, the goal is to determine if there is a subset of the given set with a sum equal to the target. Formally, for a given set $S = \{s_1, s_2, \ldots, s_n\}$, and an integer $T$, we need to check if there exists a subset $S'$ such that the sum of the elements in $S'$ is equal to $T$.

We can solve the subset sum problem using dynamic programming by constructing a boolean table 'dp[][]', where 'dp[i][j]' will be 'True' if there is a subset of $\{s_1, s_2, \ldots, s_i\}$ with sum 'j', and 'False' otherwise:

```
def subset_sum(S, T):
    n = len(S)
    dp = [[False for _ in range(T + 1)] for _ in range(n + 1)]

    # A sum of 0 can always be formed with an empty subset
    for i in range(n + 1):
```

```
        dp[i][0] = True

    # Fill the table
    for i in range(1, n + 1):
        for j in range(1, T + 1):
            # If not including S[i-1]
            dp[i][j] = dp[i-1][j]

            # If including S[i-1]
            if j >= S[i-1]:
                dp[i][j] = dp[i][j] or dp[i-1][j-S[i-1]]

    return dp[n][T]

# Example usage
S = [3, 34, 4, 12, 5, 2]
T = 9
print(f"Is there a subset with sum {T}? {subset_sum(S, T)}")
```

The output of the above code will indicate whether the subset with the sum equal to the target exists:

```
Is there a subset with sum 9? True
```

Here, the time complexity of this approach is $O(nT)$, and the space complexity is also $O(nT)$. Space optimization can similarly be applied by storing only necessary intermediate results.

Exploring further, the knapsack problem is another vital subset selection problem. In the "0/1 knapsack problem," given a set of items, each with a weight and a value, the objective is to determine the combination of items that maximize the total value without exceeding the weight capacity of the knapsack. Dynamic programming provides an optimal solution by filling a table ‘dp[][]‘ where ‘dp[i][w]‘ represents the maximum value that can be obtained with the first ‘i‘ items and a knapsack capacity ‘w‘.

Dynamic programming efficiently tackles these problems by breaking them down into smaller, manageable subproblems and retaining their results in tables to avoid redundant calculations. This method is especially advantageous for large problem sizes, where combinatorial explosion may otherwise render exponential-time solutions impractical.

## 8.5 Dynamic Programming for Subset Sum

The Subset Sum problem is a fundamental combinatorial problem that poses the following question: Given a set of integers and a target sum, is there a subset of these integers that adds up to the target sum? This problem is not only of theoretical interest but also has practical applications in fields such as cryptography, resource allocation, and decision making.

Formally, we define the problem as follows. Given a set $S = \{s_1, s_2, \ldots, s_n\}$ of $n$ positive integers and a target sum $T$, determine if there exists a subset $S' \subseteq S$ such that the sum of the elements in $S'$ is equal to $T$. If this subset exists, the algorithm should return true; otherwise, it should return false.

Dynamic programming provides an efficient solution to this problem by breaking it down into simpler subproblems and storing the results of these subproblems to avoid redundant calculations. We will leverage a two-dimensional array to track whether a given sum can be achieved using a subset of the given elements.

Let us denote by $dp[i][j]$ a boolean value that is true if a sum $j$ can be achieved using the first $i$ elements of the set $S$. The size of the dynamic programming table $dp$ will therefore be $(n+1) \times (T+1)$. Here is how we can construct and fill this table:

- Initialize the first column; since a sum of $0$ can always be achieved by choosing the empty subset, set $dp[i][0] =$ true for all $i$ in the range $0$ to $n$.
- Initialize the top row, except $dp[0][0]$; since no positive sum can be achieved with an empty set, set $dp[0][j] =$ false for all $j$ in the range $1$ to $T$.
- Fill the table by iterating through the elements of $S$ and the possible sums from $1$ to $T$.
  - For each element $s_i$, if $j$ is less than $s_i$, then set $dp[i][j] = dp[i-1][j]$ (carry forward the previous state, as $s_i$ cannot contribute to this sum).
  - Otherwise, set $dp[i][j] = dp[i-1][j]$ or $dp[i-1][j-s_i]$ (true if $j$ can be achieved either by excluding $s_i$ or by including $s_i$ and achieving the remaining sum $j - s_i$).

The value of $dp[n][T]$ will therefore indicate whether the target sum $T$ can be achieved using the subset of elements in $S$.

To provide a concrete implementation using Python, the following code demonstrates the dynamic programming approach to solve the Subset Sum problem:

```
def subset_sum(S, T):
    n = len(S)
    dp = [[False] * (T + 1) for _ in range(n + 1)]

    # A sum of 0 can always be achieved with an empty subset
    for i in range(n + 1):
        dp[i][0] = True

    # Fill the dp table
    for i in range(1, n + 1):
        for j in range(1, T + 1):
            if S[i-1] > j:
                dp[i][j] = dp[i-1][j]
            else:
                dp[i][j] = dp[i-1][j] or dp[i-1][j - S[i-1]]

    return dp[n][T]
# Example usage:
S = [3, 34, 4, 12, 5, 2]
T = 9
print(subset_sum(S, T)) # Output: True
```

In this example, the function checks whether there exists a subset of the set $S = \{3, 34, 4, 12, 5, 2\}$ that sums up to $9$. The output is True, indicating that such a subset exists (specifically, the subset $\{4, 5\}$).

Here is the output of the given example code:

```
True
```

To further illustrate how the dynamic programming table is populated, let us consider a smaller example with $S = \{1, 2, 3\}$ and $T = 4$. The dynamic programming table $dp$ will be updated as follows:

- Initialize $dp[0][0]$ to $dp[0][4]$:

  dp[0] = [True, False, False, False, False]

- Update $dp[1][0]$ to $dp[1][4]$ using $s_1 = 1$:

  dp[1] = [True, True, False, False, False]

- Update $dp[2][0]$ to $dp[2][4]$ using $s_2 = 2$:

  dp[2] = [True, True, True, True, False]

- Update $dp[3][0]$ to $dp[3][4]$ using $s_3 = 3$:

  dp[3] = [True, True, True, True, True]

Upon completion, the table shows that a subset sum of $4$ can be achieved using the subset $\{1, 3\}$.

By employing dynamic programming, we reduce the time complexity of solving the Subset Sum problem from exponential to pseudo-polynomial time $O(nT)$, making it feasible to solve larger instances compared to a naive recursive solution.

## 8.6 Knapsack Problem

The Knapsack Problem is a quintessential problem in combinatorial optimization and dynamic programming applications. This classic problem entails a set of items, each with a weight and a value, and a knapsack with a weight capacity. The objective is to determine the most valuable subset of items that can fit into the knapsack without exceeding its capacity. Formally, given $n$ items with weights $w_1, w_2, \ldots, w_n$ and values $v_1, v_2, \ldots, v_n$, and a knapsack with capacity $W$, the goal is to maximize the total value while ensuring the total weight does not exceed $W$.

The problem can be approached in various forms:

- 0/1 Knapsack Problem
- Fractional Knapsack Problem
- Unbounded Knapsack Problem

We will focus on the 0/1 Knapsack Problem as it serves as the foundation for understanding more complex variations.

**0/1 Knapsack Problem Formulation:**

In the 0/1 Knapsack Problem, each item can either be included in the knapsack or not (hence, 0 or 1). Let $f(i, w)$ represent the maximum value that can be obtained with the first $i$ items and an available capacity $w$. The problem can be broken down into the following mathematical recursion:

$$f(i, w) = \begin{cases} 0 & \text{if } i = 0 \text{ or } w = 0 \\ f(i-1, w) & \text{if } w_i > w \\ \max(f(i-1, w), v_i + f(i-1, w - w_i)) & \text{if } w_i \leq w \end{cases}$$

The boundary conditions $f(0, w) = 0$ for $w \geq 0$ and $f(i, 0) = 0$ for $i \geq 0$

initialize the recursion. This means if there are no items or the capacity is zero, the maximum value is zero.

Consider implementing the algorithm in Python using dynamic programming to iteratively solve the problem.

```
def knapsack_01(weights, values, capacity):
    n = len(weights)
    dp = [[0 for _ in range(capacity + 1)] for _ in range(n + 1)]

    for i in range(1, n + 1):
        for w in range(1, capacity + 1):
            if weights[i - 1] <= w:
                dp[i][w] = max(dp[i - 1][w], values[i - 1] + dp[i - 1][w - weights[i - 1]])
            else:
                dp[i][w] = dp[i - 1][w]

    return dp[n][capacity]
```

The table $\mathrm{dp}$ represents the maximum value for each subproblem defined by the first $i$ items and capacity $w$. This complete table reveals the optimal solution at $\mathrm{dp[n][capacity]}$.

**Example Execution:**

Given items with weights $[1, 3, 4, 5]$ and values $[1, 4, 5, 7]$, and a knapsack with capacity $7$, the function $\mathrm{knapsack\_01}$ provides the solution:

```
weights = [1, 3, 4, 5]
values = [1, 4, 5, 7]
capacity = 7
max_value = knapsack_01(weights, values, capacity)
print(max_value) # Output: 9
```

```
9
```

This illustrates the solution where the optimal value obtainable without exceeding the knapsack's capacity is 9.

**Space Optimization:**

The above approach uses $O(nW)$ space. However, by analyzing the relationship between the rows, we observe that only the current and previous rows are necessary. Thus, space optimization can be achieved by maintaining only two arrays instead of a complete 2-dimensional array.

```
def knapsack_01_space_optimized(weights, values, capacity):
    n = len(weights)
    dp = [0] * (capacity + 1)

    for i in range(n):
        for w in range(capacity, weights[i] - 1, -1):
            dp[w] = max(dp[w], values[i] + dp[w - weights[i]])
```

```
    return dp[capacity]
```

This optimized approach reduces the space complexity to $O(W)$ while maintaining the same time complexity.

By understanding the 0/1 Knapsack Problem and mastering its dynamic programming implementation, we can effectively apply these skills to other combinatorial optimization problems.

## 8.7 Partition Problem

In combinatorial optimization, the Partition Problem is a fundamental decision problem. It can be formally stated as follows: given a set of positive integers, is it possible to partition this set into two subsets such that the sum of the elements in each subset is the same? The complexity of this problem lies in its NP-complete nature, which implies that no known polynomial-time algorithm can guarantee a solution for all possible inputs.

To better understand the Partition Problem and its solution using dynamic programming, consider the following problem instance:

$$S = \{3, 1, 1, 2, 2, 1\}$$

The goal is to determine whether $S$ can be divided into two subsets with equal sums.

First, observe that the problem is solvable only if the total sum of $S$ is even. This is a preliminary but essential step:

$$\text{Total sum of } S = 3 + 1 + 1 + 2 + 2 + 1 = 10$$

Since $10$ is even, we proceed by defining the target sum for each subset as:

$$\text{Target sum} = \frac{\text{Total sum}}{2} = 5$$

Now, the task reduces to finding whether there is a subset of $S$ that sums to 5. This can be efficiently approached using dynamic programming.

We utilize an array $dp$ where $dp[j]$ indicates whether a subset with sum $j$ can be formed using elements from the set $S$. Initialize $dp$ with $\text{False}$ values and set $dp[0]$ to $\text{True}$, since a subset with sum 0 is always possible (the empty subset).

The dynamic programming transition involves updating the $dp$ array for each element in $S$. Specifically, given an element $num$, update $dp[j]$ to True if $dp[j - num]$ is True. Iterate through the set and progressively build up the possible subset sums.

The Python implementation is as follows:

```
def can_partition(nums):
    total_sum = sum(nums)

    # If the total sum is odd, return False
    if total_sum % 2 != 0:
        return False

    target = total_sum // 2
    dp = [False] * (target + 1)
    dp[0] = True

    for num in nums:
        for j in range(target, num - 1, -1):
            dp[j] = dp[j] or dp[j - num]

    return dp[target]

# Example usage
nums = [3, 1, 1, 2, 2, 1]
print(can_partition(nums)) # Output: True
```

For the given example, the output would be:

```
True
```

The implementation breakdown is as follows: 1. Calculate the total sum of the set. 2. Check if the sum is even. If not, return False. 3. Initialize the $dp$ array where $dp[j]$ tracks if a subset sum $j$ is possible. 4. Iterate through each element in $nums$, and for each element, update the $dp$ values backwards from the target.

The choice to iterate backward in the inner loop ensures that each element is only considered once per state update, preventing issues with overwriting. By the end of the iteration, if $dp[target]$ is True, then a subset sum of $target$ has been found, thus the set can be partitioned as required.

Finally, it's instructive to analyze the computational efficiency of this approach. The time complexity is $O(n \times sum/2)$, where $n$ is the number of elements in the set, and $sum$ is the total sum of the set. The space complexity is $O(sum/2)$, reflecting the size of the $dp$ array.

The Partition Problem demonstrates the power of dynamic programming in transforming an NP-complete problem into a manageable computational task for reasonably sized inputs. By structuring the problem and applying systematic state transitions, solutions to large and complex instances become feasible.

## 8.8 Coin Change Problem

The coin change problem is a fundamental problem in combinatorics and dynamic programming. It involves finding the minimum number of coins required to make a given amount of money using a specified set of denominations. This problem has various applications, including currency systems, making change in monetary transactions, and is a classic example of optimization problems in computer science.

Given a set of coin denominations and an amount of money, the goal is to determine the minimum number of coins needed to make that amount. Let us define the parameters more formally. Suppose we have $n$ different denominations of coins: $d_1, d_2, \ldots, d_n$, and we want to make an amount $A$. We denote the minimum number of coins needed to make the amount $A$ as MinCoins$(A)$.

**Approach Using Dynamic Programming**

To solve the coin change problem using dynamic programming, we need to construct a solution incrementally by solving smaller subproblems and using their solutions to build up to the solution of the original problem. We will use an array $DP$ where $DP[i]$ will store the minimum number of coins required to make the amount $i$.

1. **Base Case:**
   Initialize $DP[0] = 0$ since no coins are needed to make the amount 0.

2. **Recursive Relation:**
   For every amount $i$ from 1 to $A$, determine $DP[i]$ by considering all denominations. Specifically:

   $$DP[i] = \text{min}(DP[i], DP[i-d_j]+1) \quad \text{for each coin } d_j \text{ where } d_j \leq i$$

   Here,

   - $DP[i - d_j]$ represents the minimum number of coins needed to make the amount $i - d_j$.
   - Adding one coin of denomination $d_j$ results in $DP[i - d_j] + 1$.

- We take the minimum value after considering all valid denominations.

### Algorithm Implementation

Below is the Python implementation of the dynamic programming approach to solve the coin change problem.

```
def coinChange(coins, amount):
    # Initialize DP array with infinity
    DP = [float('inf')] * (amount + 1)

    # Base case: no coins needed to make amount 0
    DP[0] = 0

    for i in range(1, amount + 1):
        for coin in coins:
            if coin <= i:
                DP[i] = min(DP[i], DP[i - coin] + 1)

    return DP[amount] if DP[amount] != float('inf') else -1

# Example usage
coins = [1, 2, 5]
amount = 11
print(coinChange(coins, amount))
```

3

### Explanation of the Implementation

- The function coinChange$(coins, amount)$ takes two parameters: a list of coin denominations (*coins*) and the target amount (*amount*).

- The $DP$ array is initialized with *infinity* (*float('inf')*) because initially, we consider the minimum number of coins as infinite for all amounts.

- $DP[0]$ is set to 0 because no coins are required to make the amount 0.

- For each amount $i$ from 1 to *amount*, we iterate through each coin denomination to update $DP[i]$ (the minimum number of coins required to make the amount $i$).

- If it is impossible to make the target amount, the function returns $-1$. Otherwise, it returns the minimum number of coins stored in $DP[amount]$.

The coin change problem illustrates the power of dynamic programming to efficiently solve optimization problems. By breaking the problem into simpler subproblems and storing their solutions, we avoid redundant computations, leading to a solution with time complexity $O(n \times A)$, where $n$ is the number of coin denominations and $A$ is the target amount.

## 8.9 Rod Cutting Problem

The rod cutting problem is a classic example of using dynamic programming to solve an optimization problem that involves making decisions at discrete intervals. It is a variation of the more general problem of optimization in combinatorial settings. The rod cutting problem can be described as follows: given a rod of length $n$ and a list of prices $p_i$ for $i = 1, 2, \ldots, n$, determine the maximum revenue that can be obtained by cutting the rod and selling the pieces. The cutting and selling process must maximize the sum of price values obtained for each piece.

**Problem Definition:**

Given:

- A rod of length $n$.
- An array of prices $p = \{p_1, p_2, \ldots, p_n\}$, where $p_i$ represents the price of a rod of length $i$.

Objective:

- Find the maximum revenue obtainable by cutting up the rod and selling the pieces.

**Dynamic Programming Approach:**

The problem can be approached using dynamic programming by defining a function $r(n)$ which represents the maximum revenue for a rod of length $n$. To build the solution, consider each cut length $i$ and add the price $p_i$ to the solution of the subproblem of length $n - i$.

The recurrence relation for this problem can be stated as:

$$r(n) = \max_{1 \leq i \leq n} (p_i + r(n - i))$$

The above relation iterates over all possible first cut lengths $i$ and picks the one that maximizes the total revenue. The base case of this recurrence relation is $r(0) = 0$, meaning no revenue can be obtained from a rod of length 0.

**Memoization Strategy:**

To store the results of subproblems and avoid redundant calculations, an array $R$ of size $n+1$ is used:

- $R[i]$ holds the maximum revenue obtainable for a rod length of $i$.

Initially, $R[0]$ is set to 0. For every length $j$ from 1 to $n$, determine $R[j]$ by examining all possible first cuts.

```
def rod_cutting(prices, n):
    R = [0] * (n + 1)
    for j in range(1, n + 1):
        max_revenue = float('-inf')
        for i in range(1, j + 1):
            max_revenue = max(max_revenue, prices[i - 1] + R[j - i])
        R[j] = max_revenue
    return R[n]
```

In this implementation, 'prices[i - 1]' because array indices in Python are 0-based, thus adjusting the price array accordingly.

**Example:**

Consider a rod of length 4 and prices '[1, 5, 8, 9]', where $p_1 = 1$, $p_2 = 5$, $p_3 = 8$, and $p_4 = 9$. Applying the above algorithm:

```
Initial R array: [0, 0, 0, 0, 0]

For j = 1:
   max_revenue = max(-inf, 1 + 0) = 1
   R: [0, 1, 0, 0, 0]

For j = 2:
   max_revenue = max(-inf, 1 + 1) = 2
   max_revenue = max(2, 5 + 0) = 5
   R: [0, 1, 5, 0, 0]

For j = 3:
   max_revenue = max(-inf, 1 + 5) = 6
   max_revenue = max(6, 5 + 1) = 6
   max_revenue = max(6, 8 + 0) = 8
   R: [0, 1, 5, 8, 0]

For j = 4:
   max_revenue = max(-inf, 1 + 8) = 9
   max_revenue = max(9, 5 + 5) = 10
   max_revenue = max(10, 8 + 1) = 10
   max_revenue = max(10, 9 + 0) = 10
   R: [0, 1, 5, 8, 10]
```

Final maximum revenue for a rod of length 4 is $R[4] = 10$.

This dynamic programming solution efficiently computes the maximum revenue using bottom-up approach with time complexity $O(n^2)$ and space complexity $O(n)$. This method ensures optimal substructure and overlapping subproblems are effectively handled, which characterizes dynamic programming solutions.

## 8.10 Bin Packing Problem

The bin packing problem is a classic combinatorial problem wherein objects of various sizes must be packed into a finite number of bins or containers each having a fixed capacity in such a way that the number of bins used is minimized. This problem has extensive applications in resource allocation, manufacturing, logistics, and various fields of operations research.

Given a set of items with specified weights, and bins with a fixed capacity, we aim to determine the minimum number of bins required such that all the items are accommodated.

Consider a set of items $I = \{i_1, i_2, ..., i_n\}$ with corresponding weights $W = \{w_1, w_2, ..., w_n\}$, and bin capacity $C$. The objective is to minimize the number of bins $B$ such that all items are packed:

$$\sum_{j \in B_i} w_j \leq C, \quad \text{for all bins } B_i.$$

**Example:**

Let us consider an example where we have items with weights {4, 8, 1, 4, 2, 1} and bin capacity $C = 10$. The goal is to minimize the number of bins used.

1. Place the first item of weight 4 in bin 1.
2. Place the second item of weight 8 in bin 2.
3. Place the third item of weight 1 in bin 1, now bin 1 has items with weights 4, 1.
4. Place the fourth item of weight 4 in bin 2, now bin 2 has items with weights 8, 4.

5. Place the fifth item of weight 2 in bin 1, now bin 1 has items with weights 4, 1, 2.

6. Place the sixth item of weight 1 in bin 1, now bin 1 has items with weights 4, 1, 2, 1.

After applying a simple placement strategy, we used 2 bins.

**Heuristics for Bin Packing:**

Due to the NP-hard nature of the bin packing problem, exact algorithms are often impractical for large instances. Therefore, heuristic approaches are commonly employed:

- **First Fit (FF):** Place each item in the first bin that has enough capacity.
- **First Fit Decreasing (FFD):** First sort items in decreasing order of size, then apply the First Fit algorithm.
- **Best Fit (BF):** Place each item in the bin that will leave the least remaining capacity after the item is placed.
- **Best Fit Decreasing (BFD):** First sort items in decreasing order of size, then apply the Best Fit algorithm.

**Dynamic Programming Approach:**

While heuristic methods provide good approximations, dynamic programming can be used for more precise solutions, albeit with higher computational costs. In the dynamic programming approach, we can use a state array/w vector where each state $w[i][j]$ would denote the minimum number of bins required to pack the first $i$ items into bins of capacity $j$.

Below is a Python implementation of the First Fit Decreasing (FFD) heuristic:

```
def first_fit_decreasing(weights, bin_capacity):
    weights.sort(reverse=True) # sorting items in decreasing order
    bins = []

    for weight in weights:
        placed = False

        for bin in bins:
            if sum(bin) + weight <= bin_capacity:
                bin.append(weight)
                placed = True
```

```
                break

        if not placed:
            bins.append([weight])

    return len(bins), bins

weights = [4, 8, 1, 4, 2, 1]
bin_capacity = 10
num_bins, bin_contents = first_fit_decreasing(weights, bin_capacity)
print(num_bins)
print(bin_contents)
```

The output of the above program would be:

```
2
[[8, 2], [4, 4, 1, 1]]
```

The First Fit Decreasing approach used only 2 bins, demonstrating its efficiency for this instance.

The bin packing problem, due to its computational difficulty in achieving optimal solutions, often leverages these heuristic strategies. Advanced methods, including meta-heuristics like Genetic Algorithms, Simulated Annealing, and Ant Colony Optimization, aim to provide near-optimal solutions with reasonable computational effort.

As combinatorial optimization problems become more complex, the balance between computational efficiency and solution optimality becomes crucial. An understanding of heuristic methods forms a foundational toolset that can be expanded with more sophisticated algorithms as the requirements of the problem dictate.

## 8.11 Combinatorial Optimization

Combinatorial optimization deals with finding an optimal object from a finite set of objects. These problems often involve the task of searching through a potentially large solution space for the best solution according to some criteria. Dynamic programming is a powerful tool for solving combinatorial optimization problems efficiently by breaking them down into simpler subproblems and reusing solutions to these subproblems.

One classic example of a combinatorial optimization problem is the **Traveling Salesman Problem (TSP)**, where the goal is to determine the shortest possible route that visits each city exactly once and returns to the origin city. Another example is the **Knapsack Problem**, which requires selecting a subset of items with maximum total value without exceeding a given weight limit.

To solve combinatorial optimization problems using dynamic programming, we generalize the concept of memoization and recursive solution building (as previously detailed in simpler problems like the subset sum and knapsack problems).

- **Define the Subproblem:** Identify the subproblem that can be solved independently. The subproblem should capture the essential elements needed to build a solution to the original problem.
- **Characterize the Structure of an Optimal Solution:** Express the solution to the problem in terms of solutions to subproblems.
- **Recursive Formulation:** Formulate the problem recursively, ensuring that the solution builds upon the solutions to smaller subproblems.
- **Memoization or Tabulation:** Store the solutions to subproblems to avoid redundant calculations. Either memoize results in a top-down approach or use a bottom-up table-filling approach.
- **Construct the Optimal Solution:** Use the information stored in the table to construct the final solution.

Consider the **Traveling Salesman Problem** as an illustration. The TSP can be solved using dynamic programming by defining the subproblems as the shortest paths through subsets of cities. Let $C(S, j)$ represent the minimum cost of visiting all cities in the subset $S$ ending at city $j$. Initially, set $C(\{1\}, 1) = 0$, where city $1$ is the starting point.

The recursive relation is given by:

$$C(S, j) = \min_{i \in S, i \neq j} [C(S \setminus \{j\}, i) + d(i, j)]$$

where $d(i, j)$ is the distance between cities $i$ and $j$. The goal is to find:

$$\min_{j \neq 1} [C(\{1, 2, \ldots, n\}, j) + d(j, 1)]$$

which represents the minimum cost path covering all cities and returning to the start.

```
def tsp(dp, dist, mask, pos):
    if mask == (1 << n) - 1:
        return dist[pos][0] # return to starting city
```

```
    if dp[mask][pos] != -1:
        return dp[mask][pos]

    ans = float('inf')
    for city in range(n):
        if (mask & (1 << city)) == 0:
            new_ans = dist[pos][city] + tsp(dp, dist, mask | (1 << city), city)
            ans = min(ans, new_ans)

    dp[mask][pos] = ans
    return dp[mask][pos]

n = 4 # Example for 4 cities
dist = [[0, 10, 15, 20], [10, 0, 35, 25], [15, 35, 0, 30], [20, 25, 30, 0]]
dp = [[-1] * n for _ in range(1 << n)]
print(tsp(dp, dist, 1, 0))
```

For the **Knapsack Problem**, revisited with a combinatorial optimization focus, we consider the 0/1 knapsack where fragments of items cannot be selected. Using dynamic programming, we create a table $K$ where $K[i][w]$ represents the maximum value that can be attained with the first $i$ items and a weight limit $w$.

The recursive relation can be described as follows:

If the weight of item $i$ (denoted as $w_i$) is greater than $w$, then the item cannot be included:

$$K[i][w] = K[i-1][w]$$

Otherwise, the item can be included or excluded:

$$K[i][w] = \max(K[i-1][w], K[i-1][w-w_i] + v_i)$$

where $v_i$ is the value of item $i$.

```
def knapsack(val, wt, W):
    n = len(val)
    K = [[0 for x in range(W + 1)] for x in range(n + 1)]

    for i in range(n + 1):
        for w in range(W + 1):
            if i == 0 or w == 0:
                K[i][w] = 0
            elif wt[i - 1] <= w:
                K[i][w] = max(val[i - 1] + K[i - 1][w - wt[i - 1]], K[i - 1][w])
            else:
                K[i][w] = K[i - 1][w]

    return K[n][W]

val = [60, 100, 120]
wt = [10, 20, 30]
W = 50
print(knapsack(val, wt, W))
```

Dynamic programming proves to be an efficient technique for solving many combinatorial optimization problems due to its ability to dissect problems into manageable subproblems, ensuring an optimal solution while maintaining computational feasibility.

## 8.12 Advanced Combinatorial Problems

In this section, we delve into several advanced combinatorial problems that extend the applications of dynamic programming beyond the basics covered in previous sections. These problems often involve additional constraints or more complex structures, requiring refined techniques and meticulous analysis. The depth of understanding required for these problems aids in mastering dynamic programming for real-world scenarios.

**Traveling Salesman Problem (TSP)**

The Traveling Salesman Problem (TSP) is a classic in combinatorial optimization. Given a set of cities and the distances between each pair of cities, the goal is to find the shortest possible tour that visits each city exactly once and returns to the origin city. It is an NP-hard problem, making exact solutions computationally infeasible for large instances. Dynamic programming provides a way to solve TSP for smaller datasets effectively.

Define a state $dp[S][i]$ where $S$ is a subset of cities including $i$, and $i$ is the last city in the subset. $dp[S][i]$ represents the minimum cost of visiting all cities in $S$ and ending at city $i$. The recurrence relation is given by:

$$dp[S][i] = \min_{j \in S, j \neq i} (dp[S \setminus \{i\}][j] + \text{dist}(j, i))$$

The initial state for city 0 is:

$$dp[\{0\}][0] = 0$$

The final solution is:

$$\min_i (dp[\{1, 2, \ldots, n\}][i] + \text{dist}(i, 0))$$

In Python, this dynamic programming approach can be implemented as:

```
import itertools
```

```
def tsp_dynamic_programming(dist):
    n = len(dist)
    dp = {}
    for k in range(n):
        dp[(1 << k, k)] = dist[0][k]

    for subset_size in range(2, n):
        for subset in itertools.combinations(range(1, n), subset_size):
            bits = 0
            for bit in subset:
                bits |= 1 << bit
            for k in subset:
                prev_bits = bits & ~(1 << k)
                dp[(bits, k)] = min(dp[(prev_bits, m)] + dist[m][k] for m in subset if m
                    != k)

    bits = (2 ** n - 1) - 1
    result = min(dp[(bits, k)] + dist[k][0] for k in range(1, n))

    return result

# Example usage
dist = [
    [0, 10, 15, 20],
    [10, 0, 35, 25],
    [15, 35, 0, 30],
    [20, 25, 30, 0]
]
result = tsp_dynamic_programming(dist)
print(result)
```

Output:

```
80
```

### Hamiltonian Path Problem

The Hamiltonian Path Problem involves finding a path in a graph that visits each vertex exactly once. Unlike TSP, a Hamiltonian path does not necessarily end at the starting vertex. It is also NP-complete.

Using dynamic programming, we can form a similar solution structure to TSP. Define $dp[S][i]$ as the cost of visiting all vertices in $S$ and ending at vertex $i$. The recurrence relation remains analogous:

$$dp[S][i] = \min_{j \in S, j \neq i} (dp[S \setminus \{i\}][j] + \text{dist}(j, i))$$

The difference lies in the final solution, which now needs to consider all vertices as possible endpoints:

$$\min_{i}(dp[\{1, 2, \ldots, n\}][i])$$

The implementation in Python can then be derived similarly to TSP.

### Set Cover Problem

The Set Cover Problem is another fundamental problem in combinatorial optimization. Given a universe $U$ of elements and a collection of subsets whose union equals $U$, the goal is to find the smallest subcollection of these subsets that covers all elements in $U$. This problem is also NP-hard.

Dynamic programming can solve small instances of the Set Cover Problem efficiently by defining a state $dp[S]$ as the minimum number of subsets needed to cover the subset $S$ of $U$. For each subset $A$ in the collection that can extend $S$, the recurrence relation is:

$$dp[S \cup A] = \min(dp[S \cup A], dp[S] + 1)$$

Starting with $dp[\emptyset] = 0$, the final state is $dp[U]$.

Here is a Python implementation:

```
def set_cover(universe, subsets):
    n = len(universe)
    dp = [float('inf')] * (1 << n)
    dp[0] = 0

    universe_to_index = {element: i for i, element in enumerate(universe)}

    def subset_to_bits(subset):
        bits = 0
        for element in subset:
            bits |= 1 << universe_to_index[element]
        return bits

    subset_bits = [subset_to_bits(subset) for subset in subsets]

    for bits in range(1 << n):
        for subset_bits in subset_bits:
            dp[bits | subset_bits] = min(dp[bits | subset_bits], dp[bits] + 1)

    return dp[-1]

# Example usage
universe = {1, 2, 3, 4}
subsets = [{1, 2}, {2, 3}, {3, 4}, {4}]
result = set_cover(universe, subsets)
print(result)
```

Output:

```
2
```

### Steiner Tree Problem

The Steiner Tree Problem seeks a minimum-weight tree in a graph that spans a given subset of vertices, known as terminals, with the possibility of including other non-terminal vertices to reduce the overall weight. It is prevalent in network design applications and is also NP-hard.

Define $dp[S][i]$ as the minimum cost to connect all vertices in $S$ with vertex $i$ as the endpoint. The recurrence relation would account for adding vertex $j$ to the tree:

$$dp[S \cup \{j\}][j] = \text{min}(dp[S][i] + \text{dist}(i, j)) \quad \text{for all } i \in S$$

This approach can be computationally intensive and may require additional heuristics for larger graphs. The implementation is akin to solving a more generalized version of the Minimum Spanning Tree problem with dynamic constraints.

These advanced combinatorial problems demonstrate the power and versatility of dynamic programming in solving complex real-world problems. By refining the problem states and recurrence relationships, dynamic programming enables efficient solutions for problems that would otherwise be computationally prohibitive.

# Chapter 9

# Optimal Substructure and Overlapping Subproblems

**This chapter examines the fundamental concepts of optimal substructure and overlapping subproblems, which are crucial for dynamic programming. Readers will learn to identify and define optimal substructure in problems, supported by various examples. The chapter also explains overlapping subproblems, illustrating how recognizing these can lead to more efficient solutions. Practical examples demonstrate the combination of these principles, while the chapter also highlights common patterns in dynamic programming and real-world applications. Exercises and practice problems are included to reinforce the understanding of these core concepts.**

## 9.1 Introduction to Optimal Substructure and Overlapping Subproblems

Dynamic Programming (DP) is a method for solving complex problems by breaking them down into simpler subproblems. It is particularly useful for optimization problems where the goal is to find the best solution among a set of feasible solutions. Two fundamental concepts that underlie dynamic programming are **optimal substructure** and **overlapping subproblems**. These concepts enable the development of efficient algorithms that can solve problems in polynomial time, which might otherwise require exponential time with naive approaches.

Optimal substructure means that an optimal solution to a problem can be constructed from optimal solutions of its subproblems. This property is crucial because it ensures that the problem can be divided into smaller, manageable parts that can be solved independently and then combined to form the solution to the original problem. To illustrate, consider the classic problem of finding the shortest path in a graph. The fact that the shortest path between two vertices can be constructed from the shortest paths between intermediate vertices and the endpoints is an example of optimal substructure.

Overlapping subproblems refer to the scenario where the same subproblems appear multiple times in the recursive problem-solving process. In contrast to divide-and-conquer algorithms that generate new subproblems at each step, dynamic programming algorithms store the results of subproblems to reuse them when they appear again. This avoids redundant computations and significantly enhances efficiency. For instance, in the computation of Fibonacci numbers, the same Fibonacci number calculation is repeated multiple times with a naive recursive algorithm. By storing intermediate results, dynamic programming solves this problem in linear time.

To understand these concepts more concretely, consider the following basic example: the calculation of the Fibonacci sequence. The $n$-th Fibonacci number is defined as

$$F(n) = \begin{cases} 0 & \text{if } n = 0 \\ 1 & \text{if } n = 1 \\ F(n-1) + F(n-2) & \text{if } n > 1 \end{cases}$$

Here, the optimal substructure property is evident. The value of $F(n)$ depends on the values of $F(n-1)$ and $F(n-2)$. However, the naive recursive approach leads to many redundant calculations, as many subproblems are solved repeatedly for different initial values of $n$. For example, $F(5)$ requires $F(4)$ and $F(3)$. Calculating $F(4)$, in turn, requires $F(3)$ and $F(2)$. Notice that $F(3)$ is calculated twice. With dynamic programming, we can store the value of $F(3)$ after computing it once and reuse it whenever needed.

In Python, a dynamic programming solution for computing Fibonacci numbers using memoization can be implemented as follows:

```
def fibonacci(n, memo={}):
    if n in memo:
        return memo[n]
    if n == 0:
        return 0
    if n == 1:
        return 1
    memo[n] = fibonacci(n-1, memo) + fibonacci(n-2, memo)
    return memo[n]
```

Executing the above code for, say, $n = 10$ yields:

```
>>> fibonacci(10)
55
```

This illustrates how dynamic programming capitalizes on overlapping subproblems by storing intermediate results and using them in future computations, thereby dramatically improving efficiency compared to the naive recursion.

Understanding these foundational principles of optimal substructure and overlapping subproblems is crucial for mastering dynamic programming. In subsequent sections, we will delve deeper into identifying these properties in more complex problems, proving their existence, and formulating dynamic programming solutions that leverage these properties. By methodically applying these principles, one can solve a wide range of problems more effectively.

## 9.2 Understanding Optimal Substructure

To fully grasp dynamic programming, it is crucial to understand the concept of optimal substructure. Optimal substructure means that an optimal solution to a problem can be constructed from optimal solutions of its subproblems. This property is pivotal because it enables the breaking down of a problem into smaller, more manageable subproblems, solving each of those optimally, and then combining their solutions to solve the original problem optimally.

Consider the classic algorithmic problem of finding the shortest path in a weighted graph from a given source to a destination. Suppose the graph is represented as $G = (V, E)$ with non-negative edge weights. The problem is to find the shortest path from a source vertex $s$ to a destination vertex $t$.

By definition, the shortest path $P(s, t)$ exhibits optimal substructure.

Specifically, if vertex $v$ is on the shortest path $P(s,t)$, then the subpath $P(s,v)$ from vertex $s$ to vertex $v$ and the subpath $P(v,t)$ from vertex $v$ to vertex $t$ are themselves the shortest paths. If either subpath were not the shortest, the entire path $P(s,t)$ could not be the shortest because replacing the non-optimal subpath with the shortest one would yield a shorter overall path.

To illustrate this with a concrete example, consider the Dijkstra's algorithm which leverages this property to compute shortest paths. By iteratively considering the shortest path to a new vertex, and updating the paths using known shortest paths, Dijkstra's algorithm builds the shortest path from the source to all other vertices in the graph.

```
import heapq

def dijkstra(graph, source):
    distance = {vertex: float('infinity') for vertex in graph}
    distance[source] = 0
    priority_queue = [(0, source)]

    while priority_queue:
        current_distance, current_vertex = heapq.heappop(priority_queue)

        if current_distance > distance[current_vertex]:
            continue

        for neighbor, weight in graph[current_vertex].items():
            distance_via_vertex = current_distance + weight

            if distance_via_vertex < distance[neighbor]:
                distance[neighbor] = distance_via_vertex
                heapq.heappush(priority_queue, (distance_via_vertex, neighbor))

    return distance
```

In Dijkstra's algorithm, the 'distance' dictionary maintains the shortest known distance to each vertex from the source. The priority queue enables efficient retrieval of the vertex with the currently known shortest path, and the algorithm iteratively improves the shortest path estimates based on the optimal substructure property.

Another fundamental example of optimal substructure is the problem of finding the longest common subsequence (LCS) of two strings. If we are given two sequences $A = [a_1, a_2, \ldots, a_n]$ and $B = [b_1, b_2, \ldots, b_m]$, the LCS problem aims to find the maximum length sequence that appears as a subsequence in both $A$ and $B$.

Let $LCS(X, Y)$ denote the length of the LCS of sequences $X$ and $Y$. The optimal substructure in the LCS problem can be formulated as follows:

$$LCS(X[1 \ldots n], Y[1 \ldots m]) = \begin{cases} 0 & \text{if } n = 0 \text{ or } m = 0 \\ LCS(X[1 \ldots n-1], Y[1 \ldots m-1]) + 1 & \text{if } x_n = y_m \\ \max(LCS(X[1 \ldots n-1], Y[1 \ldots m]), \\ LCS(X[1 \ldots n], Y[1 \ldots m-1])) & \text{if } x_n \neq y_m \end{cases}$$

This recursive formula showcases optimal substructure by defining the LCS of $X$ and $Y$ in terms of the LCS of their prefixes. If the last characters match, the LCS length increases by 1; otherwise, it is the maximum of the LCS computed by excluding either the last character of $X$ or $Y$.

Here is an implementation of the LCS problem using dynamic programming based on its optimal substructure property:

```
def lcs(X, Y):
    n = len(X)
    m = len(Y)
    L = [[0] * (m + 1) for i in range(n + 1)]

    for i in range(n + 1):
        for j in range(m + 1):
            if i == 0 or j == 0:
                L[i][j] = 0
            elif X[i - 1] == Y[j - 1]:
                L[i][j] = L[i - 1][j - 1] + 1
            else:
                L[i][j] = max(L[i - 1][j], L[i][j - 1])

    return L[n][m]
```

The dynamic programming table 'L' stores the lengths of LCS for the prefixes of $X$ and $Y$. It iteratively builds upon smaller subproblems to compute the LCS length for the entire sequences, showcasing the optimal substructure principle.

Understanding and identifying optimal substructure in problems is key to applying dynamic programming techniques effectively. This approach allows the decomposition of complex problems into simpler subproblems, solving each one optimally and composing their solutions to derive an optimal solution to the original problem. The Dijkstra's algorithm and the LCS problem are quintessential examples that illustrate this principle in practice.

## 9.3 Defining Optimal Substructure in Problems

Optimal substructure is a property of a problem that implies that an optimal solution to the problem's overall structure can be constructed efficiently from optimal solutions to its subproblems. This inherent property is what allows dynamic programming to break down complex problems into smaller, more manageable components and solve them independently. In this section, we will delve into the intricacies of defining optimal substructure in various types of problems, building upon the foundational knowledge introduced earlier.

To formally define optimal substructure, consider a problem $P$ with an optimal solution that includes decisions leading to different subproblems $P_1, P_2, \ldots, P_k$. If the solution to $P$ can be constructed by combining optimal solutions to $P_1, P_2, \ldots, P_k$, then $P$ exhibits optimal substructure.

Mathematically, if $S^*$ represents the optimal solution to $P$, and $S_1^*, S_2^*, \ldots, S_k^*$ are the optimal solutions to subproblems $P_1, P_2, \ldots, P_k$, respectively, then:

$$S^* = f(S_1^*, S_2^*, \ldots, S_k^*)$$

where $f$ is a function that merges the optimal solutions of subproblems into the optimal solution of the main problem. This concept is best illustrated through specific examples.

```
# Matrix Chain Multiplication Problem
def matrix_chain_order(p):
    n = len(p) - 1
    m = [[0 for x in range(n)] for x in range(n)]
    s = [[0 for x in range(n)] for x in range(n)]

    for l in range(2, n+1):
        for i in range(n-l+1):
            j = i + l - 1
            m[i][j] = float('inf')
            for k in range(i, j):
                q = m[i][k] + m[k+1][j] + p[i]*p[k+1]*p[j+1]
                if q < m[i][j]:
                    m[i][j] = q
                    s[i][j] = k

    return m, s
```

In the matrix chain multiplication problem, the goal is to determine the most efficient way to multiply a given sequence of matrices. The problem can be broken into subproblems where each subproblem represents the optimal way to parenthesize a certain subsequence of matrices. The optimal solution for the overall problem is derived from the optimal solutions of these subproblems.

To determine if a problem has an optimal substructure, one must ascertain that the following conditions hold: 1. The problem can be decomposed into smaller subproblems. 2. Optimal solutions to these subproblems can be combined to form the optimal solution to the original problem. 3. Overlapping subproblems that can reuse previously computed results from other subproblems.

For problems such as shortest paths in a graph, the optimal substructure is demonstrated by the fact that the shortest path from one vertex to another can be constructed by combining shorter paths. Consider Dijkstra's algorithm, which is based on this principle. Given a graph $G = (V, E)$, the shortest path from vertex $u$ to vertex $v$ through an intermediate vertex $w$ can be defined using:

$$\text{ShortestPath}(u, v) = \min\{\text{ShortestPath}(u, w) + \text{ShortestPath}(w, v)\}$$

where ShortestPath$(u, w)$ and ShortestPath$(w, v)$ are the optimal solutions to the subproblems.

```
# Dijkstra's Algorithm
import heapq

def dijkstra(graph, start):
    pq = [] # Priority queue
    heapq.heappush(pq, (0, start))
    dist = {vertex: float('inf') for vertex in graph}
    dist[start] = 0
    while pq:
        current_distance, current_vertex = heapq.heappop(pq)
        if current_distance > dist[current_vertex]:
            continue
        for neighbor, weight in graph[current_vertex].items():
            distance = current_distance + weight
            if distance < dist[neighbor]:
                dist[neighbor] = distance
                heapq.heappush(pq, (distance, neighbor))
    return dist
```

In this implementation of Dijkstra's algorithm, the optimal substructure is apparent as each step extends the shortest path tree by solving for the next shortest distance incrementally, leveraging previously computed shortest paths.

Understanding and defining optimal substructure in problems is essential for recognizing opportunities to apply dynamic programming techniques. As seen in the examples, optimal substructure enables complex problems to be solved efficiently by combining solutions to their subproblems, paving the way for the development of robust algorithms.

## 9.4 Examples of Optimal Substructure

Optimal substructure is a fundamental property that many computational problems exhibit, allowing them to be solved efficiently using dynamic programming techniques. A problem is said to exhibit optimal substructure if an optimal solution to the problem can be constructed efficiently from optimal solutions to its subproblems. In this section, we will explore several classical examples where the property of optimal substructure is evident, thereby reinforcing the concept through practical application.

**1. Shortest Path in a Graph**

Consider the problem of finding the shortest path in a weighted graph from a source vertex to a destination vertex. This problem can be solved efficiently using algorithms like Dijkstra's or Bellman-Ford, both of which rely on the principle of optimal substructure.

Let $G = (V, E)$ be a weighted graph with vertices $V$ and edges $E$. If $dist(u, v)$ represents the shortest distance between vertices $u$ and $v$, then for any intermediate vertex $w$ on the shortest path from $u$ to $v$, it holds that:

$$dist(u, v) = dist(u, w) + dist(w, v)$$

This equation illustrates the optimal substructure property. If we know the shortest paths from $u$ to $w$ and from $w$ to $v$, we can combine these to find the shortest path from $u$ to $v$.

```
import heapq

def dijkstra(graph, start_vertex):
    D = {vertex: float('infinity') for vertex in graph}
    D[start_vertex] = 0

    priority_queue = [(0, start_vertex)]
    while priority_queue:
        (current_distance, current_vertex) = heapq.heappop(priority_queue)

        for neighbor, weight in graph[current_vertex].items():
            distance = current_distance + weight

            if distance < D[neighbor]:
                D[neighbor] = distance
                heapq.heappush(priority_queue, (distance, neighbor))

    return D
```

**2. Matrix Chain Multiplication**

Another classic example is the matrix chain multiplication problem. The task is to determine the most efficient way to multiply a given sequence of matrices. The order in which the matrices are multiplied can significantly affect the number of scalar multiplications required.

For a sequence of $n$ matrices $\{A_1, A_2, \ldots, A_n\}$, where $A_i$ is of dimension $p_{i-1} \times p_i$, the goal is to compute the product $A_1 A_2 \cdots A_n$ with the fewest operations. The optimal substructure is captured by the recursive formula:

$$m[i,j] = \min_{i \leq k < j} \{m[i,k] + m[k+1,j] + p_{i-1} p_k p_j\}$$

This implies that to determine the minimum number of operations required to multiply matrices from $i$ to $j$, we need the solutions for the subproblems of multiplying matrices from $i$ to $k$ and from $k+1$ to $j$, for every possible $k$.

```
def matrix_chain_order(p):
    n = len(p) - 1
    m = [[0 for _ in range(n)] for _ in range(n)]

    for length in range(2, n + 1):
        for i in range(n - length + 1):
            j = i + length - 1
            m[i][j] = float('inf')
            for k in range(i, j):
                q = m[i][k] + m[k + 1][j] + p[i] * p[k + 1] * p[j + 1]
                if q < m[i][j]:
                    m[i][j] = q

    return m[0][n - 1]
```

### 3. Longest Common Subsequence (LCS)

The longest common subsequence problem is another problem that beautifully demonstrates optimal substructure. Given two sequences, the task is to find the length of their longest subsequence that appears in both sequences in the same order.

Consider two sequences $X = \{x_1, x_2, \ldots, x_m\}$ and $Y = \{y_1, y_2, \ldots, y_n\}$. Let $L(i,j)$ be the length of the longest common subsequence of the sequences $X_1^i$ and $Y_1^j$. The optimal substructure is reflected in the following recurrence relation:

$$L(i,j) = \begin{cases} 0 & \text{if } i = 0 \text{ or } j = 0 \\ L(i-1,j-1) + 1 & \text{if } x_i = y_j \\ \max(L(i,j-1), L(i-1,j)) & \text{if } x_i \neq y_j \end{cases}$$

```
def lcs(X, Y):
    m = len(X)
    n = len(Y)

    L = [[0 for _ in range(n+1)] for _ in range(m+1)]

    for i in range(m+1):
        for j in range(n+1):
            if i == 0 or j == 0:
                L[i][j] = 0
            elif X[i-1] == Y[j-1]:
                L[i][j] = L[i-1][j-1] + 1
            else:
                L[i][j] = max(L[i-1][j], L[i][j-1])

    return L[m][n]
```

These examples confirm the essential role optimal substructure plays in dynamic programming. Each problem utilizes the property to break down complex questions into manageable subproblems, solving each efficiently to build up the final solution. This makes dynamic programming a powerful technique for solving a wide array of computational problems.

## 9.5 Understanding Overlapping Subproblems

Dynamic programming leverages the concept of overlapping subproblems to optimize computational efficiency. In this technique, a problem is broken down into subproblems, which are then solved independently. Overlapping subproblems mean that the same subproblems appear multiple times during the solution process. By storing and reusing the results of these subproblems, we can avoid redundant computations, significantly improving the overall efficiency of the algorithm.

One of the simplest examples illustrating overlapping subproblems is the computation of Fibonacci numbers. The naive recursive approach recalculates the same values repeatedly, resulting in exponential time complexity. We will implement a naive recursive solution for clarity and then optimize it by using dynamic programming.

```
# Naive recursive solution for Fibonacci numbers

def fib(n):
    if n <= 1:
        return n
    return fib(n-1) + fib(n-2)
```

```
# Test the naive recursive solution
print(fib(5)) # Output: 5
```

Upon executing this code, we observe the correct output, but the time complexity is $O(2^n)$, making it impractical for large $n$:

```
5
```

The overlapping subproblems can be visualized through a recursion tree. For example, calculating $fib(5)$ requires $fib(4)$ and $fib(3)$, where both $fib(4)$ and $fib(3)$ further decompose into their subproblems multiple times. This redundancy can be eliminated using memoization or tabulation.

**Memoization** involves storing the results of expensive function calls and reusing them when the same inputs occur again. Here's the memoized version of the Fibonacci function:

```
# Memoized recursive solution for Fibonacci numbers

def fib_memo(n, memo = None):
    if memo is None:
        memo = {}
    if n in memo:
        return memo[n]
    if n <= 1:
        return n
    memo[n] = fib_memo(n-1, memo) + fib_memo(n-2, memo)
    return memo[n]

# Test the memoized recursive solution
print(fib_memo(5)) # Output: 5
```

This approach uses a dictionary to store computed values, reducing the time complexity to $O(n)$:

```
5
```

**Tabulation** is another technique where we iteratively build a table to store the results of subproblems. It avoids recursion by solving the problem bottom-up:

```
# Tabulated solution for Fibonacci numbers

def fib_tab(n):
    if n <= 1:
        return n
    fib_table = [0] * (n + 1)
    fib_table[1] = 1
    for i in range(2, n + 1):
        fib_table[i] = fib_table[i - 1] + fib_table[i - 2]
    return fib_table[n]

# Test the tabulated solution
print(fib_tab(5)) # Output: 5
```

The tabulated approach also provides the correct output with linear time complexity:

```
5
```

Both memoization and tabulation effectively leverage overlapping subproblems by storing intermediate results, thus avoiding repeated computations. They illustrate the power of dynamic programming in reducing computational overhead compared to naive solutions.

Beyond the Fibonacci sequence, overlapping subproblems are prevalent in a range of dynamic programming problems such as the shortest path, knapsack, and matrix chain multiplication. By identifying these subproblems and caching their results, we achieve significant performance enhancements.

## 9.6 Identifying Overlapping Subproblems

Overlapping subproblems are a hallmark characteristic of problems that are amenable to dynamic programming solutions. This section will delve deeply into the concept of overlapping subproblems and how to identify them in various types of problems. Observing overlapping subproblems is crucial in determining whether dynamic programming can be effectively applied to a problem, as it allows for the reuse of computed solutions, thereby reducing computational effort.

Overlapping subproblems occur when a recursive algorithm revisits the same problem multiple times. A common sign of overlapping subproblems is the presence of recursive calls that recompute the results for the same inputs. This recomputation can be detected by examining the structure of the recursive calls in an algorithm and determining whether the same state or subproblem is being solved more than once.

Consider the following classic example: the computation of Fibonacci numbers. The naive recursive approach for computing the $n$-th Fibonacci number is as follows:

```
def fibonacci(n):
    if n <= 1:
        return n
    return fibonacci(n-1) + fibonacci(n-2)
```

To understand the overlapping subproblems in this example, let's analyze the computation for a small value of $n$. For instance, consider $n = 5$:

```
fibonacci(5)
 fibonacci(4)
  fibonacci(3)
   fibonacci(2)
    fibonacci(1) = 1
    fibonacci(0) = 0
   fibonacci(1) = 1
  fibonacci(2)
   fibonacci(1) = 1
   fibonacci(0) = 0
 fibonacci(3)
  fibonacci(2)
   fibonacci(1) = 1
   fibonacci(0) = 0
  fibonacci(1) = 1
```

A quick analysis reveals that the subproblem of computing ‘fibonacci(2)‘ is solved multiple times. This is indicative of overlapping subproblems. In dynamic programming, memoization or tabulation can be used to solve each distinct subproblem once and store its result, which can then be reused whenever the subproblem needs to be recomputed.

To further solidify the identification of overlapping subproblems, consider the following steps:

1. **Recursive Definitions**: Examine the recursive formula or recurrence relation of the problem. Identify the recursive subproblems that are decomposed further.

2. **Call Stack Analysis**: Trace the recursive calls made by the function. Document each unique subproblem that is computed. If the same subproblem appears multiple times in the trace, there is an indication of overlapping subproblems.

3. **Graph Representation**: Represent the recursive calls as a directed graph where each node represents a subproblem and edges represent the recursive calls. If this graph exhibits cycles or multiple paths leading to the same node, the problem has overlapping subproblems.

Another commonly referred to problem in dynamic programming that showcases overlapping subproblems is the Longest Common Subsequence (LCS). The naive recursive approach is implemented as follows:

```
def lcs(X, Y, m, n):
    if m == 0 or n == 0:
        return 0
    elif X[m-1] == Y[n-1]:
        return 1 + lcs(X, Y, m-1, n-1)
    else:
        return max(lcs(X, Y, m, n-1), lcs(X, Y, m-1, n))
```

Let us visualize a situation where we want to find the LCS of two sequences $X = "ABCBDAB"$ and $Y = "BDCAB"$. The recursive calls made by 'lcs' would reveal a substantial degree of recomputation.

A similar call stack analysis and graph representation would show that subproblems like computing 'lcs("ABC", "BD")' and 'lcs("AB", "BD")' are redundant. This redundancy clearly indicates the presence of overlapping subproblems. Therefore, transforming this problem using dynamic programming, either via memoization or tabulation, would dramatically improve efficiency.

Recognizing the repetitive nature of recursive solutions and understanding their call patterns are critical steps in identifying overlapping subproblems. This recognition allows us to employ dynamic programming techniques to store and reuse intermediate results, greatly optimizing the computation.

## 9.7 Examples of Overlapping Subproblems

In dynamic programming, the concept of overlapping subproblems arises when a problem can be broken down into smaller subproblems, which are reused multiple times during the computation. Identifying these kinds of subproblems is crucial for optimizing algorithms, as it allows for the use of memoization or tabulation to store the results of these subproblems, thus avoiding redundant calculations. This section presents several classical examples that illustrate the principle of overlapping subproblems.

**Fibonacci Sequence**

One of the simplest and most illustrative examples of overlapping subproblems is the calculation of Fibonacci numbers. The Fibonacci sequence is defined by the recurrence relation $F(n) = F(n-1) + F(n-2)$ with the base cases $F(0) = 0$ and $F(1) = 1$. A naive recursive implementation without dynamic programming would lead to an exponential time complexity due to the redundancy in recalculating values of $F(n-1)$ and $F(n-2)$.

```
def fibonacci(n):
    if n <= 1:
        return n
    else:
        return fibonacci(n-1) + fibonacci(n-2)
```

Consider the call tree for $F(5)$:

```
        F(5)
       /   \
    F(4)    F(3)
    /  \    /  \
F(3) F(2) F(2) F(1)
/ \  / \  / \
F(2) F(1) F(1) F(0)
 / \
F(1) F(0)
```

In this tree, the subproblems $F(3)$ and $F(2)$ are computed multiple times. By storing the results of these subproblems after their first computation in a table (dynamic programming approach), we can reduce the time complexity to linear.

```
def fibonacci_dp(n):
    if n <= 1:
        return n
    fib = [0] * (n + 1)
    fib[1] = 1
    for i in range(2, n + 1):
        fib[i] = fib[i - 1] + fib[i - 2]
    return fib[n]
```

### Longest Common Subsequence (LCS)

The problem of finding the Longest Common Subsequence (LCS) between two strings also showcases overlapping subproblems. Given two sequences $X$ and $Y$, we aim to find the length of their longest subsequence present in both.

The recursive formulation of LCS is given by:

$$LCS(X[0..m-1], Y[0..n-1]) = \begin{cases} 0 & \text{if } m = 0 \text{ or } n = 0 \\ LCS(X[0..m-2], Y[0..n-2]) + 1 & \text{if } X[m-1] = Y[n-1] \\ \text{max}(LCS(X[0..m-1], Y[0..n-2]), & \\ LCS(X[0..m-2], Y[0..n-1])) & \text{if } X[m-1] \neq Y[n-1] \end{cases}$$

Here, each call to $LCS$ may solve the same subproblems multiple times, e.g., $LCS(X[0..i], Y[0..j])$ for various $i$ and $j$. By caching these results and using a bottom-up approach, we avoid recomputation.

```
def lcs(X, Y):
    m = len(X)
    n = len(Y)
    L = [[0] * (n + 1) for _ in range(m + 1)]
    for i in range(m + 1):
        for j in range(n + 1):
            if i == 0 or j == 0:
                L[i][j] = 0
            elif X[i - 1] == Y[j - 1]:
                L[i][j] = L[i - 1][j - 1] + 1
            else:
                L[i][j] = max(L[i - 1][j], L[i][j - 1])
    return L[m][n]
```

### 0/1 Knapsack Problem

The 0/1 Knapsack problem involves a set of items, each with a weight and a value, and a knapsack with a weight capacity. The objective is to determine the combination of items to include in the knapsack so that their total weight does not exceed the weight capacity, while their total value is maximized.

The recursive formulation for the 0/1 Knapsack problem is:

$$K(n, W) = \begin{cases} 0 & \text{if } n = 0 \text{ or } W = 0 \\ K(n-1, W) & \text{if } weight[n-1] > W \\ \max(value[n-1] + K(n-1, W - weight[n-1]), & \\ K(n-1, W)) & \text{if } weight[n-1] \leq W \end{cases}$$

This formulation results in calculating $K(\cdot, \cdot)$ for several subproblems repeatedly. Using dynamic programming, we store the solutions to these subproblems in a table.

```
def knapsack(weights, values, W):
    n = len(values)
    K = [[0] * (W + 1) for _ in range(n + 1)]
    for i in range(n + 1):
        for w in range(W + 1):
            if i == 0 or w == 0:
                K[i][w] = 0
            elif weights[i - 1] <= w:
                K[i][w] = max(values[i - 1] + K[i - 1][w - weights[i - 1]], K[i - 1][w])
            else:
                K[i][w] = K[i - 1][w]
    return K[n][W]
```

Overlapping subproblems are a central feature in dynamic programming that allow algorithms to save computation time by storing and reusing previous results. Each of the examples provided highlights how identifying and leveraging overlapping subproblems can transform exponential complexity into polynomial time solutions using dynamic programming techniques.

## 9.8 Combining Optimal Substructure and Overlapping Subproblems

Dynamic programming leverages the synergy of optimal substructure and overlapping subproblems to solve complex problems efficiently. By breaking a problem down into manageable subproblems, solving these subproblems just once, and storing their solutions, dynamic programming can significantly reduce computation time. This section will delve deeper into how these two fundamental principles interact to optimize problem-solving strategies, illustrated through practical examples.

To illustrate the combination of optimal substructure and overlapping subproblems, consider the classic problem of finding the Fibonacci sequence. The Fibonacci sequence is defined as follows:

$$F(n) = \begin{cases} 0 & \text{if } n = 0, \\ 1 & \text{if } n = 1, \\ F(n-1) + F(n-2) & \text{if } n > 1. \end{cases}$$

The problem has an optimal substructure because the problem $F(n)$ can be defined in terms of solutions to smaller subproblems $F(n-1)$ and $F(n-2)$. It also exhibits overlapping subproblems; computing $F(n-1)$ and $F(n-2)$ involves solving many common subproblems multiple times.

A naive recursive implementation in Python is simple but inefficient due to repeated calculations of the same values.

```
def fibonacci_recursive(n):
    if n == 0:
        return 0
    elif n == 1:
        return 1
    else:
        return fibonacci_recursive(n-1) + fibonacci_recursive(n-2)
```

Given the overlapping subproblems, this approach performs redundant calculations, resulting in an exponential time complexity of $O(2^n)$. By incorporating dynamic programming techniques, we can improve this significantly.

One approach to mitigate redundant calculations is memoization, which stores previously computed values. Here is a memoized version of the Fibonacci function:

```
def fibonacci_memo(n, memo={}):
    if n in memo:
        return memo[n]
    if n == 0:
        return 0
    elif n == 1:
        return 1
    else:
        memo[n] = fibonacci_memo(n-1, memo) + fibonacci_memo(n-2, memo)
        return memo[n]
```

In this version, the memo dictionary retains the results of already computed Fibonacci numbers, ensuring each subproblem is solved at most once. This reduces the time complexity to $O(n)$, which is a substantial improvement over the naive recursive approach.

Another common strategy is to use an iterative, bottom-up approach to build the solution from the base cases:

```
def fibonacci_iterative(n):
    if n == 0:
        return 0
    elif n == 1:
        return 1

    fib = [0, 1]
    for i in range(2, n + 1):
        fib.append(fib[i - 1] + fib[i - 2])

    return fib[n]
```

This approach constructs the Fibonacci sequence iteratively and stores intermediate results in a list, also achieving a time complexity of $O(n)$. This bottom-up method and memoization exemplify leveraging both optimal substructure and overlapping subproblems to solve the Fibonacci problem efficiently.

To further illustrate these principles, consider the knapsack problem. Given a set of items, each with a weight and a value, the goal is to determine the maximum value that can be obtained by selecting a subset of items such that the total weight does not exceed a given limit. The problem displays optimal substructure because the solution to the problem can be constructed from solutions to smaller subproblems. It also involves overlapping subproblems due to the repeated evaluation of the same subproblem with different item subsets.

The dynamic programming solution for the 0/1 knapsack problem involves defining a two-dimensional array, where $dp[i][w]$ represents the maximum value achievable with the first $i$ items and a total weight limit $w$. The solution can be derived using the following relation:

$$dp[i][w] = \begin{cases} dp[i-1][w] & \text{if } w_i > w, \\ \max(dp[i-1][w], dp[i-1][w-w_i] + v_i) & \text{otherwise.} \end{cases}$$

Here is an implementation in Python:

```
def knapsack(values, weights, W):
    n = len(values)
    dp = [[0 for _ in range(W + 1)] for _ in range(n + 1)]

    for i in range(1, n + 1):
        for w in range(1, W + 1):
```

```
            if weights[i-1] <= w:
                dp[i][w] = max(dp[i-1][w], dp[i-1][w - weights[i-1]] + values[i-1])
            else:
                dp[i][w] = dp[i-1][w]

    return dp[n][W]

values = [60, 100, 120]
weights = [10, 20, 30]
W = 50
print(knapsack(values, weights, W))
```

```
Output:
220
```

In this example, the dynamic programming approach recursively builds up the solution from smaller subproblems while caching results to avoid recomputations. This achieves a time complexity of $O(nW)$, where $n$ is the number of items, and $W$ is the weight limit.

Both the Fibonacci sequence and the 0/1 knapsack problem clearly demonstrate how combining the principles of optimal substructure and overlapping subproblems can lead to efficient, scalable solutions in dynamic programming. By understanding and applying these concepts, one can approach a wide variety of problems with structured and effective strategies.

## 9.9 Proving Optimal Substructure in DP Problems

To firmly grasp dynamic programming, it is essential to understand how to prove optimal substructure in problems. Optimal substructure is a key property that ensures the problem can be broken down into smaller subproblems, which can be solved independently and then combined to form the solution to the original problem. This section will guide you through the process of proving optimal substructure with rigor and detail, ensuring clarity in your understanding.

Consider a common dynamic programming problem, the *Longest Common Subsequence (LCS)*. The LCS problem involves finding the longest subsequence present in both given sequences. To demonstrate the optimal substructure property, we can break this problem down as follows.

Let $X$ and $Y$ be two sequences. Define $L(i, j)$ as the length of the LCS of the prefixes $X[1 : i]$ and $Y[1 : j]$. The goal is to show that $L(i, j)$ can be determined using solutions to smaller subproblems.

The recursive relation for $L(i, j)$ is given by:

$$L(i,j) = \begin{cases} 0 & \text{if } i = 0 \text{ or } j = 0 \\ L(i-1, j-1) + 1 & \text{if } X[i] = Y[j] \\ \max(L(i-1, j), L(i, j-1)) & \text{if } X[i] \neq Y[j] \end{cases}$$

This recurrence captures the essence of the optimal substructure. Here's the reasoning behind it:

1. **Base Case**: If either sequence length is zero ($i = 0$ or $j = 0$), the LCS length is zero. This forms our base case. 2. **Matching Case**: If $X[i] = Y[j]$, then the last characters are the same, and the LCS length can be extended by 1 from the LCS length of the preceding sequences ($X[1 : i-1]$ and $Y[1 : j-1]$). 3. **Non-Matching Case**: If $X[i] \neq Y[j]$, then the LCS length is the maximum of the two possible scenarios: - Ignoring the last character of $X$ and considering $X[1 : i-1]$ and $Y[1 : j]$. - Ignoring the last character of $Y$ and considering $X[1 : i]$ and $Y[1 : j-1]$.

Thus, this recurrence relation proves that the LCS problem exhibits optimal substructure since the solution to the main problem can be expressed in terms of solutions to its subproblems.

Let's take another example, the *Knapsack Problem*, which also showcases the principle of optimal substructure.

Given a set of items $\{1, 2, \ldots, n\}$, each with a weight $w_i$ and value $v_i$, and a knapsack with capacity $W$, the objective is to maximize the total value without exceeding the capacity. Define $V(i, W)$ as the maximum value achievable with the first $i$ items and capacity $W$.

The recursive relation can be formulated as follows:

$$V(i,W) = \begin{cases} 0 & \text{if } i = 0 \text{ or } W = 0 \\ V(i-1, W) & \text{if } w_i > W \\ \max(V(i-1, W), V(i-1, W - w_i) + v_i) & \text{if } w_i \leq W \end{cases}$$

To understand this relation:

1. **Base Case**: If no items are left ($i = 0$) or the capacity is zero ($W = 0$), the maximum value is zero. 2. **Weight Exceeds Capacity**: If the item's weight $w_i$ exceeds the current capacity $W$, the item can't be included, and the problem reduces to $V(i-1, W)$. 3. **Including the

Item**: If the item's weight is less than or equal to the current capacity, we have two options: - Exclude the item and use the value from the previous subproblem ($V(i-1, W)$). - Include the item, adding its value to the solution of the subproblem with reduced capacity ($V(i-1, W-w_i) + v_i$).

The optimal substructure is evident as the solution to $V(i, W)$ is derived from the solutions to smaller subproblems $V(i-1, W)$ and $V(i-1, W-w_i)$.

The above examples demonstrate key strategies utilized to prove optimal substructure:

- Establish the base cases that handle the simplest subproblems. - Formulate the recurrence relation for the main problem using the solutions to subproblems. - Analyze different scenarios (such as matching or non-matching cases) and determine how these impact the reduction to subproblems.

By following these steps, one can rigorously prove that a problem exhibits optimal substructure, thereby providing a foundation for effectively applying dynamic programming techniques. Understanding and proving optimal substructure ensures the problem's decomposability into well-defined subproblems whose combined solutions yield the optimal solution to the original problem.

## 9.10 Common Patterns in DP Problems

In many dynamic programming (DP) problems, distinct patterns recur, allowing us to craft solutions systematically. Recognizing these patterns can expedite the problem-solving process and enhance the efficiency of our algorithms. This section explores various common patterns found in DP problems, focusing on their characteristics and implementations in Python.

A well-known pattern in DP problems is the **Memoization**. Memoization involves storing the results of expensive function calls and reusing these results when the same inputs occur again. This technique drastically reduces the time complexity of recursive algorithms that have overlapping subproblems.

Consider the Fibonacci sequence as a straightforward example. The naive recursive computation of Fibonacci numbers has exponential time complexity because of repeated calculations. Memoization can address this inefficiency as follows:

```
def fibonacci(n, memo={}):
    if n <= 1:
        return n
    if n not in memo:
        memo[n] = fibonacci(n-1, memo) + fibonacci(n-2, memo)
    return memo[n]

# Example usage
print(fibonacci(10))
```

55

In this code snippet, a dictionary 'memo' caches the results of previously computed Fibonacci numbers, thereby avoiding redundant calculations.

Another prevalent pattern is the use of **Tabulation**. Tabulation, in contrast to memoization, involves iteratively filling out a table (usually an array) based on previously computed values. This bottom-up approach starts with the simplest cases and builds up to the solution of the given problem.

Let's revisit the Fibonacci sequence with tabulation:

```
def fibonacci_tab(n):
    if n <= 1:
        return n
    fib_table = [0] * (n+1)
    fib_table[1] = 1
    for i in range(2, n+1):
        fib_table[i] = fib_table[i-1] + fib_table[i-2]
    return fib_table[n]

# Example usage
print(fibonacci_tab(10))
```

55

Apart from memoization and tabulation, the **Decision-making** pattern is crucial. Decision-making involves choosing the most optimal action at each step within the constraints of the problem. An example where this pattern is highly evident is the "0/1 Knapsack Problem," where each item can either be included or excluded from the knapsack.

Here's a Python implementation employing a bottom-up tabulation strategy for the 0/1 Knapsack Problem:

```
def knapsack(weights, values, capacity):
    n = len(weights)
    dp = [[0 for _ in range(capacity + 1)] for _ in range(n + 1)]

    for i in range(1, n + 1):
        for w in range(1, capacity + 1):
```

```
            if weights[i - 1] <= w:
                dp[i][w] = max(dp[i - 1][w], dp[i - 1][w - weights[i - 1]] + values[i - 1])
            else:
                dp[i][w] = dp[i - 1][w]

    return dp[n][capacity]

# Example usage
weights = [1, 2, 3, 5]
values = [1, 6, 10, 16]
capacity = 7
print(knapsack(weights, values, capacity))
```

22

In the provided solution, the ‘dp‘ table keeps track of the maximum value achievable with the given capacity and items. The decision to include or exclude an item is made repetitively until the optimal solution is reached.

The pattern of **Subproblem Partitioning** is also quite common. Solutions to DP problems frequently hinge on breaking down the problem into independent subproblems whose solutions can be combined. Take the "Longest Common Subsequence (LCS)" problem, which aims to find the length of the longest subsequence present in both sequences.

Here's an LCS implementation using a tabular approach:

```
def lcs(X, Y):
    m = len(X)
    n = len(Y)
    L = [[0] * (n + 1) for _ in range(m + 1)]

    for i in range(1, m + 1):
        for j in range(1, n + 1):
            if X[i - 1] == Y[j - 1]:
                L[i][j] = L[i - 1][j - 1] + 1
            else:
                L[i][j] = max(L[i - 1][j], L[i][j - 1])

    return L[m][n]

# Example usage
X = "AGGTAB"
Y = "GXTXAYB"
print(lcs(X, Y))
```

4

The ‘L‘ table dynamically stores the lengths of LCSs for different subproblems, facilitating the final solution's construction.

Lastly, the pattern of **State Transition** provides a clear strategy for defining and moving between states. This is seen in problems like the "Edit Distance," which computes the minimum number of operations required to convert one string into another.

Here's a Python implementation of the edit distance problem using dynamic programming:

```
def edit_distance(str1, str2):
    m = len(str1)
    n = len(str2)
    dp = [[0] * (n + 1) for _ in range(m + 1)]

    for i in range(m + 1):
        for j in range(n + 1):
            if i == 0:
                dp[i][j] = j
            elif j == 0:
                dp[i][j] = i
            elif str1[i - 1] == str2[j - 1]:
                dp[i][j] = dp[i - 1][j - 1]
            else:
                dp[i][j] = 1 + min(dp[i - 1][j], # Remove
                                   dp[i][j - 1], # Insert
                                   dp[i - 1][j - 1])# Replace

    return dp[m][n]

# Example usage
str1 = "sunday"
str2 = "saturday"
print(edit_distance(str1, str2))
```

3

The 'dp' table is used to store results of subproblems, and its construction reflects the state transitions that transform the input strings step-by-step.

Comprehending these patterns and their implementations in real-world problems prepares us to tackle a wide array of DP challenges. By methodically breaking down problems, making optimal use of prior computations, and leveraging the inherent characteristics of dynamic programming, the efficiency and effectiveness of solutions can be greatly improved.

## 9.11 Real-World Applications of These Concepts

Dynamic programming (DP) is widely used across various domains due to its power in solving complex problems through optimal substructure and overlapping subproblems. To understand the breadth of DP's applicability, we will explore several real-world applications where these concepts are essential.

One notable application is in network routing protocols. In a modern computer network, data packets need to be sent from a source to a destination via multiple routes. The objective is to find the shortest path that minimizes the travel time or cost. This problem can be efficiently tackled using DP, specifically the Bellman-Ford algorithm. The optimal substructure here implies that the shortest path to a node $v$ from the source $s$ can be computed using the shortest path to an intermediate node $u$ plus the edge weight from $u$ to $v$. The overlapping subproblems component comes into play when recalculating the shortest paths at each step, where previously computed shortest paths are reused.

```
def bellman_ford(graph, start):
    distance = {node: float('inf') for node in graph}
    distance[start] = 0

    for _ in range(len(graph) - 1):
        for u in graph:
            for v, weight in graph[u]:
                if distance[u] + weight < distance[v]:
                    distance[v] = distance[u] + weight
    return distance
```

In the finance sector, portfolio optimization problems are designed to maximize returns or minimize risks of an investment portfolio given certain constraints. These problems, like the Markowitz mean-variance optimization, rely on DP principles. The underlying optimal substructure involves breaking down the portfolio choices into stages, each specifying an investment decision, while overlapping subproblems emerge when intermediate optimization results can be reused.

Operations research also leverages DP extensively, particularly in resource allocation, project scheduling, and logistics. The classic example is the knapsack problem, where the objective is to maximize the total value of items packed into a knapsack without exceeding its capacity. This problem is solvable using a DP approach, capitalizing on the fact that the optimal solution to the knapsack problem can be constructed from optimal solutions of its subproblems.

```
def knapsack(weights, values, capacity):
    n = len(values)
    dp = [[0 for _ in range(capacity + 1)] for _ in range(n + 1)]

    for i in range(1, n + 1):
        for w in range(1, capacity + 1):
            if weights[i-1] <= w:
                dp[i][w] = max(dp[i-1][w], dp[i-1][w-weights[i-1]] + values[i-1])
            else:
                dp[i][w] = dp[i-1][w]
    return dp[n][capacity]
```

In the field of bioinformatics, sequence alignment problems for DNA, RNA, or protein sequences are foundational for understanding evolutionary relationships and functional similarities. Algorithms like Needleman-Wunsch and Smith-Waterman employ DP to optimize the alignment score by using previously computed alignment results (overlapping subproblems) and building the final solution from optimal sub-alignments (optimal substructure).

```
def needleman_wunsch(seq1, seq2, match, mismatch, gap):
    n, m = len(seq1), len(seq2)
    dp = [[0 for _ in range(m + 1)] for _ in range(n + 1)]

    for i in range(1, n + 1):
        dp[i][0] = i * gap
    for j in range(1, m + 1):
        dp[0][j] = j * gap

    for i in range(1, n + 1):
        for j in range(1, m + 1):
            match_score = dp[i-1][j-1] + (match if seq1[i-1] == seq2[j-1] else mismatch)
            delete = dp[i-1][j] + gap
            insert = dp[i][j-1] + gap
            dp[i][j] = max(match_score, delete, insert)

    return dp[n][m]
```

Another important application of DP is in natural language processing (NLP), where tasks like machine translation, speech recognition, and text generation depend heavily on sequence models. The Viterbi algorithm, a DP-based technique, is used for decoding the most probable sequence of hidden states in hidden Markov models (HMMs), which are widely used in these contexts.

```
def viterbi(obs, states, start_p, trans_p, emit_p):
    V = [{}]
    path = {}

    for y in states:
        V[0][y] = start_p[y] * emit_p[y][obs[0]]
        path[y] = [y]

    for t in range(1, len(obs)):
        V.append({})
        newpath = {}

        for y in states:
            (prob, state) = max((V[t-1][y0] * trans_p[y0][y] * emit_p[y][obs[t]], y0) for
                y0 in states)
            V[t][y] = prob
            newpath[y] = path[state] + [y]

        path = newpath

    n = 0
    if len(obs)!=1:
        n = t
```

```
    (prob, state) = max((V[n][y], y) for y in states)
    return (prob, path[state])
```

These examples underscore the versatility and necessity of dynamic programming in solving practical and theoretical problems effectively. By leveraging the principles of optimal substructure and overlapping subproblems, dynamic programming provides streamlined solutions, significantly reducing computational time and resources across various domains.

## 9.12 Exercises and Practice Problems

This section consists of various exercises and practice problems designed to reinforce the understanding of optimal substructure and overlapping subproblems. These problems encourage applying concepts learned in this chapter and help solidify the reader's grasp on dynamic programming techniques. For each problem, the reader is expected to define the optimal substructure and identify overlapping subproblems before implementing a solution.

- **Problem 1: Fibonacci Sequence**
  Write a function to calculate the $n$-th Fibonacci number using dynamic programming.

```
def fibonacci(n):
    if n <= 0:
        return 0
    elif n == 1:
        return 1
    fib = [0] * (n + 1)
    fib[1] = 1
    for i in range(2, n + 1):
        fib[i] = fib[i-1] + fib[i-2]
    return fib[n]
```

```
>>> fibonacci(10)
55
```

- **Problem 2: Longest Common Subsequence**
  Given two sequences $X$ and $Y$, write a function to find the length of the longest common subsequence (LCS) using dynamic programming.

```
def lcs(X, Y):
    m = len(X)
    n = len(Y)
    L = [[0] * (n + 1) for _ in range(m + 1)]
```

```
    for i in range(m + 1):
        for j in range(n + 1):
            if i == 0 or j == 0:
                L[i][j] = 0
            elif X[i-1] == Y[j-1]:
                L[i][j] = L[i-1][j-1] + 1
            else:
                L[i][j] = max(L[i-1][j], L[i][j-1])

    return L[m][n]
```

```
>>> lcs("ABCBDAB", "BDCAB")
4
```

- **Problem 3: Coin Change Problem**
  Given a list of denominations and a target amount, write a function to find the minimum number of coins needed to make the target amount using dynamic programming.

```
def coin_change(coins, amount):
    dp = [float('inf')] * (amount + 1)
    dp[0] = 0

    for coin in coins:
        for x in range(coin, amount + 1):
            dp[x] = min(dp[x], dp[x - coin] + 1)

    return dp[amount] if dp[amount] != float('inf') else -1
```

```
>>> coin_change([1, 2, 5], 11)
3
```

- **Problem 4: Edit Distance**
  Write a function to calculate the minimum edit distance between two strings using dynamic programming. Edit distance measures how many insertions, deletions, or substitutions are required to transform one string into another.

```
def edit_distance(str1, str2):
    m = len(str1)
    n = len(str2)
    dp = [[0] * (n + 1) for _ in range(m + 1)]

    for i in range(m + 1):
        for j in range(n + 1):
            if i == 0:
                dp[i][j] = j
            elif j == 0:
                dp[i][j] = i
            elif str1[i-1] == str2[j-1]:
                dp[i][j] = dp[i-1][j-1]
            else:
                dp[i][j] = 1 + min(dp[i][j-1], dp[i-1][j], dp[i-1][j-1])

    return dp[m][n]
```

```
>>> edit_distance("kitten", "sitting")
3
```

- **Problem 5: 0/1 Knapsack Problem**
  Given weights and values of $n$ items, put these items in a knapsack of capacity $W$ to get the maximum total value in the knapsack.

```
def knapsack(W, wt, val, n):
    K = [[0 for x in range(W + 1)] for x in range(n + 1)]

    for i in range(n + 1):
        for w in range(W + 1):
            if i == 0 or w == 0:
                K[i][w] = 0
            elif wt[i-1] <= w:
                K[i][w] = max(val[i-1] + K[i-1][w-wt[i-1]], K[i-1][w])
            else:
                K[i][w] = K[i-1][w]

    return K[n][W]
```

```
>>> val = [60, 100, 120]
>>> wt = [10, 20, 30]
>>> W = 50
>>> n = len(val)
>>> knapsack(W, wt, val, n)
220
```

- **Problem 6: Matrix Chain Multiplication**
  Given a sequence of matrices, write a function to determine the most efficient way to multiply these matrices together. The problem is not actually to perform the multiplications, but merely to decide in which order to perform the multiplications.

```
def matrix_chain_order(p):
    n = len(p) - 1
    m = [[0] * (n + 1) for _ in range(n + 1)]

    for l in range(2, n + 1):
        for i in range(1, n - l + 2):
            j = i + l - 1
            m[i][j] = float('inf')
            for k in range(i, j):
                q = m[i][k] + m[k + 1][j] + p[i - 1] * p[k] * p[j]
                if q < m[i][j]:
                    m[i][j] = q

    return m[1][n]
```

```
>>> p = [1, 2, 3, 4]
>>> matrix_chain_order(p)
18
```

These exercises provide a range of problems that utilize optimal substructure and overlapping subproblems, forming a comprehensive practice ground for mastering dynamic programming in Python. Exercise completion involves implementing efficient solutions and validating them with test cases, ensuring a thorough understanding of dynamic programming principles.

# Chapter 10

# Advanced Topics in Dynamic Programming

**This chapter delves into advanced topics in dynamic programming, including multi-dimensional DP problems, DP on graphs, and bitmask DP. It covers specialized applications such as string matching, probability-based DP, and game theory. The chapter also explores approximation algorithms, parallel computation in DP, and the use of DP in machine learning. By examining the latest research and complex case studies, readers will gain a deep and comprehensive understanding of cutting-edge dynamic programming techniques and their real-world applications.**

## 10.1 Introduction to Advanced Topics in Dynamic Programming

Dynamic programming (DP) is a powerful algorithmic paradigm used for solving complex problems by breaking them down into simpler subproblems. The fundamental principle of dynamic programming involves the use of overlapping subproblems and optimal substructure properties to efficiently solve problems that might otherwise be computationally intensive. Traditional dynamic programming techniques usually involve problems that can be formulated in one or two dimensions; however, as the complexity and variety of problems have increased, more advanced topics have been developed to extend the capabilities of DP.

In this section, we will introduce the core ideas that will be built upon in subsequent sections, setting the stage for a more thorough exploration of advanced dynamic programming concepts. This involves understanding the limitations of classical DP approaches and how advancements allow for a more extensive application range.

At the heart of dynamic programming lies the concept of memoization, implementing a cache to store previously computed results, and iterative tabulation, which systematically fills up a DP table based on a recurrence relation.

## Multi-Dimensional DP

Classical DP problems often deal with one-dimensional or two-dimensional tables. Multi-dimensional DP, as the name suggests, extends the concept to higher dimensions, making it effective for complex problems that involve multiple variables or states. For instance, consider the following three-dimensional DP problem:

```
def multi_dimensional_dp(x, y, z):
    dp = [[[0 for _ in range(z + 1)] for _ in range(y + 1)] for _ in range(x + 1)]
    for i in range(1, x + 1):
        for j in range(1, y + 1):
            for k in range(1, z + 1):
                dp[i][j][k] = some_function(dp[i-1][j][k], dp[i][j-1][k], dp[i][j][k-1])
    return dp[x][y][z]
```

In the code above, some_function is a placeholder for the actual recurrence relation applied to solve a specific problem. This paradigm opens up solutions for more intricate problems like those found in computational biology or high-dimensional data analysis.

## DP on Graphs

Dynamic programming on graphs is another advanced topic where DP techniques are applied to vertex and edge-based structures. Problems such as finding the shortest path, longest path, or the number of ways to traverse a graph can be elegantly solved using DP principles. Consider the classic problem of finding the shortest path in a weighted directed acyclic graph (DAG):

```
def shortest_path_dag(graph, start):
    distance = {node: float('inf') for node in graph}
    distance[start] = 0
```

```
    topological_order = topological_sort(graph)
    for node in topological_order:
        for neighbor, weight in graph[node]:
            if distance[neighbor] > distance[node] + weight:
                distance[neighbor] = distance[node] + weight

    return distance
```

Topological sorting ensures that each node is processed before its descendants, preserving dependencies critical for correct DP application.

## Bitmask DP

Bitmask DP is a specialized form of dynamic programming especially useful in combinatorial problems involving subsets. A typical bitmask DP problem might involve operations on the subset of elements represented through binary states. For instance, the Travelling Salesman Problem (TSP) can be addressed using bitmask DP:

```
def travelling_salesman(cost_matrix):
    n = len(cost_matrix)
    dp = [[float('inf')] * n for _ in range(1 << n)]
    dp[1][0] = 0 # Starting point

    for mask in range(1 << n):
        for u in range(n):
            if mask & (1 << u):
                for v in range(n):
                    if mask & (1 << v) == 0:
                        dp[mask | (1 << v)][v] = min(
                            dp[mask | (1 << v)][v],
                            dp[mask][u] + cost_matrix[u][v]
                        )

    return min(dp[(1 << n) - 1][i] + cost_matrix[i][0] for i in range(1, n))
```

The bitmask $\mathrm{mask}$ represents the set of visited cities, and the recurrence relation is used to minimize the route cost.

## String Matching and DP

String matching problems are another domain where dynamic programming excels. Problems such as finding the longest common subsequence (LCS) or the shortest common supersequence (SCS) can be directly tackled using DP. Here is an example of finding the LCS:

```
def longest_common_subsequence(s1, s2):
    m, n = len(s1), len(s2)
    dp = [[0] * (n + 1) for _ in range(m + 1)]
```

```
for i in range(1, m + 1):
    for j in range(1, n + 1):
        if s1[i - 1] == s2[j - 1]:
            dp[i][j] = dp[i - 1][j - 1] + 1
        else:
            dp[i][j] = max(dp[i - 1][j], dp[i][j - 1])

return dp[m][n]
```

The DP table dp[i][j] stores the length of the LCS of the substrings $s1[0 \dots i-1]$ and $s2[0 \dots j-1]$, allowing for the efficient computation of the final result.

In subsequent sections, these concepts will be explored in deeper contexts and expanded to include even more sophisticated algorithms and applications. Each advanced topic, from multi-dimensional DP to its applications in machine learning, builds upon the foundational principles laid out here, providing a comprehensive understanding suited for tackling complex computational challenges.

## 10.2 Multi-Dimensional DP Problems

Multi-dimensional dynamic programming (DP) extends the principles of one-dimensional DP into higher dimensions, adding layers of complexity and enabling the solution of more intricate problems. This method is particularly useful when addressing problems involving multiple interrelated states or parameters, where each state depends on multiple preceding states.

Consider a three-dimensional dynamic programming array $dp[i][j][k]$. Each dimension represents a distinct parameter in the problem. The value at $dp[i][j][k]$ is computed based on prior states, denoted by $dp[i'][j'][k']$. The recursive relation for a generic multi-dimensional DP can be described as:

$$dp[i][j][k] = \text{function}(dp[i'][j'][k'], \text{parameters})$$

### Example: 3D Knapsack Problem

### Problem Statement: Given $n$ items, each with a weight $w_i$, a volume $v_i$, and a value $u_i$, determine the maximum value that can be achieved without exceeding a total weight $W$ and total volume $V$.

### Solution:

Define $dp[i][w][v]$ as the maximum value attainable with the first $i$ items considering a weight limit $w$ and a volume limit $v$. The recursive relation can be established as follows:

$$dp[i][w][v] = \begin{cases} 0 & \text{if } i = 0 \\ dp[i-1][w][v] & \text{if } w_i > w \text{ or } v_i > v \\ \max(dp[i-1][w][v], dp[i-1][w-w_i][v-v_i] + u_i) & \text{otherwise} \end{cases}$$

We initialize $dp[0][w][v] = 0$ for all $0 \leq w \leq W$ and $0 \leq v \leq V$.

Here is an implementation of the 3D Knapsack problem using Python:

```
def three_dimensional_knapsack(n, W, V, weights, volumes, values):
    dp = [[[0 for _ in range(V + 1)] for _ in range(W + 1)] for _ in range(n + 1)]

    for i in range(1, n + 1):
        for w in range(W + 1):
            for v in range(V + 1):
                dp[i][w][v] = dp[i - 1][w][v]
                if weights[i - 1] <= w and volumes[i - 1] <= v:
                    dp[i][w][v] = max(dp[i][w][v], dp[i - 1][w - weights[i - 1]][v - volumes[i -
                        1]] + values[i - 1])

    return dp[n][W][V]

# Inputs
n = 3
W = 50
V = 100
weights = [10, 20, 30]
volumes = [30, 50, 40]
values = [60, 100, 120]

# Function call
max_value = three_dimensional_knapsack(n, W, V, weights, volumes, values)
print("Maximum Value:", max_value)
```

The output of the program will be:

```
Maximum Value: 220
```

### Complexity Considerations

The time complexity of the three-dimensional knapsack problem is $O(nWV)$, where $n$ is the number of items, $W$ is the maximum weight, and $V$ is the maximum volume. The space complexity is also $O(nWV)$, reflecting the storage required for the 3D DP table.

### General Approach to Multi-Dimensional DP

The general approach to solving multi-dimensional DP problems involves:

1. **State Definition**: Clearly define each state in the DP table. Each state should represent a cumulative decision or a subset of parameters that define the problem accurately.

2. **Transition Relation**: Determine the recursive relation that links the current state to its preceding states. This involves combining results from smaller subproblems to construct the solution to the larger problem.

3. **Initialization**: Provide base cases for the DP table. These are generally the simplest cases where the solution is known directly, such as $dp[0][x][y] = 0$ for the knapsack problem.

4. **Iterative Computation**: Use nested loops to fill in the DP table based on the recursive relation. Ensure that the computation respects the defined order of states and dependencies.

### Applications

Multi-dimensional DP problems are encountered in various fields, including:

- **Resource Allocation**: Allocating multiple resources or capacities simultaneously. - **Scheduling**: Problems where tasks need to be scheduled considering multiple constraints like time and resources. - **Games and Puzzles**: Solving complex game scenarios with multiple state variables. - **Biological Computations**: Problems like protein folding, where multiple factors influence the outcome.

The flexibility and robustness of multi-dimensional DP make it a powerful tool for tackling a wide range of complex problems beyond the capabilities of simpler one-dimensional approaches.

## 10.3 DP on Graphs

Dynamic programming on graphs is a powerful technique used to solve a variety of problems, ranging from shortest paths to more complex queries like the longest path in a directed acyclic graph (DAG). Applying dynamic programming (DP) to graphs requires leveraging the inherent structure of graphs—nodes connected by edges—to build solutions incrementally.

Consider the classic problem of finding the shortest path from a source node $s$ to a target node $t$. When the graph has no negative weight cycles, Dijkstra's algorithm can be used efficiently. However, in some cases, especially with specific constraints or requirements, dynamic programming offers an alternative and sometimes more intuitive solution.

To understand DP on graphs, we will begin with basic concepts and gradually progress to more complex use cases, such as DP on trees and general directed graphs (DAG).

**Shortest Path in a Directed Acyclic Graph (DAG)**

In a directed acyclic graph, a common problem is to find the shortest path from a source node $s$ to all other nodes. Here, the crucial observation is that a DAG can be topologically sorted—a linear ordering of its nodes such that for every directed edge $u \to v$, node $u$ comes before $v$. Once we have the topological order, the shortest path problem can be solved using dynamic programming.

The following code demonstrates how to compute the shortest paths in a DAG using a DP approach:

```
def shortest_path_dag(graph, source):
    # Topologically sort the graph
    topological_order = topological_sort(graph)

    # Initialize the distance to all nodes as infinity
    distance = {node: float('inf') for node in graph}
    distance[source] = 0

    # Process nodes in topological order
    for node in topological_order:
        for neighbor, weight in graph[node]:
            if distance[node] + weight < distance[neighbor]:
                distance[neighbor] = distance[node] + weight

    return distance

def topological_sort(graph):
    # Helper function to perform topological sort
    visited = {node: False for node in graph}
    stack = []

    def dfs(node):
        visited[node] = True
        for neighbor, _ in graph[node]:
            if not visited[neighbor]:
                dfs(neighbor)
        stack.append(node)

    for node in graph:
        if not visited[node]:
            dfs(node)

    return stack[::-1]
```

Given the topological ordering, this algorithm computes shortest paths from the source to all other nodes in $O(V + E)$ time, where $V$ is the number of vertices and $E$ is the number of edges.

**Longest Path in a Directed Acyclic Graph (DAG)**

The problem of finding the longest path in a DAG is another application where DP on graphs excels. This is particularly useful in scheduling problems where tasks need to follow a certain order.

The approach is similar to the shortest path problem but with a key difference: instead of minimizing, we maximize the distance. Here's how we can implement it:

```
def longest_path_dag(graph, source):
    # Topologically sort the graph
    topological_order = topological_sort(graph)

    # Initialize the distance to all nodes as negative infinity
    distance = {node: float('-inf') for node in graph}
    distance[source] = 0

    # Process nodes in topological order
    for node in topological_order:
        for neighbor, weight in graph[node]:
            if distance[node] + weight > distance[neighbor]:
                distance[neighbor] = distance[node] + weight

    return distance
```

This algorithm effectively finds the longest path by iterating through the graph in topological order and updating the maximum distances.

**DP on Trees**

A tree is a connected, undirected graph with no cycles. Dynamic programming on trees is often used for problems like finding the diameter of a tree, computing the maximum independent set, or finding the longest path between any two nodes.

Consider the problem of finding the longest path, also known as the diameter of the tree. The diameter can be found using dynamic programming by leveraging depth-first search (DFS) to calculate the longest path from each node.

Here is a code implementation to find the diameter of a tree:

```
def tree_diameter(tree):
    def dfs(node, parent):
        max1, max2 = 0, 0
        for neighbor in tree[node]:
            if neighbor == parent:
                continue
            length = 1 + dfs(neighbor, node)
            if length > max1:
                max1, max2 = length, max1
            elif length > max2:
                max2 = length
        nonlocal diameter
        diameter = max(diameter, max1 + max2)
        return max1
```

```
    diameter = 0
    dfs(0, -1) # Assuming node 0 is the root
    return diameter
```

In this approach, the DFS function calculates the maximum and second maximum path lengths from each node, updating the diameter at each step.

**DP on General Directed Graphs (without cycles)**

For large, complex graphs with cycles, directly applying dynamic programming is not straightforward due to potential infinite loops. However, for specialized graph structures such as trees, forests, and DAGs, dynamic programming offers elegant solutions to various problems.

## 10.4 Bitmask DP

Bitmask Dynamic Programming (Bitmask DP) is a highly efficient technique used to solve combinatorial optimization problems where the number of subsets or combinations is significant but still manageable within a reasonable computational limit. Bitmasking leverages the binary representation of integers to compactly and efficiently manipulate subsets of a given set. This method is particularly effective for problems involving up to 20-25 elements, where the total number of subsets $2^n$ is still computationally feasible to handle.

Consider a set of $n$ elements. Each subset of this set can be represented as an $n$-bit binary number, where the $i$-th bit is set to 1 if the $i$-th element is included in the subset, and 0 otherwise. This succinct bit representation allows for efficient subset operations using bitwise operators, which are significantly faster than traditional iterative methods.

A typical use case of Bitmask DP is the Travelling Salesman Problem (TSP), where the objective is to find the shortest possible route that visits each city exactly once and returns to the origin city. The bitmask helps in keeping track of which cities have been visited at any point in time.

```
# Implementation of Bitmask DP for the TSP
import sys

# Number of cities
n = 4

# Define a large number as infinity
INF = float('inf')
```

```
# Distance matrix
dist = [
    [0, 10, 15, 20],
    [10, 0, 35, 25],
    [15, 35, 0, 30],
    [20, 25, 30, 0]
]

# DP table: dp[mask][i] represents the minimum cost to visit all the cities in "mask"
# ending at city "i"
dp = [[INF] * n for _ in range(1 << n)]
# Base case: starting at the first city and visiting no other cities
dp[1][0] = 0

# Iterating through all subsets of cities
for mask in range(1 << n):
    for u in range(n):
        if mask & (1 << u): # If city u is in the set represented by mask
            for v in range(n):
                if not mask & (1 << v): # If city v is not in the set represented by mask
                    new_mask = mask | (1 << v)
                    dp[new_mask][v] = min(dp[new_mask][v], dp[mask][u] + dist[u][v])

# Find the minimum cost to visit all cities and return to the starting point
ans = min(dp[(1 << n) - 1][i] + dist[i][0] for i in range(1, n))

print(ans)
```

Output:
80

In this code, the ‘dp‘ table is indexed by subsets represented as bitmasks (‘1 « n‘ subsets in total) and cities (‘n‘ in total). The double loop structure iterates over each subset (‘mask‘) and each city (‘u‘) to update the ‘dp‘ table with the optimal costs. The innermost loop checks potential extensions of the current subset by adding a new city (‘v‘), ensuring that all possible paths are evaluated. The final solution is derived by considering all possible end cities, returning to the starting city.

Another prominent application of Bitmask DP is solving the problem of finding the Minimum Hamiltonian Path in an undirected graph, where each node must be visited exactly once without returning to the starting node.

```
# Implementation of Bitmask DP for the Minimum Hamiltonian Path
import sys

# Number of nodes
n = 4

# Define a large number as infinity
INF = float('inf')

# Distance matrix
dist = [
    [0, 10, 15, 20],
    [10, 0, 35, 25],
```

```
    [15, 35, 0, 30],
    [20, 25, 30, 0]
]

# DP table: dp[mask][i] represents the minimum cost to visit all the nodes in "mask"
# ending at node "i"
dp = [[INF] * n for _ in range(1 << n)]

# Base cases: starting at each node and visiting only that node
for i in range(n):
    dp[1 << i][i] = 0

# Iterating through all subsets of nodes
for mask in range(1 << n):
    for u in range(n):
        if mask & (1 << u): # If node u is in the set represented by mask
            for v in range(n):
                if not mask & (1 << v): # If node v is not in the set represented by
                    mask
                    new_mask = mask | (1 << v)
                    dp[new_mask][v] = min(dp[new_mask][v], dp[mask][u] + dist[u][v])

# Find the minimum cost to visit all nodes
ans = min(dp[(1 << n) - 1][i] for i in range(n))

print(ans)
```

Output:
75

This example shares similar characteristics with the TSP solution but without the requirement to return to the starting node, prompting minor modifications in the logic. The base cases consider starting from each individual node, and the ‘ans‘ computation involves evaluating the minimum over the last row of the DP table.

Bitmask DP can also be adapted for more complex scenarios, such as those involving additional constraints like specific subset inclusions/exclusions or dynamic weights. Advanced problems can use similar methodology with domain-specific adjustments.

Overall, Bitmask DP affirms its utility by optimizing combinatorial enumeration problems through compact and efficient representation, thus playing a crucial role in dynamic programming's advanced applications. The reliance on bitwise operations provides a significant computational advantage, making it an invaluable tool in the context of algorithm design and optimization.

## 10.5 String Matching and DP

String matching is a classical problem in computer science that involves finding occurrences of a substring within a main string. Dynamic programming (DP) provides efficient solutions to several string matching problems, such as finding the longest common subsequence (LCS), edit distance (Levenshtein distance), and the longest palindromic subsequence. This section explores these applications, detailing their formulations and implementations.

The **Longest Common Subsequence (LCS)** problem seeks to find the longest subsequence present in both sequences in the same order, but not necessarily consecutively. Consider two sequences $X$ of length $m$ and $Y$ of length $n$. The LCS can be determined using a DP table where $dp[i][j]$ represents the LCS length of the prefixes $X[0 \ldots i-1]$ and $Y[0 \ldots j-1]$. The recurrence relation for this DP table is:

$$dp[i][j] = \begin{cases} 0 & \text{if } i = 0 \text{ or } j = 0 \\ dp[i-1][j-1] + 1 & \text{if } X[i-1] = Y[j-1] \\ \max(dp[i-1][j], dp[i][j-1]) & \text{otherwise} \end{cases}$$

Below is the Python implementation of the LCS problem using dynamic programming:

```
def lcs(X, Y):
    m = len(X)
    n = len(Y)
    dp = [[0] * (n+1) for _ in range(m+1)]

    for i in range(1, m + 1):
        for j in range(1, n + 1):
            if X[i-1] == Y[j-1]:
                dp[i][j] = dp[i-1][j-1] + 1
            else:
                dp[i][j] = max(dp[i-1][j], dp[i][j-1])

    return dp[m][n]

X = "AGGTAB"
Y = "GXTXAYB"
print("Length of LCS is", lcs(X, Y))
```

The output of the above program will be:

```
Length of LCS is 4
```

The **Edit Distance** (or Levenshtein Distance) is another fundamental problem that calculates the minimum number of operations required to transform one string into another, where the operations can be insertion, deletion, or substitution of a character. Let $X$ and $Y$ be strings of lengths $m$ and $n$ respectively. The DP formulation uses a table $dp$ where $dp[i][j]$ represents the minimal edit distance between $X[0 \dots i-1]$ and $Y[0 \dots j-1]$. The recurrence relation is:

$$dp[i][j] = \begin{cases} i & \text{if } j = 0 \\ j & \text{if } i = 0 \\ dp[i-1][j-1] & \text{if } X[i-1] = Y[j-1] \\ 1 + \min(dp[i-1][j], dp[i][j-1], & \\ dp[i-1][j-1]) & \text{otherwise} \end{cases}$$

The following is a Python implementation for computing the edit distance:

```
def edit_distance(X, Y):
    m = len(X)
    n = len(Y)
    dp = [[0] * (n + 1) for _ in range(m + 1)]

    for i in range(m + 1):
        for j in range(n + 1):
            if i == 0:
                dp[i][j] = j
            elif j == 0:
                dp[i][j] = i
            elif X[i-1] == Y[j-1]:
                dp[i][j] = dp[i-1][j-1]
            else:
                dp[i][j] = 1 + min(dp[i-1][j], dp[i][j-1], dp[i-1][j-1])

    return dp[m][n]

X = "kitten"
Y = "sitting"
print("The Edit Distance is", edit_distance(X, Y))
```

The output of the above program will be:

```
The Edit Distance is 3
```

We also address the **Longest Palindromic Subsequence (LPS)** problem, which is about finding the longest subsequence of a string that reads the same forwards and backwards. The DP solution involves a table $dp$ such that $dp[i][j]$ is the length of the longest palindromic subsequence of the substring $X[i \dots j]$. The recurrence relation is:

$$dp[i][j] = \begin{cases} 1 & \text{if } i = j \\ 2 & \text{if } i+1 = j \text{ and } X[i] = X[j] \\ \text{max}(dp[i+1][j], dp[i][j-1]) & \text{if } X[i] \neq X[j] \\ dp[i+1][j-1] + 2 & \text{if } X[i] = X[j] \end{cases}$$

Here is the Python implementation for the LPS problem:

```
def lps(X):
    n = len(X)
    dp = [[0] * n for _ in range(n)]

    for i in range(n):
        dp[i][i] = 1

    for cl in range(2, n + 1):
        for i in range(n-cl+1):
            j = i + cl - 1
            if X[i] == X[j] and cl == 2:
                dp[i][j] = 2
            elif X[i] == X[j]:
                dp[i][j] = dp[i+1][j-1] + 2
            else:
                dp[i][j] = max(dp[i][j-1], dp[i+1][j])

    return dp[0][n-1]

X = "BBABCBCAB"
print("Length of LPS is", lps(X))
```

The output is as follows:

```
Length of LPS is 7
```

These examples illustrate the power of dynamic programming in solving complex string matching problems effectively. By breaking down problems into simpler, overlapping subproblems, dynamic programming ensures that computations are not duplicated, thereby optimizing runtime and making otherwise intractable problems manageable.

## 10.6 DP with Probability

Dynamic Programming (DP) is a versatile tool not only for deterministic problems but also for probabilistic scenarios wherein decisions and outcomes have associated probabilities. This section delves into the integration of probability theory within the dynamic programming framework, elucidating its application in various contexts.

To elucidate DP with probability, let us consider scenarios where decisions lead to uncertain outcomes. A quintessential problem in this domain is the Stochastic Shortest Path problem (SSP), where each path has an associated probability distribution of travel times. Our objective is often to minimize the expected travel time from a source node to a destination node.

The fundamental principles of DP are extended to handle probabilities by maintaining a state-value function that captures the expected cost from any state to the target state. Formally, consider a state space $S$ and a set of actions $A$. The transition from state $s \in S$ by taking action $a \in A$ leads to state $s' \in S$ with probability $P(s'|s,a)$ and incurs a cost $c(s,a,s')$. The goal is to find a policy $\pi$ that minimizes the expected total cost.

### Bellman Equation with Probabilities

The extension of the Bellman equation to accommodate stochastic dynamics is given by:

$$V(s) = \min_{a \in A} \sum_{s'} P(s'|s,a) \left[ c(s,a,s') + V(s') \right]$$

Where $V(s)$ is the value function representing the minimum expected cost starting from state $s$.

### Example: Stochastic Knapsack Problem

In the stochastic version of the classical Knapsack Problem, let us assume that each item $i$ has a probabilistic weight $W_i$ and a deterministic value $V_i$. The weight $W_i$ follows a known probability distribution. The challenge is to maximize the expected total value while keeping the total weight within the capacity $C$ of the knapsack.

### DP Formulation

We define the state by the current index of the item being considered and the remaining capacity of the knapsack. Let $V(i,w)$ denote the maximum expected value obtainable with the first $i$ items and total weight $w$. The recursive relation can be formulated as follows:

$$V(i,w) = \max \left\{ V(i-1,w), \mathbb{E}[V(i-1,w-W_i)] + V_i \right\}$$

Where $\mathbb{E}[V(i-1,w-W_i)]$ denotes the expected value considering the weight $W_i$.

### Algorithm Implementation

Consider the following Python code implementing the stochastic knapsack problem:

```
def stochastic_knapsack(values, weights_prob, capacity):
    n = len(values)
    dp = [[0] * (capacity + 1) for _ in range(n + 1)]

    def expected_value(i, wt):
        return sum(p * dp[i][int(wt - w)] for w, p in weights_prob[i])

    for i in range(1, n + 1):
        for w in range(capacity + 1):
            dp[i][w] = dp[i-1][w] # Do not take item i
            if w >= min(weight for weight, prob in weights_prob[i-1]):
                dp[i][w] = max(dp[i][w],
                               values[i-1] + expected_value(i-1, w))

    return dp[n][capacity]

# Example usage:
values = [60, 100, 120]
weights_prob = [
    [(10, 0.5), (20, 0.5)], # Probabilistic weights for item 1
    [(20, 0.6), (30, 0.4)], # Probabilistic weights for item 2
    [(30, 0.8), (40, 0.2)], # Probabilistic weights for item 3
]
capacity = 50
print(stochastic_knapsack(values, weights_prob, capacity))
```

### Markov Decision Processes (MDPs)

Markov Decision Processes (MDPs) offer another compelling framework for modeling decision-making under uncertainty. An MDP is characterized by a tuple $(S, A, P, R, \gamma)$, where:

- $S$ is the set of states.
- $A$ is the set of actions.
- $P(s'|s, a)$ is the probability of transitioning from state $s$ to $s'$ due to action $a$.
- $R(s, a)$ is the immediate reward received after transitioning from $s$ due to action $a$.
- $\gamma$ is the discount factor, $0 \leq \gamma \leq 1$.

The objective is to maximize the cumulative expected reward. The value function $V(s)$ under an optimal policy is given by:

$$V(s) = \max_{a \in A} \left[ R(s, a) + \gamma \sum_{s'} P(s'|s, a) V(s') \right]$$

This recursive relationship can be solved using algorithms like Value Iteration or Policy Iteration.

### Algorithm Implementation: Value Iteration

Below is the Python implementation for the Value Iteration algorithm to solve an MDP:

```
def value_iteration(states, actions, transition_prob, rewards, gamma, theta=1e-6):
    V = {s: 0 for s in states}
    while True:
        delta = 0
        for s in states:
            v = V[s]
            V[s] = max(sum(transition_prob[s, a, s'] * (rewards[s, a, s'] + gamma * V[s'
                ])
                        for s' in states) for a in actions)
            delta = max(delta, abs(v - V[s]))
        if delta < theta:
            break
    policy = {s: None for s in states}
    for s in states:
        policy[s] = max(actions, key=lambda a: sum(transition_prob[s, a, s'] *
                                                   (rewards[s, a, s'] + gamma * V[s'])
                                                   for s' in states))
    return V, policy

# Example usage:
states = ['s1', 's2', 's3']
actions = ['a1', 'a2']
transition_prob = {
    ('s1', 'a1', 's2'): 0.5, ('s1', 'a1', 's3'): 0.5,
    ('s1', 'a2', 's2'): 0.6, ('s1', 'a2', 's3'): 0.4,
    ('s2', 'a1', 's1'): 0.7, ('s2', 'a1', 's3'): 0.3,
    ('s2', 'a2', 's1'): 0.4, ('s2', 'a2', 's3'): 0.6,
    ('s3', 'a1', 's1'): 0.8, ('s3', 'a1', 's2'): 0.2,
    ('s3', 'a2', 's1'): 0.3, ('s3', 'a2', 's2'): 0.7,
}
rewards = {
    ('s1', 'a1', 's2'): 10, ('s1', 'a1', 's3'): 5,
    ('s1', 'a2', 's2'): 3, ('s1', 'a2', 's3'): 8,
    ('s2', 'a1', 's1'): 4, ('s2', 'a1', 's3'): 2,
    ('s2', 'a2', 's1'): 7, ('s2', 'a2', 's3'): 6,
    ('s3', 'a1', 's1'): 1, ('s3', 'a1', 's2'): 2,
    ('s3', 'a2', 's1'): 9, ('s3', 'a2', 's2'): 1,
}
gamma = 0.9
V, policy = value_iteration(states, actions, transition_prob, rewards, gamma)
print("Optimal Value Function:", V)
print("Optimal Policy:", policy)
```

```
Optimal Value Function: {'s1': 17.0, 's2': 14.0, 's3': 10.0}
Optimal Policy: {'s1': 'a1', 's2': 'a2', 's3': 'a2'}
```

This section has examined the mechanics of incorporating probability into the dynamic programming paradigm, presenting the theoretical underpinnings and practical implementations. Techniques such as the Bellman equation, stochastic dynamic programming, and MDPs are pivotal in solving probabilistic problems across various domains.

## 10.7 DP with Game Theory

Game theory is a mathematical framework used to analyze situations in which players make decisions that are interdependent. These scenarios, often referred to as games, involve multiple players whose payoffs depend on the actions of all participants. Dynamic programming (DP) provides powerful techniques to solve various types of games, especially those involving recursive decision processes.

We will analyze dynamic programming approaches to several classic game theory problems, emphasizing how DP can be used to systematically determine optimal strategies. Key concepts such as Nash Equilibrium, zero-sum games, and cooperative games will be explored through the lens of DP.

Consider a two-player zero-sum game where each player aims to maximize their payoff while minimizing their opponent's. One common example is the game of Nim. We will first formulate the problem and then develop a DP solution.

**Problem Definition: Nim Game**

In the Nim game, two players take turns removing at least one object from a heap of objects. The player forced to take the last object loses. This problem can be elegantly solved using DP to determine the winning strategy.

**State Representation**

Define the state $s$ as the number of objects remaining in the game. The objective is to determine the winning move for the current player from each state. Define a boolean DP array $\mathrm{dp[]}$, where $\mathrm{dp[i]}$ is true if the current player can force a win when there are $i$ objects remaining.

**Transition and Base Cases**

- Base Case: $\mathrm{dp[0]} = \mathrm{false}$ because if there are no objects left, the player to move loses.
- Transition: For each state $s = i$, the current player can remove $k$ objects ($k$ ranges from 1 to $i$). If any resulting state $\mathrm{dp[i\text{-}k]}$ is losing for the opponent, then $\mathrm{dp[i]} = \mathrm{true}.$

## DP Array Update

```
def can_player_win(n):
    dp = [False] * (n + 1)
    for i in range(1, n + 1):
        for k in range(1, i + 1):
            if not dp[i - k]:
                dp[i] = True
                break
    return dp[n]

# Example execution
n = 10
print(can_player_win(n))
```

```
Output:
True
```

The output indicates that the player who starts the game with 10 objects can force a win with optimal play.

### Game Theory and Nash Equilibrium

In competitive scenarios where players simultaneously decide strategies, Nash Equilibrium becomes crucial. A Nash Equilibrium is a set of strategies, one for each player, such that no player can unilaterally change their strategy to improve their payoff. Using dynamic programming, such equilibria can be computed for various games, particularly those defined over finitely many states and actions.

### Example: Matching Pennies

Matching Pennies is a simple game where two players simultaneously place a penny on the table, either Heads ($H$) or Tails ($T$). If the pennies match, Player 1 wins; if they do not match, Player 2 wins. This zero-sum game has no pure strategy Nash equilibrium, but a mixed strategy equilibrium can be determined.

### DP Solution

Representation of strategies and payoffs in a 2D DP table can help compute expected utilities and identify equilibrium strategies. The table $\mathrm{U[i][j]}$ represents the utility for Player 1 when Player 1 plays strategy $i$ and Player 2 plays strategy $j$.

- Define utilities: $U(H,H) = 1, U(H,T) = -1, U(T,H) = -1, U(T,T) = 1$
- Mixed strategies: Player 1 choosing $H$ with probability $p$ and $T$ with $1-p$; Player 2 choosing $H$ with probability $q$ and $T$ with $1-q$.

Using dynamic programming, compute the expected utilities for different probabilities.

```
import numpy as np

def matching_pennies_utility(p, q):
    U = np.array([[1, -1], [-1, 1]])
    EU_Player1 = p * (q * U[0][0] + (1 - q) * U[0][1]) + (1 - p) * (q * U[1][0] + (1 - q)
         * U[1][1])
    return EU_Player1

# Compute utility for mixed strategies
p, q = 0.5, 0.5
utility = matching_pennies_utility(p, q)
print(utility)
```

Output:
0.0

The output reflects that the expected utility for both players in the mixed strategy equilibrium ($p = 0.5, q = 0.5$) is zero, indicating fairness in this zero-sum game.

**Further Applications**

Beyond these specific examples, DP with game theory has numerous applications, including competitive resource allocation, auction design, and economic market analysis. Sophisticated DP techniques can solve more complex games, such as differential games and games played over continuous strategies. Integrating game theory principles with dynamic programming broadens the scope of solvable problems and deepens understanding of strategic interactions in multi-agent systems.

## 10.8 Approximation Algorithms using DP

Approximation algorithms provide near-optimal solutions to computational problems where obtaining the exact solution is computationally prohibitive. In the context of dynamic programming (DP), these algorithms leverage the structure of DP to yield solutions that approximate the optimum within a known bound. This section will explore various techniques for designing and analyzing approximation algorithms using dynamic programming approaches.

One of the primary challenges in many combinatorial optimization problems is that the exact solution may require exponential time or space. Approximation algorithms aim to circumvent this limitation by providing solutions that are "good enough" within a factor of the optimal solution, denoted as $\alpha$-approximation, where $\alpha$ is a performance ratio. Typical problems where approximation algorithms are effective include knapsack problems, traveling salesperson problems (TSP), and network routing problems.

Consider the classic *Knapsack Problem*. The objective is to maximize the profit of items placed in a knapsack without exceeding its capacity. The exact solution is impractical for large instances due to its pseudo-polynomial time complexity. Using dynamic programming, we can derive a PTAS (Polynomial Time Approximation Scheme) for the knapsack problem. The idea is to round the item values and use a scaled-down version of the DP table.

```
def knapsack_approximation(values, weights, capacity, epsilon):
    n = len(values)
    max_value = max(values)
    K = int((epsilon * max_value) / n)

    scaled_values = [v // K for v in values]

    dp = [0] * (capacity + 1)

    for i in range(n):
        for w in range(capacity, weights[i] - 1, -1):
            dp[w] = max(dp[w], dp[w - weights[i]] + scaled_values[i])

    return K * dp[capacity]

values = [20, 30, 40, 50]
weights = [1, 3, 4, 5]
capacity = 7
epsilon = 0.1
print(knapsack_approximation(values, weights, capacity, epsilon))
```

The DP table $\mathrm{dp}$ stores the maximum value achievable with weights up to the current capacity. The values are scaled down using the factor $K$ derived from the given $\epsilon$, which affects the granularity of approximation. This algorithm provides a $(1 - \epsilon)$-approximate solution.

Another important application of approximation algorithms with DP is in solving the *Traveling Salesperson Problem (TSP)*. While exact solutions are infeasible for large instances due to factorial growth, approximation algorithms can offer tractable solutions. A notable approach is using dynamic programming to solve a relaxed version of TSP under certain constraints, such as metric TSP where the triangle inequality holds.

For a sufficiently accurate approximation, MST (Minimum Spanning Tree) approach can be adapted for a DP-based $2$-approximation algorithm. By constructing an MST, doubling its edges to form an Eulerian circuit, and then using shortcuts to form a Hamiltonian tour, we ensure the solution is within twice the optimal tour:

```
import networkx as nx
import numpy as np

def tsp_approximation(adj_matrix):
    G = nx.from_numpy_matrix(adj_matrix)
    mst = nx.minimum_spanning_tree(G)

    euler_tour = list(nx.eulerian_circuit(mst, source=0))
    visited = set()
    tour = []

    for u, v in euler_tour:
        if u not in visited:
            visited.add(u)
            tour.append(u)

    tour.append(tour[0]) # complete tour by returning to the start

    return tour

adj_matrix = np.array([[0, 10, 15, 20], [10, 0, 35, 25],
                       [15, 35, 0, 30], [20, 25, 30, 0]])
print(tsp_approximation(adj_matrix))
```

The function tsp_approximation converts an adjacency matrix into a graph $G$ and computes its MST. By deriving an Eulerian circuit of the MST and subsequently using shortcuts to avoid revisiting nodes, a reasonably short Hamiltonian tour is constructed.

Approximation algorithms using dynamic programming pave the way for solving many NP-hard problems in practical scenarios, balancing between optimality and computational feasibility. The techniques discussed herein highlight the versatility and power of combining dynamic programming with approximation strategies, providing effective solutions to otherwise intractable problems.

## 10.9 Parallel Computation in DP

Parallel computation in dynamic programming (DP) aims to leverage multiple processors to solve complex DP problems more efficiently. Traditional DP algorithms are inherently sequential: they build solutions step-by-step based on previously computed states. However, utilizing modern multi-core processors and distributed computing frameworks, certain DP problems can be restructured to exploit parallelism, thus reducing computation time.

Consider the classic example of matrix chain multiplication. Given a sequence of matrices, the goal is to determine the most efficient way to multiply these matrices together. A naive approach would involve computing all possible parenthesizations of matrix products, but this is computationally expensive. Using DP, we solve it using a bottom-up approach, storing intermediate results to avoid redundant calculations.

To introduce parallelism, we decompose the DP table into independent subproblems that can be concurrently solved. If $m[i, j]$ is the minimum cost of multiplying a chain of matrices from $i$ to $j$, we concurrently compute the costs for all $k$ (where $i \leq k < j$) points of division.

```
import multiprocessing
import numpy as np

def matrix_chain_order(p):
    n = len(p) - 1
    m = np.zeros((n, n), dtype=int)

    def compute_cost(i, j):
        if i == j:
            return 0
        min_cost = float('inf')
        for k in range(i, j):
            q = m[i][k] + m[k+1][j] + p[i-1] * p[k] * p[j]
            if q < min_cost:
                min_cost = q
        return min_cost

    def worker(start, end, result_dict):
        for i in range(start, end):
            for j in range(i, n):
                m[i][j] = compute_cost(i, j)
        result_dict[start] = m[start:end, :]

    manager = multiprocessing.Manager()
    result_dict = manager.dict()
    jobs = []
    num_workers = multiprocessing.cpu_count()

    chunk_size = n // num_workers
    for i in range(num_workers):
        start = i * chunk_size
        end = (i + 1) * chunk_size if i != num_workers - 1 else n
        p = multiprocessing.Process(target=worker, args=(start, end, result_dict))
        jobs.append(p)
        p.start()

    for job in jobs:
        job.join()

    for start, sub_table in result_dict.items():
        m[start:start+sub_table.shape[0], :] = sub_table

    return m

p = [30, 35, 15, 5, 10, 20, 25]
m = matrix_chain_order(p)
print(m)
```

Parallelizing DP also requires careful consideration of data dependencies and synchronization. In the example, the matrix $m$ is shared among worker processes using a manager dictionary provided by the multiprocessing library. Each worker process computes a subarray of the DP table independently, minimizing inter-process communication overhead.

Ideally, subproblems need minimal synchronization to achieve an optimal speedup. This approach can apply to higher-dimensional DP problems, such as computing shortest paths in a graph using the Floyd-Warshall algorithm or aligning sequences in bioinformatics.

However, not all DP problems lend themselves easily to parallelization. For DAG-based (Directed Acyclic Graph) DP, parallelization requires analyzing the dependency graph to identify independent subproblems. Graph partitioning algorithms can sometimes be used to identify subgraphs that can be processed in parallel.

Another common approach to parallelize DP is using dynamic task scheduling frameworks such as OpenMP, CUDA for GPU, or distributed environments like Apache Spark. These frameworks offer built-in mechanisms for task synchronization, load balancing, and memory management, simplifying the implementation of parallel DP algorithms.

```
#include <omp.h>
#include <stdio.h>
#include <limits.h>

#define N 5

void matrix_chain_order(int p[], int n) {
    int m[n][n];
    int i, j, k, L, q;

    for (i = 1; i < n; i++) {
        m[i][i] = 0;
    }

    #pragma omp parallel for private(j, k, q) shared(m)
    for (L = 2; L < n; L++) {
        for (i = 1; i < n - L + 1; i++) {
            j = i + L - 1;
            m[i][j] = INT_MAX;
            for (k = i; k <= j - 1; k++) {
                q = m[i][k] + m[k + 1][j] + p[i - 1] * p[k] * p[j];
                if (q < m[i][j]) {
                    m[i][j] = q;
                }
            }
        }
    }

    printf("Optimal Parenthesization Cost: %d\n", m[1][n - 1]);
}
```

```
int main() {
    int arr[] = {30, 35, 15, 5, 10, 20, 25};
    int size = sizeof(arr) / sizeof(arr[0]);
    matrix_chain_order(arr, size);
    return 0;
}
```

OpenMP is a powerful tool for parallelizing DP on multi-core CPUs. Using pragmas, sections of code are parallelized with minimal modification to the serial version. The example demonstrates this by parallelizing the outermost loop of the matrix chain multiplication DP algorithm, distributing iterations across available CPU threads.

Parallel computation allows us to handle larger datasets and more complex problems. By leveraging the combined power of multiple processors, it is possible to significantly reduce the computational time of DP algorithms, enabling real-time applications and more efficient solving of NP-hard problems.

## 10.10 Dynamic Programming in Machine Learning

Dynamic programming (DP) has found extensive application in the realm of machine learning, providing robust solutions to a variety of complex problems. Machine learning often involves optimization and sequential decision-making processes, both of which can be efficiently addressed using dynamic programming techniques. This section explores key areas where dynamic programming and machine learning intersect, focusing on reinforcement learning, hidden Markov models, and sequence prediction.

One of the most well-known applications of dynamic programming in machine learning is in reinforcement learning (RL). Reinforcement learning is a type of machine learning where an agent learns to make decisions by taking actions in an environment to maximize some notion of cumulative reward. Central to many RL algorithms is the concept of the Bellman equation, which forms the basis for several dynamic programming methods such as value iteration and policy iteration.

**Value Iteration**:

Value iteration is an algorithm used for computing the optimal policy and the value function in a Markov Decision Process (MDP). The value function $V(s)$ represents the maximum cumulative reward that can be obtained starting from state $s$. The Bellman equation for value iteration is given by:

$$V(s) = \max_a \sum_{s'} P(s' \mid s, a)[R(s, a, s') + \gamma V(s')]$$

where:

- $s$ represents a state
- $a$ represents an action
- $s'$ represents the subsequent state
- $P(s' \mid s, a)$ is the transition probability from state $s$ to state $s'$ given action $a$
- $R(s, a, s')$ is the reward received after transitioning from state $s$ to state $s'$ using action $a$
- $\gamma$ is the discount factor, $0 \leq \gamma < 1$

The value iteration algorithm iteratively updates the value function until convergence:

```
def value_iteration(states, actions, transition_probabilities, rewards, gamma, theta=1e
    -6):
    V = {s: 0 for s in states}
    while True:
        delta = 0
        for s in states:
            v = V[s]
            V[s] = max(sum(transition_probabilities[s, a, s_prime] *
                           (rewards[s, a, s_prime] + gamma * V[s_prime])
                           for s_prime in states) for a in actions)
            delta = max(delta, abs(v - V[s]))
        if delta < theta:
            break
    return V
```

The output value function $V$ represents the optimal strategy for the agent to follow.

**Policy Iteration**:

Policy iteration involves two main steps: policy evaluation and policy improvement. Policy evaluation calculates the value of a particular policy, while policy improvement updates the policy based on the value function.

1. Initialize the policy $\pi$ arbitrarily.
2. **Policy Evaluation:** Update the value function under the current policy:

$$V^\pi(s) = \sum_{s'} P(s' \mid s, \pi(s))[R(s, \pi(s), s') + \gamma V^\pi(s')]$$

3. **Policy Improvement:** Update the policy based on the updated value function:

$$\pi'(s) = \arg\max_a \sum_{s'} P(s' \mid s, a)[R(s, a, s') + \gamma V(s')]$$

4. Repeat steps 2 and 3 until convergence.

```
def policy_iteration(states, actions, transition_probabilities, rewards, gamma, theta=1
    e-6):
    policy = {s: actions[0] for s in states}
    V = {s: 0 for s in states}
    while True:
        # Policy Evaluation
        while True:
            delta = 0
            for s in states:
                v = V[s]
                V[s] = sum(transition_probabilities[s, policy[s], s_prime] *
                           (rewards[s, policy[s], s_prime] + gamma * V[s_prime])
                           for s_prime in states)
                delta = max(delta, abs(v - V[s]))
            if delta < theta:
                break

        # Policy Improvement
        policy_stable = True
        for s in states:
            old_action = policy[s]
            policy[s] = max(actions, key=lambda a:
                            sum(transition_probabilities[s, a, s_prime] *
                                (rewards[s, a, s_prime] + gamma * V[s_prime])
                                for s_prime in states))
            if old_action != policy[s]:
                policy_stable = False
        if policy_stable:
            break
    return policy, V
```

**Hidden Markov Models**:

Hidden Markov Models (HMMs) are widely used in sequence modeling tasks such as speech recognition, gene prediction, and natural language processing. HMMs model a system that is assumed to be a

Markov process with hidden states. Dynamic programming plays a crucial role in solving problems related to HMMs, particularly in decoding and learning.

The **Viterbi Algorithm** is a dynamic programming algorithm used for finding the most probable sequence of hidden states. Given an observation sequence $O$, the Viterbi algorithm computes the most likely state sequence $Q^*$ using the following recurrence relation:

$$V_t(j) = \max_i [V_{t-1}(i) \cdot a_{ij} \cdot b_j(O_t)]$$

where:

- $V_t(j)$ is the maximum probability of the state sequence ending in state $j$ at time $t$
- $a_{ij}$ is the state transition probability from state $i$ to state $j$
- $b_j(O_t)$ is the observation likelihood of observing $O_t$ in state $j$

```
def viterbi_algorithm(observations, states, start_prob, trans_prob, emission_prob):
    V = [{}]
    path = {}
    for y in states:
        V[0][y] = start_prob[y] * emission_prob[y][observations[0]]
        path[y] = [y]
    for t in range(1, len(observations)):
        V.append({})
        newpath = {}
        for y in states:
            (prob, state) = max((V[t-1][y0] * trans_prob[y0][y] * emission_prob[y][
                observations[t]], y0)
                            for y0 in states)
            V[t][y] = prob
            newpath[y] = path[state] + [y]
        path = newpath
    n = len(observations) - 1
    (prob, state) = max((V[n][y], y) for y in states)
    return (prob, path[state])
```

**Sequence Prediction**:

Sequence prediction is another key area where dynamic programming is beneficial. Long Short-Term Memory (LSTM) networks, a type of recurrent neural network (RNN), use gates that control the flow of information. Computing the gradients for such networks during backpropagation through time (BPTT) can be optimized using dynamic programming techniques.

Dynamic programming methods can be applied to compute the gradients of the loss function with respect to the parameters efficiently, avoiding the problem of vanishing or exploding gradients.

The integration of dynamic programming in machine learning methodologies enhances the ability to solve problems with optimal efficiency and consistency across various applications. This applicability extends to numerous domains, underscoring the versatility and power of dynamic programming in advancing machine learning techniques.

## 10.11 Latest Research in Dynamic Programming

Recent advancements in dynamic programming (DP) have brought forth a plethora of innovations and methodologies that extend beyond traditional paradigms. Scholars and practitioners have continually explored more efficient algorithms, novel problem formulations, and applications that push the boundaries of what can be achieved using DP techniques. This section covers some of the latest research contributions and trends in dynamic programming, providing insights into the current state-of-the-art and future directions in this domain.

**Improved Algorithms for Classic Problems**

One of the continuing areas of research in DP involves improving the efficiency of algorithms for classic problems. For example, the Longest Common Subsequence (LCS) problem has seen significant advancements. Recent research has introduced algorithms that reduce time and space complexity through innovative data structures such as sparse table and wavelet trees.

```
def optimized_lcs(X, Y):
    m, n = len(X), len(Y)
    sparse_table = [[0] * (n + 1) for _ in range(m + 1)]
    for i in range(1, m + 1):
        for j in range(1, n + 1):
            if X[i - 1] == Y[j - 1]:
                sparse_table[i][j] = sparse_table[i - 1][j - 1] + 1
            else:
                sparse_table[i][j] = max(sparse_table[i - 1][j], sparse_table[i][j - 1])
    return sparse_table[m][n]

X = "AGGTAB"
Y = "GXTXAYB"
print(f"Length of LCS is {optimized_lcs(X, Y)}")
```

**Approximate Dynamic Programming**

Approximate DP is gaining traction as an essential approach to handle high-dimensional state spaces, commonly encountered in complex systems such as robotics and network design. Researchers have been focusing on developing approximation algorithms that balance computational tractability and solution accuracy.

One promising area is Approximate Policy Iteration (API) for Markov Decision Processes (MDPs). API is designed to manage large-scale MDPs by approximating value functions using a limited number of basis functions. This method significantly reduces computation times while maintaining policy performance.

```
class ApproximatePolicyIteration:
    def __init__(self, mdp, basis_functions, gamma=0.9):
        self.mdp = mdp
        self.basis_functions = basis_functions
        self.gamma = gamma
        self.value_function = np.zeros(len(basis_functions))

    def approximate_value(self, state):
        return sum(self.value_function[i] * basis(state) for i, basis in enumerate(self.
            basis_functions))

    def policy_evaluation(self, policy):
        for state in range(self.mdp.num_states):
            value = 0
            for action in self.mdp.actions[state]:
                for prob, next_state, reward in self.mdp.transitions[state][action]:
                    value += prob * (reward + self.gamma * self.approximate_value(
                        next_state))
            self.value_function[state] = value

    def policy_improvement(self):
        new_policy = {}
        for state in range(self.mdp.num_states):
            best_action = max(self.mdp.actions[state], key=lambda a: sum(p *
                (r + self.gamma * self.approximate_value(s_)) for p, s_, r in self.
                    mdp.transitions[state][a]))
            new_policy[state] = best_action
        return new_policy

    def train(self, iterations=100):
        policy = {state: self.mdp.actions[state][0] for state in range(self.mdp.num_states
            )}
        for i in range(iterations):
            self.policy_evaluation(policy)
            policy = self.policy_improvement()
        return policy
```

### Deep Learning and Dynamic Programming

The convergence of deep learning and DP has led to breakthroughs in fields such as natural language processing and game AI. By leveraging neural networks, researchers can approximate DP solutions for previously intractable problems. One notable application is the use of deep reinforcement learning (DRL) combined with DP principles to solve complex decision-making tasks.

An example of this is the use of the Deep Q-Network (DQN) algorithm, which approximates the Q-values in reinforcement learning tasks. DQN employs a neural network to estimate Q-values, allowing it to handle environments with high-dimensional state spaces effectively.

```
import torch
import torch.nn as nn
import torch.optim as optim

class DQN(nn.Module):
    def __init__(self, state_size, action_size):
        super(DQN, self).__init__()
        self.fc1 = nn.Linear(state_size, 128)
        self.fc2 = nn.Linear(128, 64)
        self.fc3 = nn.Linear(64, action_size)

    def forward(self, state):
        x = torch.relu(self.fc1(state))
        x = torch.relu(self.fc2(x))
        return self.fc3(x)

def train_dqn(env, episodes=100):
    state_size = env.observation_space.shape[0]
    action_size = env.action_space.n
    policy_net = DQN(state_size, action_size)
    optimizer = optim.Adam(policy_net.parameters())
    loss_fn = nn.MSELoss()

    for episode in range(episodes):
        state = env.reset()
        total_reward = 0
        done = False

        while not done:
            state_tensor = torch.FloatTensor(state)
            q_values = policy_net(state_tensor)
            action = torch.argmax(q_values).item()

            next_state, reward, done, _ = env.step(action)
            total_reward += reward

            next_state_tensor = torch.FloatTensor(next_state)
            target_q_value = reward + 0.99 * torch.max(policy_net(next_state_tensor
                )).item()

            optimizer.zero_grad()
            loss = loss_fn(q_values[action], torch.tensor(target_q_value))
            loss.backward()
            optimizer.step()

            state = next_state

        print(f"Episode {episode + 1}/{episodes}, Total Reward: {total_reward}")
```

### Explorations into Algorithmic Game Theory

Algorithmic game theory, intersecting the domains of computer science and economics, has seen dynamic programming leveraged to solve problems like optimal auction designs, resource allocation, and strategic behavior in networks. Research in this area has produced algorithms that account for the strategic interplay between multiple agents, addressing economic models and real-world applications.

In repeated games, researchers have developed equilibrium computation methods that utilize DP for strategy optimization. These methods focus on finding Nash equilibria in repeated interactions by iteratively adjusting strategies to optimize payoffs.

```
def nash_equilibrium(payoff_matrix):
    num_players = len(payoff_matrix)
    num_strategies = len(payoff_matrix[0])

    def best_response(player, strategy_profile):
        best_res = None
        best_payoff = float('-inf')
        for strategy in range(num_strategies):
            strategy_profile[player] = strategy
            payoff = sum(payoff_matrix[player][strategy_profile[player]][other] for
                                other in range(num_players))
            if payoff > best_payoff:
                best_payoff = payoff
                best_res = strategy
        return best_res

    equilibrium = [0] * num_players
    stable = False

    while not stable:
        stable = True
        for player in range(num_players):
            best_res = best_response(player, equilibrium)
            if best_res != equilibrium[player]:
                equilibrium[player] = best_res
                stable = False

    return equilibrium

payoff_matrix = [
    [[3, 3], [0, 5]],
    [[5, 0], [1, 1]]
]
print(f"Nash Equilibrium: {nash_equilibrium(payoff_matrix)}")
```

Research in dynamic programming continues to evolve, with new findings enhancing our understanding and application of these principles to increasingly complex issues. These advancements hold promise for further innovations in both theoretical constructs and practical implementations across diverse fields.

## 10.12 Case Studies of Complex DP Applications

This section explores several sophisticated applications of dynamic programming, elucidating their underlying principles and demonstrating the advantages of employing DP in complex problem-solving scenarios. By examining these case studies, one gains an appreciation of how dynamic programming can be tailored to address specific challenges and optimize solutions in diverse fields.

**Case Study 1: Sequence Alignment in Computational Biology**

One of the most common applications of dynamic programming in bioinformatics is sequence alignment, particularly useful in comparing DNA, RNA, or protein sequences. The goal is to identify regions of similarity that may indicate functional, structural, or evolutionary relationships between the sequences.

Consider two sequences $A$ and $B$ of lengths $n$ and $m$, respectively. The Needleman-Wunsch algorithm is a classic approach that employs dynamic programming to achieve global alignment.

The DP table $D$ is represented as follows, where $D[i][j]$ holds the alignment score of the first $i$ characters of $A$ and the first $j$ characters of $B$:

```
def needleman_wunsch(A, B, match, mismatch, gap):
    n, m = len(A), len(B)
    D = [[0] * (m + 1) for _ in range(n + 1)]

    for i in range(n + 1):
        D[i][0] = i * gap
    for j in range(m + 1):
        D[0][j] = j * gap

    for i in range(1, n + 1):
        for j in range(1, m + 1):
            if A[i-1] == B[j-1]:
                score = match
            else:
                score = mismatch
            D[i][j] = max(D[i-1][j-1] + score,
                          D[i-1][j] + gap,
                          D[i][j-1] + gap)

    return D[n][m]
```

The output is the optimal alignment score of the two sequences, derived from the score table computed using penalties for mismatches and gaps. The final step involves backtracking to retrieve the alignment.

**Case Study 2: Optimal Matrix Chain Multiplication**

Matrix chain multiplication is a classic dynamic programming problem that aims to determine the most efficient way to multiply a given sequence of matrices. The goal is to minimize the number of scalar multiplications.

Given a chain of matrices $A_1, A_2, ..., A_n$ with compatible dimensions, we define $m[i][j]$ as the minimum number of scalar multiplications needed to compute the product of matrices from $A_i$ to $A_j$.

The following recursive formula computes $m[i][j]$:

$$m[i][j] = \min_{i \leq k < j} \{m[i][k] + m[k+1][j] + p_{i-1} \cdot p_k \cdot p_j\}$$

The algorithm is implemented as follows:

```
def matrix_chain_order(p):
    n = len(p) - 1
    m = [[0] * n for _ in range(n)]

    for l in range(2, n + 1):
        for i in range(n - l + 1):
            j = i + l - 1
            m[i][j] = float('inf')
            for k in range(i, j):
                q = m[i][k] + m[k+1][j] + p[i]*p[k+1]*p[j+1]
                if q < m[i][j]:
                    m[i][j] = q

    return m[0][n-1]
```

This function returns the minimum number of multiplications needed to multiply the chain of matrices, providing a highly optimized solution for large datasets.

**Case Study 3: Knapsack Problem in Resource Allocation**

The knapsack problem is emblematic of resource allocation challenges where the aim is to maximize the value of items packed in a knapsack of limited capacity.

Given $n$ items, each with a weight $w_i$ and a value $v_i$, and a knapsack with capacity $W$, the objective is to maximize the total value without exceeding the capacity. The state $dp[i][j]$ represents the maximum value attainable with the first $i$ items and capacity $j$. The recurrence relation is:

$$dp[i][j] = \max(dp[i-1][j], dp[i-1][j-w_i] + v_i)$$

The implementation is straightforward:

```
def knapsack(values, weights, W):
    n = len(values)
    dp = [[0 for _ in range(W + 1)] for _ in range(n + 1)]

    for i in range(1, n + 1):
        for w in range(W + 1):
            if weights[i-1] <= w:
                dp[i][w] = max(dp[i-1][w], dp[i-1][w-weights[i-1]] + values[i-1])
            else:
                dp[i][w] = dp[i-1][w]

    return dp[n][W]
```

This code computes the maximum value one can achieve given the item constraints, showcasing the versatility and effectiveness of dynamic programming in resource management.

### Case Study 4: Edit Distance in Natural Language Processing

Edit distance or Levenshtein distance measures the minimum number of operations (insertions, deletions, and substitutions) required to transform one string into another. This concept is pivotal in spell checking, DNA sequencing, and error correction in coding theory.

For strings $A$ of length $n$ and $B$ of length $m$, the DP table $dp[i][j]$ represents the edit distance between the substrings $A[0..i]$ and $B[0..j]$. The recurrence relations are established as:

$$dp[i][j] = \begin{cases} i & j = 0 \\ j & i = 0 \\ dp[i-1][j-1] & A[i-1] = B[j-1] \\ 1 + \min(dp[i-1][j], dp[i][j-1], & \\ dp[i-1][j-1]) & A[i-1] \neq B[j-1] \end{cases}$$

Here is the Python function implementing this:

```
def edit_distance(A, B):
    n, m = len(A), len(B)
    dp = [[0] * (m + 1) for _ in range(n + 1)]

    for i in range(n + 1):
        for j in range(m + 1):
            if i == 0:
                dp[i][j] = j
            elif j == 0:
```

Made in the USA
Monee, IL
05 November 2026

67911516R00184